Artificial Intelligence for Health Professionals

Transforming Practice, Teaching, and Research

Vaikunthan Rajaratnam &

Ang Mu Liang

Copyright © 2023 Vaikunthan Rajaratnam & Ang Mu Liang
All rights reserved.
ISBN:9798853094833

DEDICATION

This book is dedicated to healthcare professionals, researchers, policymakers, and advocates who tirelessly work to advance AI in healthcare. Your commitment to patient care, groundbreaking research, ethical guidelines, and equitable access inspires us all. Together, you shape a future where AI enhances healthcare outcomes and revolutionises the field. Thank you for your unwavering dedication and passion in harnessing the power of AI to improve lives.

ACKNOWLEDGMENTS

We extend our heartfelt gratitude to NHG that have supported clinicians in expanding their knowledge of artificial intelligence (AI) in healthcare. Your commitment to advancing healthcare and embracing AI's potential has paved the way for transformative advancements in patient care. We thank KTPH for fostering a culture of lifelong learning and providing resources for clinicians to engage with AI. We also acknowledge the contributions of AI research teams and the dedication of clinicians in embracing AI opportunities.

We would like to acknowledge the use of ChatGPT, an AI language model developed by OpenAI, in assisting us with the writing process for this paper. ChatGPT has provided valuable suggestions and generated content based on the prompts and inquiries we provided. While ChatGPT has played a role in supporting our writing efforts, it is important to note that the final content, interpretations, and conclusions presented in this paper are the responsibility of the authors. The use of ChatGPT has been instrumental in enhancing our writing capabilities, but human judgment and critical thinking were exercised to ensure the accuracy, coherence, and integrity of the final manuscript.

CONTENTS

Foreword ix
Preface x
Chapter 1 Introduction to Artificial Intelligence 1
Chapter 2 Foundations of Artificial Intelligence 11
   2.1 What is artificial intelligence? 12
   2.2 AI, Machine Learning, and Deep Learning 16
   2.3 A brief history of AI in Healthcare 27
Chapter 3 AI in Clinical Practice 37
   3.1 AI applications in Diagnostics and Prognostics 37
   3.2 AI-driven Decision Support Systems (DSS) 42
   3.3 Personalised Medicine and AI 48
   3.4 Telemedicine and remote patient monitoring 50
   3.5 AI in surgical procedures and Rehabilitation 55
Chapter 4 AI in Healthcare Education and Teaching 61
   4.1 AI Use in healthcare education 64
   4.2 Example of AI use 72
   4.3 Infrastructure and Architecture for AI in healthcare education ... 75
   4.4 Simulation and virtual reality in medical education 78
   Scenario: Nursing Simulation Training 79
   Scenario: Emergency Care Training 80
   4.5 Personalised Learning with AI-driven education platforms 86
   Scenario: Administering a New Medication 88
   4.6 AI-assisted curriculum Design and Assessment 89
   4.7 AI in continuing professional development 96
   Scenario for AI in Continuing Professional Development for Radiologists
   98

Chapter 5 AI in Healthcare Research 100
   5.1 AI-powered literature reviews and evidence synthesis 103
   5.2 AI in data analysis and predictive modelling 106
   5.3 AI in drug discovery and clinical trial design 112
   AI-driven research collaboration and communication 115
Chapter 6 Ethical, Legal, and Social Implications of AI in Healthcare ... 122
   Biomedical Ethics 123
   Ethical Framework for AI in Healthcare 126
   The Intersection of Society and AI and Healthcare 131
   6.1 Data Privacy and Security 135
   6.2 Bias and Fairness in AI Algorithms 139
   6.3 Liability and accountability in AI-driven decision-making 142
   6.4 Informed consent and transparency 146
Chapter 7 Overcoming Barriers to AI Adoption in Healthcare 150
   Challenges and Barriers 150
   Mitigating Barriers 153
   Cultivating a culture of innovation and collaboration 157
   Example of Innovation in service design 157
   Example of collaboration 159
   AI workforce development and training 160
   Financial Considerations and Investment in AI Infrastructure 165
Chapter 8 Practical Implications of AI for Healthcare Professionals 175
   Introduction 175
   8.1 AI in Clinical Practice 175
      AI in Diagnostics and Decision Support 176
      ChatGPT in clinical practice 178
      AI in Treatment and Personalized Medicine 181
      Strategies for Interpreting AI-Generated Recommendations 183
      AI in Workflow Optimization and Resource Allocation 184
   8.2 AI in Healthcare Research 188
      AI in Data Analysis and Interpretation 189
      AI in Clinical Trials and Drug Discovery 191

8.3 AI in Healthcare Education and Teaching 193
   AI in Continuing Professional Development 195
   8.4 Summary 198
Chapter 9 The Future of AI in Healthcare 200
   9.1 Emerging Trends and Technologies 202
   9.2 AI's potential impact on the healthcare workforce 204
   9.3 Preparing for the future: strategies for health professionals. 207
Chapter 10 Conclusion 212
   10.1 Embracing AI 213
   10.2 Lifelong Learning and Adaptability 216
   10.3 Key takeaways 218
Bibliography 224
Index 234

Foreword

There are several inventions and discoveries in the past that revolutionized medical care. The discovery of penicillin, the introduction of sterile processes, the invention of vaccines, the invention of X-rays and advanced imaging, genomics and precision medicine and minimally invasive procedures. Artificial intelligence (AI) has the great potential to be ranked among the above and has been encroaching into the conservative medical field. It is therefore timely that a book written on how AI is impacting healthcare practice is written.

Dr Vai is an orthopaedic hand surgeon with a keen interest in medical education and technology. He has been using AI to help develop educational content and speed up research for his articles. Dr Ang is an orthopaedic spine surgeon who is an early adopter of technology as evidenced by his passion for minimally invasive endoscopic spine surgery and his involvement in the implementation of Singapore's Next Generation Electronic Medical Records (NGEMR) across all public healthcare institutions.

The book starts with definition of AI and the various areas where AI is applied in healthcare delivery, education and research. It also touches on the critical areas of biomedical ethics and medico-legal implications of AI in healthcare where data privacy, bias and transparency are discussed.

As with all new tools, there are barriers to change and challenges to incorporating AI into our decision support and workflows, the book discusses practical considerations on how to overcome these barriers. To show how it is done, several real-life examples of how AI is used clinical care, education and research are cited. It ends on a high note with the future of AI in healthcare and how we should embrace it with the correct frame of mind.

Gamaliel Tan
Group Chief Medical Informatics Officer, National University Hospital System, 2018-2023
Head of Department of Orthopaedic Surgery and Chief Medical Informatics Officer, Ng Teng Fong Hospital, 2009-2018

Preface

This book, "Artificial Intelligence for Health Professionals: Transforming Practice, Teaching, and Research," aims to bridge the knowledge gap between healthcare's clinical, educational, and research dimensions and the rapidly evolving world of AI. The role of AI in Healthcare extends beyond just clinical practice. It is reshaping how we teach, learn, and conduct research, enabling us to push the boundaries of what is possible in-patient care, medical education, and scientific exploration.

This book provides a comprehensive overview of these applications, aiming to instil a solid understanding of AI's potential within the healthcare context. "Artificial Intelligence for Health Professionals" delves into the practical applications of AI, from diagnostics and decision support systems to telemedicine and surgical procedures. It explores the transformative potential of AI in medical education, curriculum design, and professional development. The book also examines how AI can revolutionise healthcare research, foster collaboration, and enhance communication.

Discussing AI's ethical, legal, and social implications in healthcare is equally crucial. As much as AI can be a force for good, it is essential to understand its potential pitfalls and how to navigate them. This book addresses these challenges, guiding data privacy, bias, liability, and the importance of transparency and informed consent.

Furthermore, it is critical to understand the barriers to AI adoption in healthcare and strategies to overcome them. This book delves into this aspect, providing insights into organisational challenges, cultivating a culture of innovation, workforce development, and financial considerations. The future of AI in Healthcare is both exciting and daunting. This book provides a clear roadmap for this journey, discussing emerging trends, potential impacts, and strategies to prepare for a future where AI is integral to healthcare.

In conclusion, this book serves as a guide and a catalyst for positive change in healthcare. It emphasises AI as a tool that can enhance our abilities to help and heal when used wisely. As we navigate this new frontier, let us remember that the human touch in healthcare is irreplaceable, and AI is here to augment, not replace, that connection.

Drs Vaikunthan Rajaratnam & Ang Mu Liang

Chapter 1 Introduction to Artificial Intelligence

As we stand on the brink of a new era in healthcare, we find ourselves in a rapidly evolving landscape, increasingly influenced by the integration of artificial intelligence (AI). This book, "Artificial Intelligence for Health Professionals: Transforming Practice, Teaching, and Research," has been crafted to guide healthcare professionals navigating this transformative period.

AI is no longer a concept confined to science fiction or high-tech laboratories. It has become a potent tool, reshaping industries far and wide. Healthcare stands among these industries, ripe for AI-driven transformation. AI has the potential not only to revolutionise patient care but also to streamline administrative processes within providers, payers, and pharmaceutical organisations, making healthcare delivery more efficient and effective.

Moreover, we are witnessing a growing body of research suggesting that AI can perform as well as, or in some cases, even better than humans in critical healthcare tasks, such as diagnosing disease. This highlights AI's real, transformative potential beyond mere theoretical discourse.

The key categories of applications involve diagnosis and treatment recommendations, patient engagement and adherence, and administrative activities. However, the authors believe it will be years before AI replaces humans in broad medical process domains. There are also ethical implications around using AI in Healthcare, such as accountability, transparency, permission, and privacy.[1]

---

[1] Thomas Davenport and Ravi Kalakota, 'The Potential for Artificial Intelligence in Healthcare', *Future Healthcare Journal* 6, no. 2 (June 2019): 94–98, https://doi.org/10.7861/futurehosp.6-2-94.

The potential and transformative power of artificial intelligence (AI) in healthcare is vast, making it crucial for healthcare professionals to engage with this technology. AI promises to enhance patient outcomes by enabling more accurate diagnoses, personalising treatments, and offering more efficient health monitoring. Its capacity to analyse extensive data quickly and precisely can lead to earlier identification of health issues and better intervention strategies.

AI also offers avenues for efficiency and cost savings by streamlining administrative tasks. By aiding in patient record management, scheduling, and billing, AI allows healthcare professionals to dedicate more time to patient care, enhancing the overall quality of services.

One of AI's most significant potential benefits lies in its power to support medical research. AI can sift through large datasets, identify patterns and trends, and contribute meaningfully to the design and execution of clinical trials. AI's role in telemedicine and remote patient monitoring is another area of great importance, especially in the wake of increased demand due to the COVID-19 pandemic.

In surgical or other complex procedures, AI can provide real-time assistance, increasing the precision of interventions and reducing the risk of errors. Importantly, AI tools can also play a role in identifying and addressing disparities in healthcare access and outcomes by analysing data on social determinants of health.

However, as we move toward greater AI integration, addressing the ethical and legal considerations it raises, such as data privacy issues, potential bias in AI algorithms, and liability concerns, is important. These complexities underline the necessity for healthcare professionals to become literate in AI.

An algorithm is a set of detailed, step-by-step instructions or rules to solve a problem or accomplish a task. In the context of computing, algorithms guide the execution of a program, telling a computer exactly what steps to take to process data and produce a desired outcome.

It can be classified as basic or complex.

Basic Algorithms - These are simpler and involve clear, concise steps. They are used in basic data processing and computations. An example is a sorting algorithm that rearranges a sequence of objects in a particular order - numerical or lexicographical order.

Complex Algorithms - These involve more advanced computational techniques and have a greater depth of instructions. They are typically used for more complex tasks requiring deeper domain understanding. For example, algorithms in machine learning are used to identify patterns in data and make predictions or decisions without being explicitly programmed to perform the task.

In the context of Artificial Intelligence (AI), algorithms play a crucial role, particularly in machine learning and deep learning.

1. **Machine Learning Algorithms**: These are used to build models that can learn from data. The algorithm is given input and output data and tasked with finding a mathematical relationship between them. Examples include linear regression, decision trees, and support vector machines.
2. **Deep Learning Algorithms**: These are a subset of machine learning algorithms based on artificial neural networks, particularly deep neural networks. They are designed to mimic how the human brain works and are particularly good at processing large amounts of data. Examples include convolutional neural networks (CNNs) for image recognition and recurrent neural networks (RNNs) for sequential data like time series.

3. **Reinforcement Learning Algorithms**: These are another type of machine learning algorithm where an agent learns to behave in an environment by performing actions and seeing the results. It uses feedback regarding rewards and punishments to learn the best actions to perform in different states.

So, AI relies on both basic and complex algorithms for different functionalities. While basic algorithms form the foundation of many processes, complex algorithms help AI systems learn, adapt, and improve, hence enabling advanced capabilities like image recognition, natural language processing, autonomous driving, and more. The ideal healthcare algorithms should be designed to be more transparent, adaptable, accurate, unbiased, and shareable.[2]

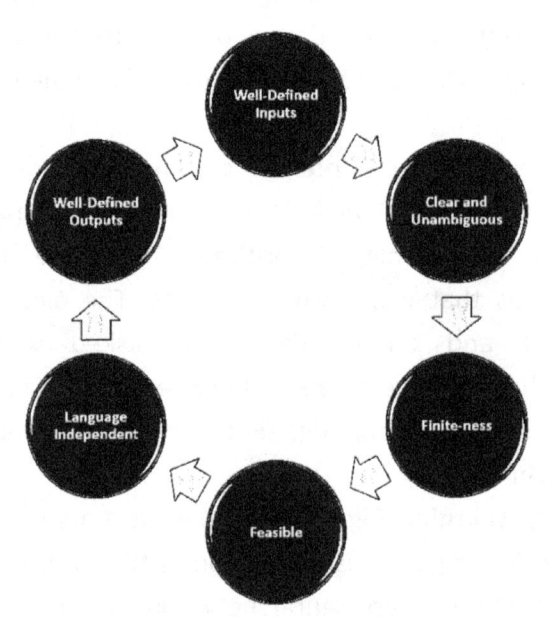

Figure 1. Algorithms in Healthcare

Incorporating artificial intelligence (AI) is rapidly redefining the landscapes of healthcare provision, education and research. Its

---
[2] Tyler J. Loftus et al., 'Ideal Algorithms in Healthcare: Explainable, Dynamic, Precise, Autonomous, Fair, and Reproducible', *PLOS Digital Health* 1, no. 1 (18 January 2022): e0000006, https://doi.org/10.1371/journal.pdig.0000006.

impact spans various dimensions of these fields, enhancing efficiency, personalisation, and overall effectiveness. Artificial Intelligence (AI) offers an array of applications that healthcare professionals can utilise in their daily practice, enhancing their ability to provide high-quality care to their patients.

The rapid incorporation of artificial intelligence (AI) is revolutionizing the landscapes of healthcare provision, education, and research. With its vast array of applications, AI is transforming these fields, boosting efficiency, personalization, and overall effectiveness. In the realm of healthcare, AI offers unprecedented opportunities for professionals to deliver high-quality care to their patients. One of the most significant areas where AI shines is diagnostics. Advanced machine learning algorithms can now analyse complex medical images, such as plain radiographs (X-rays), Computed Tomography (CT) or Magnetic Resonance Imaging (MRI) scans, to identify patterns that may indicate the presence of diseases. For instance, AI systems have showcased remarkable abilities in detecting breast and lung cancers, often rivalling, or surpassing the accuracy of human radiologists. As a result, healthcare professionals can make faster and more precise diagnoses, leading to improved patient outcomes.

In addition to diagnostics, AI transforms how healthcare professionals manage and monitor patient health. AI-powered health monitoring devices, such as smartwatches and wearable sensors, can continuously track a patient's vital signs and other health indicators, alerting healthcare professionals to any significant changes that may require intervention. For example, an AI algorithm can analyse data from a wearable device to predict the onset of conditions like heart disease or diabetes mellitus, allowing for earlier intervention and better management.

AI also plays a vital role in personalising treatment plans. It can analyse large amounts of data, such as a patient's genetic information, lifestyle factors, and past medical history, to predict how they may respond to different treatments. Healthcare professionals can tailor treatment to each patient's needs, improving treatment effectiveness and reducing side effects. For instance, oncologists are already using AI to personalise chemotherapy regimens for cancer patients based on their unique genetic makeup and the specific characteristics of their tumours.

Moreover, AI can automate administrative tasks like scheduling appointments, managing patient records, and processing insurance claims. This can save healthcare professionals significant time and allow them to focus more on direct patient care. For example, AI-powered chatbots can handle routine patient inquiries, freeing time for healthcare professionals to address more complex issues.

Thus, AI holds the potential to profoundly improve the way healthcare professionals practise medicine, allowing them to provide better care, make more informed decisions, and spend more time on patient interaction. As AI continues to evolve, it is expected to play an even more integral role in healthcare practice.

In healthcare education, AI has emerged as a powerful tool. It enables personalised learning by analysing each student's unique learning style, progress, and areas of challenge, thereby allowing the creation of customised study plans and resources. This approach fosters an individualised learning pace and enhances academic outcomes. Furthermore, AI-powered simulations and virtual reality environments offer students invaluable practical experience. They can perform complex procedures or manage rare conditions within a controlled setting, which ensures safety while promoting experiential learning. Adding to these benefits, AI's automated assessment and feedback capacity provides students with real-time performance reviews, helping them promptly identify and improve upon their deficiencies.

The influence of AI extends to healthcare research, marking notable strides in literature reviews and evidence synthesis. AI's ability to rapidly analyse vast amounts of literature to pinpoint relevant studies, extract crucial findings, and amalgamate evidence significantly reduces the time and effort required from researchers. Moreover, in data analysis and predictive modelling, AI's proficiency in pattern recognition and prediction provides profound insights that can guide research direction and inform clinical practice.[3]

AI's role in drug discovery and clinical trial design cannot be overstated. Its predictive capabilities can aid in identifying potential new drugs and crafting more effective clinical trial designs by forecasting the effects of different variables on outcomes. Lastly, AI facilitates research collaboration and communication, assisting in identifying potential collaborators, organising and sharing data, and coordinating tasks seamlessly.

While the potential of artificial intelligence (AI) in revolutionising healthcare is enormous, it has inherent risks and challenges that require careful consideration and management.

One of the paramount concerns is data privacy and security. AI systems often function on extensive data, including sensitive personal and medical information, raising important questions about privacy and the potential risk of data breaches that can expose this information to unauthorised parties.

Moreover, issues of bias and fairness are intricately linked with AI. AI algorithms, trained on specific datasets, may inadvertently perpetuate or intensify biases in the data, leading to potentially unfair outcomes. For example, an AI system introduced

---

[3] Ravi Manne and Sneha C. Kantheti, 'Application of Artificial Intelligence in Healthcare: Chances and Challenges', SSRN Scholarly Paper (Rochester, NY, 24 April 2021), https://papers.ssrn.com/abstract=4393347.

predominantly on data from one racial or ethnic group may perform sub-optimally for individuals from other groups.

When an AI system errs, such as a misdiagnosis or an incorrect treatment suggestion, liability and accountability become complex. It remains challenging to discern the party legally responsible— the AI system's creators, the healthcare professionals using it, or the institution implementing it.

There also exists a risk of over-reliance on AI, possibly leading to diminished critical thinking or overlooking the human aspect of care. AI should serve as a supportive tool, supplementing, not supplanting, the judgement of healthcare professionals.

Furthermore, issues of informed consent and transparency are of significant concern. Patients must be adequately informed and consent to using AI in their care. However, AI algorithms' sophisticated and often opaque nature can make comprehending the decision-making process challenging for patients and healthcare providers, impacting trust and acceptance.

Concerns also arise around access and equity, as AI technologies can potentially exacerbate health disparities if they are more accessible to certain groups over others, such as those with higher incomes or in specific geographic locations. Additionally, fears around job displacement due to AI exist, although many argue that AI is more likely to modify the nature of jobs rather than eliminate them outright.

Given these potential dangers, it is essential to establish robust regulation, oversight, and ethical guidelines for using AI in Healthcare. Such steps will aid in maximising the benefits of AI while minimising its potential harm.[4]

---

[4] Chokri Kooli and Hend Al Muftah, 'Artificial Intelligence in Healthcare: A Comprehensive Review of Its Ethical Concerns', *Technological Sustainability* 1, no. 2 (1 January 2022): 121–

As AI evolves, healthcare professionals must stay abreast of these changes. Engaging with AI now will ensure that healthcare systems can adapt to future changes and continue to provide high-quality care. Therefore, a call goes out to all healthcare professionals: embrace the opportunities AI offers, get literate with AI, and lead the way in shaping a future where AI and Healthcare go hand in hand for the betterment of patient care.

The book is meticulously organized to offer a comprehensive and cohesive understanding of the topic. It starts by establishing the fundamental principles of AI, serving as a strong foundation for readers. From there, it seamlessly transitions into a detailed exploration of AI's applications in clinical practice, highlighting real-world examples and success stories.

Moving beyond clinical practice, the book delves into the transformative impact of AI in healthcare education and research. It explores how AI is revolutionizing teaching methodologies, empowering learners, and fostering innovative research approaches. Moreover, it carefully addresses the complex ethical, legal, and social implications associated with AI in healthcare, underscoring the importance of responsible implementation and accountability.

To ensure practicality, the book also tackles the barriers that hinder the widespread adoption of AI in healthcare, providing insights on how to overcome them. Finally, it offers an intriguing glimpse into the future of AI, discussing emerging trends and potential advancements that will shape the healthcare landscape.

With its well-structured chapters and thought-provoking content, this book equips readers with a comprehensive understanding of AI

31, https://doi.org/10.1108/TECHS-12-2021-0029.

in healthcare while fostering critical thinking about its potential and implications.

This book is intended as a valuable resource for health professionals at all stages of their careers, whether they are just beginning to explore the realm of AI or are seasoned professionals looking to update their knowledge. With this goal in mind, each chapter is designed to be accessible, informative, and practical, drawing on the latest research and real-world examples.

By the end of this book, we hope that readers will have a solid understanding of AI in the healthcare context and will be inspired to consider how they can incorporate AI into their practice, teaching, and research. In this rapidly evolving field, embracing AI and lifelong learning is not just an option but a necessity.

Let us embark on this journey together to leverage AI to improve healthcare and better serve our patients. The future of healthcare is here, and it is infused with AI.

Chapter 2 Foundations of Artificial Intelligence

It is essential to clearly understand the fundamental concepts underpinning AI and its applications in healthcare. This chapter is the foundation upon which we build the rest of the book, providing a comprehensive exploration of AI's basic terminology and its historical evolution within the healthcare sector.

Section 2.1, "What is Artificial Intelligence?" introduces the concept of AI, a term often used but perhaps less commonly understood. We delve into its core elements and various types, offering a detailed overview to help demystify this complex field.

Section 2.2 delves further into the AI lexicon, focusing on two critical subfields - "Machine Learning" and "Deep Learning". By understanding these terminologies, we can better recognise the nuances that distinguish these areas and how they interconnect to form the broader landscape of AI.

Section 2.3 finishes the chapter by tracing the "Brief History of AI in Healthcare". Understanding AI's past and present in healthcare is crucial in contextualising its future applications. This historical lens helps us appreciate the evolution of AI, its successes, challenges, and the driving forces behind its growing importance in healthcare.

By the end of this chapter, readers will have a well-rounded understanding of AI's core concepts and its trajectory in the healthcare sector. Armed with this knowledge, we will be better positioned to explore AI's potential to revolutionise various aspects of healthcare, which we will discuss in the subsequent chapters.

2.1 What is artificial intelligence?

AI is creating systems capable of performing tasks that typically require human intelligence. These tasks include learning from experience, understanding complex content, recognising patterns, interpreting spoken or written language, and making decisions.

At its core, AI is about *developing machines that can mimic human cognitive functions.* It aims to create systems that can understand, learn, and apply knowledge, improving performance over time without being explicitly programmed.

AI can be categorised into two main types: Narrow AI and General AI.[5]

Narrow AI, also known as Weak AI, is designed to perform a specific task, such as voice/image recognition or recommendation systems. We interact with This type of AI daily, such as Siri, Amazon's Alexa, or Google's search algorithms. Although Narrow AI is incredibly

---

[5] Ragnar Fjelland, 'Why General Artificial Intelligence Will Not Be Realised', *Humanities and Social Sciences Communications* 7, no. 1 (17 June 2020): 1–9, https://doi.org/10.1057/s41599-020-0494-4.

sophisticated in its designated tasks, it operates under limited constraints and is focused solely on its specific task.

On the other hand, *General AI,* also known as Strong AI, is the type of artificial intelligence that has the potential to understand, learn, and apply knowledge across a wide range of tasks at the level of a human being. This includes reasoning, solving puzzles, making judgments, planning, and learning from previous experiences. General AI remains largely theoretical, with no existing systems reaching this level of complexity and versatility.[6]

AI technology uses various techniques, including machine learning and deep learning. Machine learning is a subset of AI that involves the development of algorithms that allow computers to learn from and make decisions or predictions based on data. Deep learning, a subset of machine learning, uses artificial neural networks to simulate human decision-making.

The evolution of AI has brought about significant advancements and capabilities, opening a world of possibilities in various fields, including healthcare. Artificial Intelligence (AI) in healthcare uses complex algorithms and software to emulate human cognition in analysing, interpreting, and comprehending complex medical and healthcare data. Specifically, AI is bringing about a paradigm shift in healthcare, driven by the

---

[6] Sofia Samoili et al., 'AI Watch. Defining Artificial Intelligence. Towards an Operational Definition and Taxonomy of Artificial Intelligence, Monograph (Joint Research Centre (Seville site), 2020), https://publications.jrc.ec.europa.eu/repository/handle/JRC118163.

increasing availability of healthcare data and rapid progress of analytics techniques.

AI in healthcare is applied in various forms, such as predictive analytics, decision support systems, and robotics. Here are a few examples:

1. **Predictive Analytics:** AI predicts patient outcomes or disease progression based on patient data. This can help healthcare providers intervene earlier and make more accurate treatment decisions.
2. **Decision Support Systems:** AI can assist doctors in making decisions, especially in complex cases where multiple factors must be considered. For example, AI can help a doctor decide the best treatment plan for a patient with cancer after considering the type and stage of cancer, past medical history, and latest research outcomes.
3. **Robotics:** In surgery, AI-enabled robots assist surgeons in performing precise and minimally invasive procedures. Inpatient care robots are used for tasks like disinfecting rooms, delivering supplies, or helping patients with rehabilitation exercises.
4. **Image Analysis:** AI can analyse medical images to detect diseases. For instance, AI algorithms can process hundreds of prints in seconds with accuracy matching or sometimes exceeding that of human experts.
5. **Personalised Medicine:** AI can analyse a person's genetic makeup and lifestyle factors to predict

their susceptibility to certain diseases and response to specific treatments. This can help in creating highly personalised treatment plans.
6. **Telemedicine:** AI provides medical consultations to patients who cannot visit healthcare facilities. AI can evaluate the patient's symptoms and medical history to provide recommendations.

AI in Healthcare

Predictive Analytics	Predict patient outcomes or diseases progression based on patient data
Decision Support Systems	Assist with the decision process in complex cases where multiple factors must be considered
Robotics	Assist in procedures with AI-enabled robots
Image Analysis	Analyse medical images to detect diseases
Personalised Medicine	Predict disease susceptibility and treatment response according to genetic / lifestyle factors
Telemedicine	Evaluate the patient's symptoms and medical history

Figure 2. Components of AI in Healthcare

While the use of AI in Healthcare holds significant promise for improving patient care and outcomes, it also comes with challenges, such as data privacy, algorithm bias, and the need for substantial infrastructure investment. These issues must be carefully managed to realise AI's potential in healthcare fully.

In subsequent sections, we will delve deeper into the specific terminologies of Machine Learning and Deep Learning and explore the rich history of AI's application in healthcare. As we navigate this journey, we will better understand how AI is revolutionising healthcare practices, enhancing patient care, and transforming the future of medicine.

2.2 AI, Machine Learning, and Deep Learning

Machine learning is a key subset of artificial intelligence that focuses on developing systems capable of learning from data, identifying patterns, and making decisions or predictions, often with minimal human intervention. Machine learning is like teaching a computer to learn from experience, much like we do as humans.

Artificial intelligence
- Development of smart systems and machines to carry out tasks of human intelligence

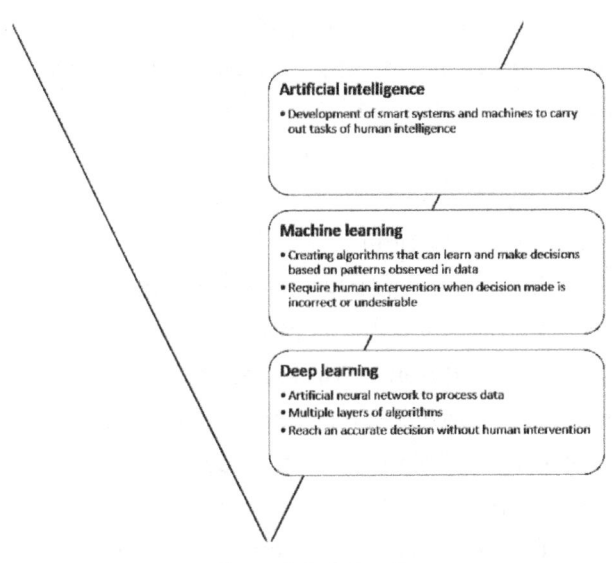

Machine learning
- Creating algorithms that can learn and make decisions based on patterns observed in data
- Require human intervention when decision made is incorrect or undesirable

Deep learning
- Artificial neural network to process data
- Multiple layers of algorithms
- Reach an accurate decision without human intervention

Figure 3. Defining AI

Imagine teaching a child to identify different types of fruits. Initially, you show the child various fruits and name them - apples, oranges, bananas, etc. Over time, the child learns to identify these fruits based on their characteristics, such as colour, shape, or size. Machine learning operates on a similar principle but is a computer program instead of a child. The program is fed large amounts of data and uses algorithms to learn how to classify or predict new data.

One significant application of machine learning in healthcare is disease diagnosis and prediction. By analysing vast quantities of data, including medical images and electronic health records, machine learning algorithms can detect subtle patterns and abnormalities that the human eye may overlook. An example is the use of machine learning to analyse medical images, such as X-rays or CT/MRI scans, to assist in diagnosing diseases or conditions, such as cancer, at an early stage, with an accuracy rate often matching or even exceeding that of experienced radiologists. Machine learning algorithms can be trained to recognise patterns in these images associated with specific diseases or conditions, which can help healthcare providers make more accurate diagnoses and develop more effective treatment plans. Predictive models can identify patients at risk of developing certain diseases or conditions. For example, machine learning algorithms can analyse and identify patient data patterns associated with a higher risk of growing conditions such as diabetes mellitus, heart disease, or cancer. This can help healthcare providers to intervene early and provide targeted interventions to prevent or manage these conditions.[7]

However, machine learning is about more than just making predictions. It can also help in understanding complex data patterns that humans may miss. For instance, vast amounts of patient data can be analysed by algorithms to identify subtle ways that can indicate the early stages of a disease and prompt earlier intervention.

The true power of machine learning lies in its ability to learn and improve over time. As more data is processed, the algorithm continues to learn and refine its predictions or classifications, becoming increasingly effective. This continual learning and adaptation make

---

[7] Irene Y. Chen et al., 'Ethical Machine Learning in Healthcare', *Annual Review of Biomedical Data Science* 4, no. 1 (2021): 123–44, https://doi.org/10.1146/annurev-biodatasci-092820-114757.

machine learning a powerful tool across numerous domains, including healthcare.

Machine learning is revolutionising the healthcare industry by offering innovative approaches to enhance patient care and operational efficiency. Its ability to learn from complex data and make informed decisions is being harnessed in numerous ways.

Personalised treatment is another area where machine learning is making a considerable impact. Every individual's response to treatment varies based on many factors, such as genetic makeup, lifestyle, and medical history. Machine learning algorithms can analyse these complex inter-relationships to predict a patient's response to treatments. This ability to tailor treatment plans to individual needs can enhance the effectiveness of treatment and reduce potential side effects.

Machine learning is also speeding up drug discovery and development. Traditional methods of identifying potential drug candidates are often time-consuming and expensive. Machine learning can analyse large amounts of data on the effects of various compounds, helping to identify potential drug candidates more quickly and efficiently.

Moreover, machine learning is pivotal in improving operational efficiency within healthcare facilities. Predictive analytics, powered by machine learning, can help predict patient volumes, manage staffing levels, and allocate resources effectively, leading to improved patient care and reduced costs.

Finally, the rise of health monitoring wearables, such as fitness trackers and smartwatches, has opened another avenue for machine learning. These devices continually collect health data, such as heart rate, sleep patterns, and activity levels. Machine learning algorithms can analyse this data to provide insights into a person's health, predict potential health risks, and guide interventions.[8]

These examples illustrate just a fraction of the potential machine learning holds in healthcare. As the technology continues to mature and more data becomes available, the possibilities for machine learning in healthcare are virtually limitless.

Deep learning, a subset of machine learning, represents the cutting edge of artificial intelligence technology, and it is significantly transforming industries, including healthcare. But what exactly is deep learning? Let us break it down in simpler terms.

Imagine embarking on an exciting journey to teach a child the art of recognizing a cat. You begin by introducing a delightful array of cat pictures, drawing their attention to distinguishing traits such as pointed ears, delicate whiskers, and a gracefully swaying tail. As

---

[8] Hafsa Habehh and Suril Gohel, 'Machine Learning in Healthcare', *Current Genomics* 22, no. 4 (16 December 2021): 291–300, https://doi.org/10.2174/1389202922666210705124359.

the child's learning progresses, these patterns become familiar, and they develop the ability to effortlessly identify a cat. Deep learning, akin to this process, operates on a grander scale, employing intricate layers of complexity and sophistication to unravel the mysteries of recognition.

Deep learning algorithms, often called "artificial neural networks," are designed to mimic the human brain's structure and function. They consist of multiple layers of interconnected nodes or "neurons." Each layer processes a part of the data and passes it on to the next. The first layer may recognise simple patterns in an image, like lines or edges. The next may identify more complex shapes, like a tail or a whisker. The deeper layers can locate even more intricate patterns, leading to cat identification.

One of the key strengths of deep learning is its ability to process vast amounts of unstructured data. This can be anything from images and audio recordings to text documents. For example, a deep learning algorithm can analyse thousands of radiological images to identify patterns indicative of a specific disease, often with remarkable accuracy. [9].

In healthcare, deep learning is used in numerous ways, including interpreting medical images for the diagnosis, analysing patient records for predictive analytics, and

---

[9] Andre Esteva et al., 'A Guide to Deep Learning in Healthcare', *Nature Medicine* 25, no. 1 (January 2019): 24–29, https://doi.org/10.1038/s41591-018-0316-z.

even in drug discovery, where it can predict the potential effectiveness of new compounds. It is also used in speech recognition technology, which powers virtual assistants in healthcare, helping to streamline administrative tasks.

It is important to note that deep learning requires significant amounts of data and computational power to work effectively. But with the ever-increasing availability of health data and advancements in computing technology, deep learning is set to revolutionise healthcare, provide valuable insights, and improve patient outcomes.

Deep learning has emerged as a groundbreaking application in healthcare, revolutionizing the field of medical imaging and significantly impacting disease diagnosis, particularly in cases like cancer. The power of deep learning algorithms lies in their ability to extract intricate patterns and features from medical images, enabling accurate and efficient identification of diseases. Therefore, one of the most impactful applications of deep learning in healthcare is in medical imaging, specifically in diagnosing diseases such as cancer.[10]

Let us take the example of diagnosing skin cancer. Traditionally, a dermatologist would examine a patient's skin, particularly any unusual moles or growths, and decide based on visual examination and experience. A biopsy can be taken for further examination under a

---

[10] A. Dascalu and E. O. David, 'Skin Cancer Detection by Deep Learning and Sound Analysis Algorithms: A Prospective Clinical Study of an Elementary Dermoscope', *EBioMedicine* 43 (1 May 2019): 107–13, https://doi.org/10.1016/j.ebiom.2019.04.055.

microscope if there is doubt. This process can be time-consuming, and the early stages of skin cancer may be missed.

This is where deep learning comes into play. Researchers have developed deep learning algorithms that can analyse images of skin lesions and moles and classify them as benign (non-cancerous) or malignant (cancerous). The algorithm is trained using thousands of photos of skin lesions that dermatologists have already diagnosed. Through this process, it learns to identify patterns and features in the images indicative of skin cancer.

A doctor or patient can take a high-quality image of a suspicious mole using a smartphone. This image is then analysed by the deep learning algorithm, which provides a real-time diagnosis. Several studies have shown that these deep-learning algorithms can match or even outperform dermatologists in diagnosing skin cancer.

The power of this technology is in its potential to provide quicker, more accessible initial screening for skin cancer, which can lead to earlier detection and treatment, hence significantly improving patient outcomes. This is just one example of how deep learning is used in healthcare, and the possibilities for future applications are limitless.

Creating a deep learning model for diagnosing skin cancer, or any disease from medical images, involves several technical steps[11] :

---

[11] Heang-Ping Chan et al., 'Deep Learning in Medical Image Analysis',

1. **Data Collection:** The first step involves collecting a large dataset of skin lesion images. These images should be labelled, where each image is associated with a diagnosis made by a dermatologist or confirmed by a biopsy. This labelled dataset is used to train and test the deep learning model.

2. **Data Pre-processing:** The images are pre-processed to make them suitable for the deep learning model. This could involve resizing the images to a standard size, normalising the pixel values, removing noise, augmenting the dataset by creating modified versions of the images (like rotated or zoomed-in images), and other steps to make the training process more efficient and the model more robust.

3. **Model Design:** A deep learning model is designed to take an image as input and provide a diagnosis as output. The model consists of multiple layers of "artificial neurons", with each layer learning to recognise different features in the image. The final layer outputs the probability of the image being cancerous.

4. **Training:** The model is trained using a large fraction of labelled images, typically 80% of the dataset as the training set. During training, the model learns to recognise patterns in the pictures associated with each diagnosis. The training involves showing the model an image, letting it make a prediction, and then adjusting its parameters based on the difference between its prediction and the actual labelled diagnosis. This process is repeated many times for all the images in the training set.

Advances in Experimental Medicine and Biology 1213 (2020): 3–21, https://doi.org/10.1007/978-3-030-33128-3_1.

5. Testing and Validation: Once the model is trained, it is tested on a remaining set of images it has not seen during training. This estimates how well the model will perform on new unseen photos.

6. Deployment: If the model performs well on the test set, it can be deployed in a real-world setting. A user can input a new skin image into the model, and it will output its predicted diagnosis.

It is important to note that while deep learning models can be powerful tools for medical diagnosis, they are not infallible and should not replace professional medical advice. They are best used to aid and augment healthcare professionals' abilities.

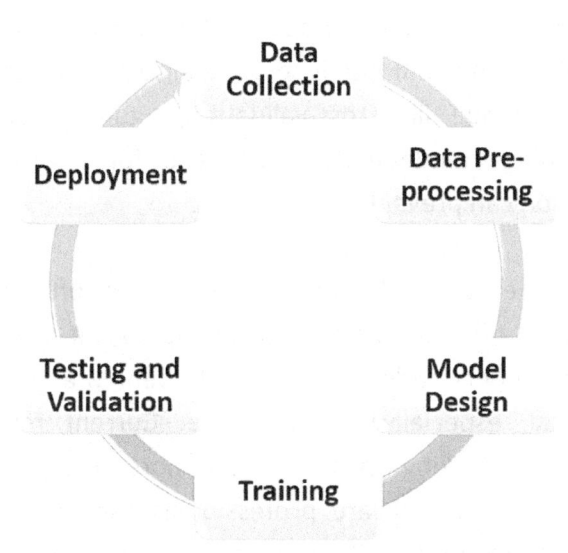

Figure 4. Creating a Deep Learning model in healthcare

While the advent of deep learning holds immense potential for the healthcare industry, it also brings challenges and risks that we must carefully consider and address.

The quality and diversity of data used to train these models can significantly impact their effectiveness. Deep learning models learn from the data they are given, and if that data is skewed or unrepresentative of the population, the models may produce biased or inaccurate predictions. For instance, a skin cancer detection model trained primarily on light-skinned individuals may not perform adequately on darker-skinned patients. Therefore, the training data must represent the diverse populations the model will serve.

Another area for improvement is over-fitting, a phenomenon where the model performs impressively on the training data but needs to generalise to new, unseen data. Techniques like cross-validation, regularisation, and maintaining an independent testing set for performance evaluation can prevent over-fitting.

The opaque nature of deep learning models, often called the "black box" problem, poses a significant challenge because understanding the rationale behind a diagnosis is critical, especially in healthcare. Current research focuses on making these models more interpretable, ensuring that healthcare professionals can understand and trust the output of these tools.

Data privacy and security are paramount in healthcare. Patient data must be de-identified and securely stored to ensure privacy. Regulatory frameworks like the Health

Insurance Portability and Accountability Act (HIPAA) in the United States (U.S.) guide how patient data can be utilised, and it is mandatory to adhere to these regulations.

Lastly, the risk of over-dependence on AI systems can lead to declining diagnostic skills among healthcare professionals. AI should be seen as a tool to augment, not replace, human expertise. Rigorous testing and validation of these models in clinical settings are necessary, and their integration into healthcare needs careful management, with continuous monitoring and adjustment to ensure fair, safe, and beneficial use for all patients.[12]

2.3 A brief history of AI in Healthcare

Artificial Intelligence's journey in healthcare is a fascinating tale of rapid evolution and transformation. The inception of AI in Healthcare began with simple tasks, primarily focused on managing healthcare data. Electronic Health Records (EHRs) were some of the earliest applications of AI, helping to digitalise patient information and making it easier to store, access, and manage.

As AI developed, so did its role in healthcare. One significant turning point was the introduction of Machine Learning (ML), a subset of AI that uses statistical

---

[12] Mohammed Yousef Shaheen, 'AI in Healthcare: Medical and Socio-Economic Benefits and Challenges', *ScienceOpen Preprints*, 25 September 2021, https://doi.org/10.14293/S2199-1006.1.SOR-.PPRQNI1.v1.

techniques to allow computers to "learn" from data. ML started to play a crucial role in predictive analytics. For example, it was used to predict patient readmissions or identify individuals at high risk of chronic diseases like diabetes mellitus or heart disease based on their health records. This allowed healthcare professionals to intervene earlier and institute preventive care.

AI further evolved with the advent of deep learning, a more sophisticated form of machine learning that can analyse vast amounts of data with a structure similar to the human brain's neural networks. Deep learning has revolutionised medical imaging, with algorithms now capable of detecting diseases such as cancers or eye diseases from medical images at accuracy rates equivalent to or surpassing human experts. For instance, Google's DeepMind developed an AI system that can diagnose Age-related Macular Degeneration and Diabetic Retinopathy from retinal scans with 94% accuracy, which matches world-leading ophthalmologists.

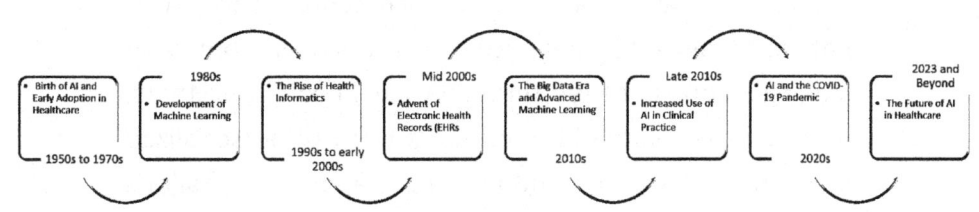

Figure 5. Evolution of AI in Healthcare

Natural language processing, another AI technology, is used to parse and interpret the colossal volumes of unstructured data in health records, clinical notes, and medical literature, helping improve patient care and drive research forward.

In the ever-evolving landscape of healthcare, the applications of AI have witnessed remarkable growth, embracing a wide range of advancements. Today, AI is not only assisting healthcare professionals but also making its presence felt through virtual health assistants, robot-assisted surgeries, and the advent of personalized medicine. This groundbreaking approach tailor's treatment plans to individual patients, considering their unique genetic makeup and lifestyle factors, ushering in a new era of precision healthcare.

However, as AI's role in healthcare continues to expand, it is critical to ensure its deployment is carefully managed to maintain patient safety, privacy, and trust and to ensure that these tools are used to augment human healthcare professionals rather than replace them. The journey of AI in Healthcare is still ongoing, and its full potential is yet to be realised. But AI has made significant strides in transforming healthcare delivery and holds great promise for the future.[13]

---

[13] Fei Jiang et al., 'Artificial Intelligence in Healthcare: Past, Present and Future', *Stroke and Vascular Neurology* 2, no. 4 (21 June 2017): 230–43, https://doi.org/10.1136/svn-2017-000101.

AI's future in healthcare is exciting and promising, with potential advancements that could transform various aspects of the industry.

Personalised Medicine: AI is poised to play a central role in the evolution of personalised medicine. By analysing a patient's genetic profile, lifestyle, and environmental factors, AI could help healthcare providers customise treatments to everyone's unique circumstances. This level of personalisation can improve treatment effectiveness and reduce unwanted side effects.

Early Disease Detection and Prevention: By integrating and analysing a wealth of health data from numerous sources, including wearables and genomics, AI can help detect diseases early or even predict their onset before symptoms appear. This can significantly improve patient outcomes and reduce healthcare costs.

Robot-Assisted Surgery: AI-driven robotics is expected to play a more significant role in surgeries by assisting surgeons with better precision and potentially performing certain procedures independently. This can minimise human error and improve patient outcomes.

Virtual Health Assistants: AI-powered virtual health assistants could become a common tool for patient care, providing health advice, reminding patients to take their medication, and monitoring patients' health parameters in real time.

Healthcare Administration: AI is set to streamline administrative tasks, such as scheduling appointments, processing insurance claims, and managing patient records, which can save healthcare providers time and money.

Drug Discovery: AI can significantly accelerate drug discovery by predicting how drugs interact with various biological systems. This can drastically cut the time and cost of bringing new medications to market.

However, alongside these advancements, there will be ongoing challenges. Ensuring data privacy, mitigating algorithmic bias, maintaining the human touch in medicine, and dealing with regulatory and ethical considerations will require constant attention. Yet, with careful management and regulation, the future of AI in Healthcare holds enormous potential to improve patient care and outcomes, making healthcare more accurate, efficient, and personalised.

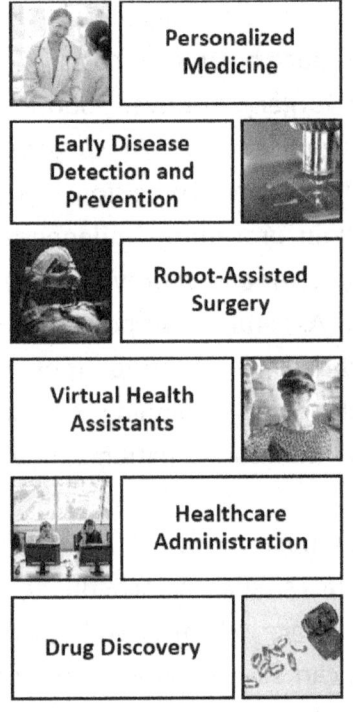

Figure 6. The Future of AI in Healthcare

As we delve into the realm of AI's transformative potential in healthcare, it becomes crucial to address the pivotal role legislators and regulators play. Public safety and trust gatekeepers are responsible for navigating the fine line between promoting innovation and ensuring ethical, safe, and fair practices. This section will illuminate the multifaceted roles of these key stakeholders, from protecting privacy and data, ensuring safety and efficacy, mitigating bias, and establishing liability and accountability standards. We will also discuss their role in fostering an environment conducive to innovation, underlining the importance of balance in regulation. In this complex dance of progress and precaution, legislators and regulators serve as the conductors, orchestrating a symphony that can redefine healthcare as we know it.

The role of legislators and regulators in the field of AI in Healthcare is of paramount importance. They are responsible for shaping policies, creating guidelines, and setting up regulations that ensure AI technologies' safe and ethical use while promoting innovation.[14] Some of the areas that need attention are as follows: -

1. Privacy and Data Protection: Legislators and regulators need to ensure that AI applications comply with existing data privacy laws and regulations, such as the Health Insurance Portability and Accountability Act (HIPAA) in the U.S. or the General Data Protection

---

[14] Sandeep Reddy et al., 'A Governance Model for the Application of AI in Health Care', *Journal of the American Medical Informatics Association* 27, no. 3 (1 March 2020): 491–97, https://doi.org/10.1093/jamia/ocz192.

Regulation (GDPR) in the European Union (EU). They may also need to update or create new laws to address unique challenges posed by AI, such as issues around data anonymisation and data sharing across borders.

2. Safety and Efficacy: Regulators like the U.S. Food and Drug Administration (FDA) are crucial in reviewing and approving AI-based medical devices and applications. They ensure these technologies are safe and effective before use in clinical practice.

3. Ethics and Bias: Guidelines need to be developed to prevent and address bias in AI algorithms, which can lead to unequal treatment or outcomes. This includes guidelines for diverse and representative data collection and transparency in AI decision-making processes.

4. Liability and Accountability: With AI, it may be difficult to determine responsibility when things go wrong. Legislators must clarify liability issues; for instance, who is responsible if an AI makes an incorrect diagnosis or treatment recommendation - the algorithm developer, the healthcare provider, or the AI itself?

5. Standards and Certification: Regulators should work on developing standards and certification processes for AI applications in healthcare to ensure their quality and reliability.

6. Encouraging Innovation: While regulation is important for safety and ethics, it is also essential that it does not stifle innovation. Legislators and regulators should work to create a regulatory environment that continues to encourage research and development in the field of AI.

Ultimately, the goal of legislators and regulators should be to create a balanced framework that safeguards patient safety, privacy, and rights, while also fostering an environment that encourages the growth and development of AI in Healthcare.

AI in healthcare holds immense potential to revolutionise the sector, offering significant improvements in personalised medicine, early disease detection, surgical assistance, patient care, administrative efficiency, and drug discovery. The transformative influence of AI in Healthcare is evident, yet this remarkable journey is still in its early stages, with the full potential yet to be uncovered.

However, this journey is challenging and calls for careful management and regulation. Key areas that require sustained attention include data privacy, algorithmic bias, maintaining the human touch in medicine, and addressing regulatory and ethical considerations. Policymakers and regulators in healthcare play a crucial role in advocating for patient safety and data privacy, yet with the creation of a conducive environment for the advancement and use of AI.

Legislators and regulators are tasked with carefully balancing the promotion of innovation with the assurance of ethical, safe, and fair practices. They should ensure that AI applications comply with existing data privacy laws, are safe and effective for clinical use, prevent and address algorithmic bias, clarify liability issues, develop standards and certification processes, and encourage innovation in AI.

While AI's role in healthcare expands, it is paramount that these tools are used to augment human healthcare professionals rather than replace them. They should serve as valuable allies, not substitutes, in delivering patient care. As we continue to navigate the path of AI in Healthcare, focusing on these guiding principles is essential to fully realise AI's benefits while ensuring patients' safety, privacy, and trust. The future of AI in Healthcare is bright, promising to usher in a new era of improved patient care and outcomes.

Chapter 3 AI in Clinical Practice

Welcome to the captivating realm where the realms of technology and medicine converge, forever altering the landscape of patient care. In this chapter, we embark on an enthralling exploration of AI's integration into clinical practice, witnessing a powerful fusion that redefines the very essence of healthcare. Through the unravelling of AI's evolution from science fiction to present-day reality, we witness its extraordinary strides in transforming the fabric of everyday healthcare delivery.

From diagnostics to prognosis, from decision support systems to personalised medicine, AI's influence permeates every nook of clinical practice. It even extends its reach to telemedicine, making healthcare accessible beyond the confines of brick-and-mortar establishments. Moreover, its role in surgical procedures and Rehabilitation signifies a new era of precision and efficiency.

However, adopting AI in clinical practice is challenging, and it is crucial to understand and address them for successful integration. This chapter aims to provide an insightful exploration of AI's role, its applications, and its potential impact on clinical practice. We will look at concrete examples, understand the underpinning technology, and discuss how it can be harnessed to its full potential. So, let us embark on this journey to understand how AI is reshaping the landscape of clinical practice by making healthcare more accurate, efficient, and personalised.

3.1 AI applications in Diagnostics and Prognostics

One of the most profound impacts of AI in clinical practice is in diagnostics and prognostics. Machine learning (ML) algorithms can now analyse medical images such as X-rays, CT and MRI scans with accuracy that matches or exceeds that of human professionals. The application of AI in diagnostics and prognostics has been gaining significant momentum in the healthcare field. Leveraging AI's ability to analyse enormous and complex data sets, these technologies can aid in the early detection of diseases, prediction of disease progression, and enhancement of patient outcomes.[15]

For example, Google's DeepMind has developed an AI system that can diagnose over 50 eye diseases with 94% accuracy by analysing retinal scans.[16] Similarly, the AI system developed by PathAI has shown promising results in diagnosing breast and prostate cancers from pathology slides.[17] By developing ML technology to assist pathologists in making more accurate diagnoses, their system can identify patterns in biopsy images that may be overlooked by the human eye, hence potentially leading to earlier and more precise diagnoses.

---

[15] Hang Qiu et al., 'Applications of Artificial Intelligence in Screening, Diagnosis, Treatment, and Prognosis of Colorectal Cancer', *Current Oncology* 29, no. 3 (March 2022): 1773–95, https://doi.org/10.3390/curroncol29030146.
[16] Jeffrey De Fauw et al., 'Clinically Applicable Deep Learning for Diagnosis and Referral in Retinal Disease', *Nature Medicine* 24, no. 9 (September 2018): 1342–50, https://doi.org/10.1038/s41591-018-0107-6.
[17] Kaustav Bera et al., 'Artificial Intelligence in Digital Pathology - New Tools for Diagnosis and Precision Oncology', *Nature Reviews. Clinical Oncology* 16, no. 11 (November 2019): 703–15, https://doi.org/10.1038/s41571-019-0252-y.

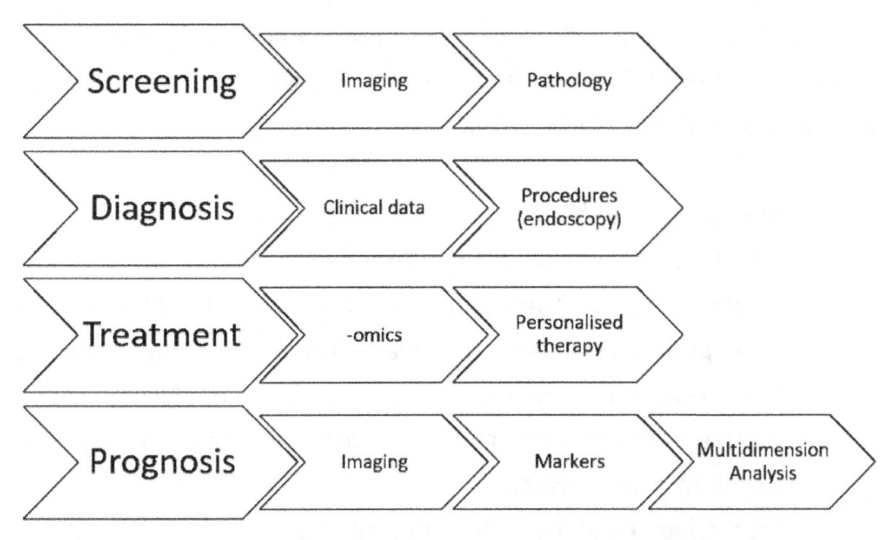

Screening	Imaging	Pathology	
Diagnosis	Clinical data	Procedures (endoscopy)	
Treatment	-omics	Personalised therapy	
Prognosis	Imaging	Markers	Multidimension Analysis

Figure 7. AI applications in diagnostics and prognostics

In the realm of prognostics, AI can predict disease progression and patient outcomes based on patterns in patient data. An example is a novel data-mining artificial intelligence method called Limitless-Arity Multiple-testing Procedure (LAMP) to identify combinations of clinical factors that predict heart failure (HF) onset in the general population. This quantitative AI method can stratify the probability of developing HF and identify the high-risk cohort for new-onset HF in the general population.[18]

Another promising application is the use of AI in predicting cancer progression. The role of AI and ML algorithms in precisely diagnosing solid and non-solid tumours and the prognosis of disease forecasted will improve cancer care and outcomes.[19]

Artificial Intelligence (AI), particularly ML and deep learning algorithms, have shown promising capabilities in handling complex

---

[18] Yohei Miyashita et al., 'Predicting Heart Failure Onset in the General Population Using a Novel Data-Mining Artificial Intelligence Method', *Scientific Reports* 13, no. 1 (16 March 2023): 4352, https://doi.org/10.1038/s41598-023-31600-0.

[19] Kritika Gaur and Miheer M Jagtap, 'Role of Artificial Intelligence and Machine Learning in Prediction, Diagnosis, and Prognosis of Cancer', *Cureus* 14, no. 11 (n.d.): e31008, https://doi.org/10.7759/cureus.31008.

and multi-dimensional data sets in healthcare. This is integral to accurately predicting patient survival and tracking disease progression.[20] It includes the following:

1. **Managing High-Dimensional Data**: AI algorithms are excellent at managing high-dimensional data - a common characteristic of healthcare data. This medium includes data from genomics, electronic health records (EHRs), imaging, and wearable devices. Integrating and analysing these diverse data sets can provide a more comprehensive view of a patient's health status.
2. **Predictive Analytics**: ML algorithms can be trained to predict patient outcomes based on historical data. These models can factor in numerous variables simultaneously, which enhances the accuracy of survival predictions. For instance, in cancer treatment, AI algorithms can predict survival rates by analysing tumour characteristics, treatment plans, patient demographics, and other relevant information.
3. **Identifying Disease Patterns**: Deep learning, a subset of AI, is particularly good at identifying patterns in complex data sets. For example, it can analyse medical imaging data to detect subtle changes that may indicate disease progression, even before symptoms become apparent. This capability is critical for conditions like cancer, neurodegenerative diseases, and heart diseases, where early intervention can significantly improve outcomes.
4. **Personalised Medicine**: AI can help create personalised treatment plans by considering a wide array of individual patient factors like genetic makeup, lifestyle habits, environmental factors, etc. This personalised approach can

---

[20] Ziad Obermayer and Ezekiel J. Emanuel, 'Predicting the Future — Big Data, Machine Learning, and Clinical Medicine', *New England Journal of Medicine* 375, no. 13 (29 September 2016): 1216–19, https://doi.org/10.1056/NEJMp1606181.

increase the effectiveness of treatments and improve patient survival and satisfaction rates.

5. **Real-time Monitoring and Prediction**: AI can create predictive models that estimate future health status and provide real-time insights into disease progression. By analysing data from wearable devices, AI can identify deviations from normal health parameters which signify potential health issues.
6. **Flexibility in Tracking Disease Progression**: AI models can be trained to be adaptable to changes in a patient's condition over time. This allows healthcare providers to adjust treatment strategies to ensure patient outcomes.
7. **Predictive Models**: AI can improve prognostic models by utilising multiple data sources to predict disease progression and survival rates. This can allow clinicians to determine the best treatment method and provide patients with a clearer understanding of their prognosis.

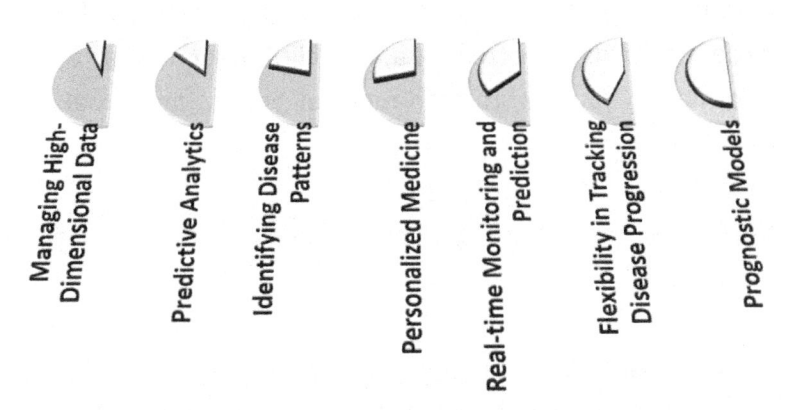

Figure 8. Steps in AI for predicting and prognostics.

Despite the promising prospects, it is crucial to remember that AI is a tool to assist healthcare providers and not replace them. Healthcare decisions should always involve human judgement while being guided by AI-generated insights. Additionally, ethical considerations, such as data privacy and algorithmic bias, require careful management as we implement AI in Healthcare.

While AI's potential in diagnostics and prognostics is enormous, it is important to note that these technologies are tools designed to support and not replace healthcare professionals. They can provide valuable insights but require careful implementation and monitoring to ensure data accuracy, reliability, and ethical use.

3.2 AI-driven Decision Support Systems (DSS)

AI-driven Decision Support Systems (DSS) are a revolutionary application of AI in Healthcare. These systems aim to support healthcare professionals in making robust clinical decisions by processing large amounts of data and providing evidence-based recommendations.

At the core of a DSS is a sophisticated AI algorithm capable of learning from and making sense of complex datasets. It can analyse patient records, research data, and clinical guidelines, among other information sources, to help medical professionals make informed decisions.[21]

Here are the steps generally involved in AI-driven DSS in Healthcare:

1. **Data Collection**: This is the process's first and most crucial step. Relevant patient data is collected from various sources, such as EHRs, medical imaging databases,

---

[21] Ploypun Narindrarangkura, Min Soon Kim, and Suzanne A. Boren, 'A Scoping Review of Artificial Intelligence Algorithms in Clinical Decision Support Systems for Internal Medicine Subspecialties', *ACI Open* 05, no. 2 (July 2021): e67–79, https://doi.org/10.1055/s-0041-1735470.

laboratory results, genomic data, patient-reported information, and wearable device data.
2. **Data Pre-processing**: The collected data needs to be cleaned, normalised, and standardised for AI algorithms. This step may involve handling missing values, removing inconsistencies or outliers, and transforming data into a format suitable for AI processing.
3. **Feature Selection and Extraction**: In this step, relevant features (variables) are identified from the data that will be useful for decision-making. For example, for a DSS predicting heart disease, relevant features may include age, sex, blood pressure, cholesterol levels, etc.
4. **Model Training**: This is where the AI algorithm is taught to identify patterns in the data. Having studied hard, the algorithm learns to make predictions or decisions based on the input data. The model is trained using some of the collected data, with the remaining data saved for testing the model.
5. **Model Testing and Validation**: After the model has been trained, it is tested on the remaining data to assess its accuracy, sensitivity, specificity, and other performance metrics. The goal is to ensure the model generalises well to new data and makes accurate predictions.
6. **Integration into Healthcare Workflow**: If the model is accurate and reliable, it can be integrated into the healthcare workflow. This may involve creating a user interface for healthcare providers to interact with the model, combining the model with EHR systems, or creating protocols for how and when the model's predictions should be used in decision-making.
7. **Continuous Monitoring and Updating**: Once the AI-driven DSS is in use, it is important to monitor its performance and update the model as needed continuously. This may involve retraining the model with new data, tweaking the algorithm

based on feedback from healthcare providers or making other adjustments to improve its relevance, usefulness and accuracy.

8. **Evaluation of Clinical Outcomes**: Finally, the impact of the AI-driven DSS on patient care and clinical outcomes should be evaluated. This can help refine the system and prove its efficacy and safety for broader adoption.

It is important to note that AI-driven DSS should always comply with relevant legal and ethical guidelines, including data privacy regulations and algorithmic fairness and transparency guidelines. Additionally, such systems should be designed to support and enhance healthcare professionals' decision-making rather than replace them. They are tools that can provide valuable insights, but trained healthcare professionals should always make the final clinical decisions.

Figure 9. Steps in AI Decision Support Systems

A Decision Support System (DSS), a computer-based system, is designed to assist healthcare professionals in making decisions. It uses data, analytical models, and user-friendly software to support decision-making. Here is a general description of how a DSS works:

1. **Data Input**: A DSS receives input from various sources. Healthcare can include patient health records, clinical guidelines, research databases, diagnostic images, laboratory test results, and other relevant information.
2. **Data Processing**: Once the data is input into the system, the DSS processes it using various algorithms. These algorithms may be based on statistical models, machine learning, or AI. They analyse the data and extract relevant information for decision-making.
3. **Decision-Making Model**: The DSS uses a decision-making model to interpret the processed data and make recommendations. This model is based on a set of rules or criteria that guide how decisions should be made. For instance, in healthcare, the model can use established medical guidelines to recommend a specific treatment plan based on the patient's data.
4. **Output**: The DSS presents its recommendations to the user in an understandable format. This can be a suggested course of action, a list of treatment options ranked by likely effectiveness, or a prediction of patient outcomes based on different treatment decisions. The output is designed to provide clear and actionable insights for users to apply in decision-making.
5. **User Interaction**: The user interacts with the DSS, reviewing the system's recommendations, providing additional inputs, or adjusting the decision-making model as needed. The goal is to support the user in making the best possible decision based on all available information.
6. **Feedback Loop**: After the user has decided and the outcomes are observed, this information can be fed back into the DSS to improve its accuracy and effectiveness over

time. This feedback loop allows the system to learn from past decisions and improve its decision-making models.

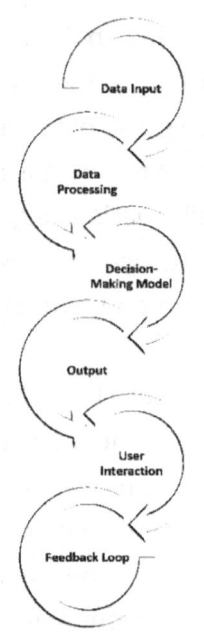

Figure 10. DSS process

One notable example of AI-driven DSS is IBM's Watson for Oncology. This AI-powered system aids oncologists in providing personalised cancer treatment. Watson for Oncology uses natural language processing to understand the medical literature, stays updated with the latest research, and learns from each patient's unique medical information. It then provides treatment options based on its analysis, thereby assisting oncologists in choosing an appropriate course of action.[22]

Another example is Google's AI for predicting patient outcomes, which can forecast a patient's length of stay and time of discharge,

---

[22] S. P. Somashekhar et al., 'Watson for Oncology and Breast Cancer Treatment Recommendations: Agreement with an Expert Multidisciplinary Tumor Board', *Annals of Oncology: Official Journal of the European Society for Medical Oncology* 29, no. 2 (1 February 2018): 418–23, https://doi.org/10.1093/annonc/mdx781.

among other things. This tool can aid healthcare providers in managing resources more effectively and improving patient care.[23]

The potential of AI-driven DSS in Healthcare is immense. However, while these systems can assist in decision-making, they are meant to supplement the judgement of healthcare professionals. Instead, they are tools that can provide insightful input to augment the decision-making capabilities of healthcare providers and allow them to deliver more personalised and effective care.

Still, AI-driven DSS come with their own set of challenges. Data privacy, transparency in how recommendations are made, and integration with existing healthcare systems must be addressed for their successful deployment. In a case study on the safety assurance of an AI-based clinical decision support system for sepsis treatment, the authors identified four hazardous clinical management in sepsis resuscitation, such as giving no fluids and no vasopressors to a patient with low blood pressure, which was unsafe, to limit the action space of the AI agent to reduce the likelihood of hazardous decisions. They demonstrated that the AI recommended fewer dangerous decisions than human clinicians in three predefined clinical scenarios. At the same time, the difference was not statistically significant in the fourth scenario. The retrained model shows enhanced safety without negatively impacting model performance.[24] As AI continues to evolve and permeate the healthcare industry, healthcare professionals must stay informed about these technologies and their implications.

---

[23] Alvin Rajkumar et al., 'Scalable and Accurate Deep Learning with Electronic Health Records', *Npj Digital Medicine* 1, no. 1 (8 May 2018): 1–10, https://doi.org/10.1038/s41746-018-0029-1.

[24] Paul Festor et al., 'Assuring the Safety of AI-Based Clinical Decision Support Systems: A Case Study of the AI Clinician for Sepsis Treatment', *BMJ Health & Care Informatics* 29, no. 1 (1 July 2022): e100549, https://doi.org/10.1136/bmjhci-2022-100549.

3.3 Personalised Medicine and AI

Personalised medicine, or precision medicine, is a medical model that proposes the customisation of healthcare, with all decisions and treatments tailored to individual patients. It emphasises the use of genetic and other biomarkers to customise treatment. Artificial Intelligence (AI) is vital in making personalised medicine a reality.[25]

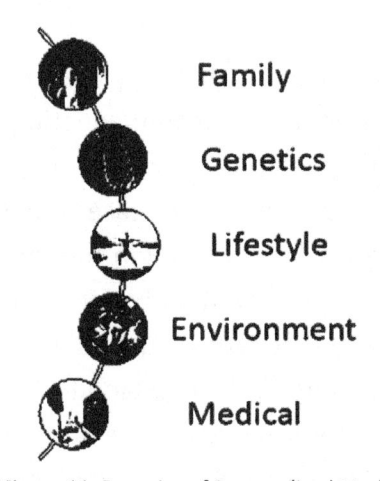

Figure 11. Domains of Personalised Medicine

AI's ability to analyse and interpret colossal amounts of data is crucial in personalised medicine. For instance, genomic data, which is often huge and complex, can be analysed more efficiently using AI. This analysis can help identify genetic markers linked to certain diseases, thus enabling early detection or prevention through tailored health plans.[26]

---

[25] Nicholas J Schork, 'Artificial Intelligence and Personalized Medicine', *Cancer Treatment and Research* 178 (1 January 2019): 265–83, https://doi.org/10.1007/978-3-030-16391-4_11.

[26] Mubashir Hassan et al., 'Innovations in Genomics and Big Data Analytics for Personalized Medicine and Health Care: A Review', *International Journal of Molecular Sciences* 23, no. 9 (January 2022): 4645, https://doi.org/10.3390/ijms23094645.

Furthermore, AI can aid in designing personalised treatment plans in oncology by analysing a patient's medical records and providing personalised treatment options based on the latest medical research.[27]

In drug discovery and development, AI can significantly reduce time and cost by predicting how different drugs may interact with an individual's unique genetic makeup. This can lead to custom-designed personalised drug therapies for effective and safer personalised treatments.[28]

AI's role in personalised medicine also extends to patient engagement and care. AI-driven applications and platforms can deliver personalised health advice, remind patients to take medications, monitor their symptoms and vital signs, and provide individualised feedback. A case study of a cross-platform mobile application for patients includes a macronutrient detection algorithm for meal recognition and a nudge-inspired meal logger. The web-based application allows the clinician to support a patient self-management regime. This platform incorporates behavioural intervention techniques from nudge theory to support and encourage a sustained change in a patient's lifestyle.[29]

However, while AI has the potential to revolutionise personalised medicine, it comes with several challenges. These include data privacy concerns, the need for diverse and representative data to avoid bias in personalised treatment, and regulatory issues related to the use of AI in Healthcare.

---

[27] Somashekhar et al., 'Watson for Oncology and Breast Cancer Treatment Recommendations'.
[28] Alex Zhavoronkov et al., 'Deep Learning Enables Rapid Identification of Potent DDR1 Kinase Inhibitors', Nature Biotechnology 37, no. 9 (September 2019): 1038–40, https://doi.org/10.1038/s41587-019-0224-x.
[29] Shane Joachim et al., 'A Nudge-Inspired AI-Driven Health Platform for Self-Management of Diabetes', Sensors 22, no. 12 (January 2022): 4620, https://doi.org/10.3390/s22124620.

As it continues to evolve and integrate into healthcare, its potential to enhance personalised medicine becomes increasingly evident. It promises a future where treatment is customised to the individual patient, leading to more effective interventions and improved health outcomes.

3.4 Telemedicine and remote patient monitoring

These are two interconnected areas where Artificial Intelligence (AI) is making significant advancements, revolutionising the delivery of healthcare services, and enabling patient care beyond traditional clinical settings.

They are part of the broad field of Telehealth that involves using digital information and communication technologies to access healthcare services remotely and manage health. These technologies facilitate many healthcare functions, such as diagnosis, treatment, patient education, health advice, and patient monitoring.

Here are some common components of a telehealth system:

1. **Live Video Conferencing (Synchronous Telehealth)**: This involves using live, two-way interaction between a person (patient, caregiver, or provider) and a provider using audio-visual technology. This is often used for patient consultations and certain types of physical examinations.
2. **Store-and-Forward (Asynchronous Telehealth)**: This involves the transmission of recorded health information (like medical images, bio-signals etc.) through a secure electronic communications system to a practitioner, usually a specialist, who uses the data to evaluate the case or render a service outside of real-time or live interaction.

3. **Remote Patient Monitoring (RPM)** includes using connected electronic tools to record personal health and medical data in one location that can be transmitted securely to a provider in a different area for assessment and recommendations. These tools can include wearables that capture and share vital signs, glucometers for diabetic patients or other devices to monitor patients with chronic illnesses.
4. **Mobile Health (mHealth):** This involves healthcare and public health practice and education supported by mobile communication devices such as smartphones, tablets, and wearable devices. mHealth can use mobile applications (apps) for various purposes, including disease tracking, medication reminders, patient education, and teleconsultations.
5. **Tele-pharmacy:** This enables pharmacists to provide pharmaceutical care and services remotely, including medication therapy management, medication adherence monitoring, prescription verification and dispensing, patient counselling, and other pharmaceutical care services.
6. **EHR (Electronic Health Records):** These digital versions of a patient's medical history are often critical to telehealth systems. They allow healthcare providers to securely access and share patient data to facilitate better coordinated and more effective care.
7. **Patient Portal:** This secure online website gives patients 24-hour access to their health information. Patients can use it to schedule appointments, view their health records, renew prescriptions, and communicate with healthcare providers.
8. **Security and Compliance Tools:** Ensuring the security and privacy of patient data is a critical aspect of Telehealth. Tools to protect data security, maintain system integrity, and ensure compliance with laws, such as the Health

Insurance Portability and Accountability Act (HIPAA) in the U.S., are vital components of a telehealth system.

Telehealth has the potential to make healthcare more accessible and efficient, especially for individuals in remote areas or those who have difficulty travelling to a healthcare provider. However, successfully implementing Telehealth involves addressing challenges like ensuring data privacy, mitigating cyber threats, and managing regulatory and licensure requirements.

Figure 12. Components of Telehealth

Telemedicine refers to providing healthcare services remotely, allowing patients and healthcare professionals to connect through digital platforms. AI plays a crucial role in enhancing telemedicine by facilitating accurate and efficient remote diagnoses, treatment recommendations, and monitoring of patients.

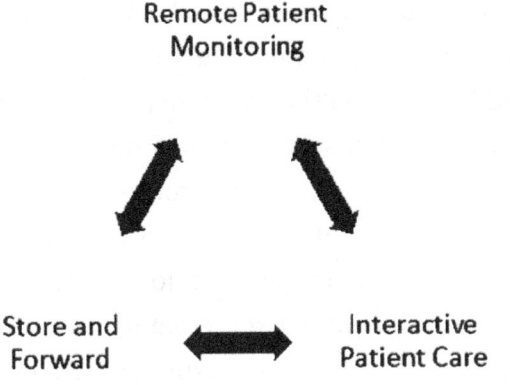

Figure 13. Components of telemedicine

AI-powered algorithms can analyse patient symptoms with their medical history and use data from connected devices to assist healthcare providers in making remote diagnoses. Healthcare providers and policymakers can use this approach to effectively implement telemedicine screening using digital technology, improving access to healthcare and reducing healthcare costs.[30] For example, AI-powered chatbot applications can engage patients in conversations, asking relevant questions and providing preliminary assessments and guidance based on the symptoms reported, as shown in a case study for hypertension. A text-based remote hypertension management program implemented a prototype chatbot to alleviate the messaging burden on clinicians. The study found that the chatbot accurately triaged 99% of patient messages, successfully addressing 1,379 out of 1,393 messages. Furthermore, most of the letters (approximately 75%) did not require escalation to a clinician, indicating the chatbot's effectiveness in handling patient inquiries independently.[31]

---

[30] Zhen Ling Teo and Daniel Shu Wei Ting, 'AI Telemedicine Screening in Ophthalmology: Health Economic Considerations', *The Lancet Global Health* 11, no. 3 (1 March 2023): e318–20, https://doi.org/10.1016/S2214-109X(23)00037-2.
[31] Natalie S. Lee et al., 'Developing a Chatbot–Clinician Model for Hypertension Management', *NEJM Catalyst* 3, no. 11 (19 October 2022): CAT.22.0228, https://doi.org/10.1056/CAT.22.0228.

Remote patient monitoring, enabled by AI, allows healthcare providers to monitor patients' health conditions in real-time outside of traditional healthcare settings. Wearable sensors can collect and transmit data, such as heart rate, blood pressure, blood glucose, and activity levels, to AI algorithms. These systems can then analyse the data and provide alerts or notifications to healthcare professionals in case of abnormal patterns or potential health risks. Pedro et al. discussed creating and utilising two rule-based chatbots in health telemonitoring settings. The chatbots were developed to aid in data collection and guide patients and those with inadequate coagulation after cardiothoracic surgery. They were designed to be user-friendly, adaptable, and directed by human input. The chatbots facilitated the collection of surgical wound photos, coagulation profiles with International Normalised Ratio (INR) values, and related questions from patients using a coagulometer. The collected data was accessible to the clinical team through a web application, which allowed them to analyse the information and interact with patients. The chatbots enhanced patient safety perception and engagement with their health status.[32]

The integration of AI in telemedicine and remote patient monitoring offers several benefits. It improves access to healthcare services, particularly for remote or underserved individuals with limited access to medical facilities. AI algorithms can quickly process large volumes of patient data, providing more accurate and timely assessments and recommendations. This can result in early detection of health issues, proactive interventions, and better management of chronic conditions.

For example, in the VESTA study (NCT04758429), AI was used to monitor heart failure (HF) through wearable and implantable devices that collect data on parameters such as heart rate, blood

---

[32] Pedro Dias et al., 'Remote Patient Monitoring Systems Based on Conversational Agents for Health Data Collection', 2021, https://doi.org/10.5220/0011011000003123.

pressure, and oxygen saturation. This data is then analysed using machine learning (ML) algorithms to create accurate prediction models for early detection of heart failure events. This is an example of a study validating an ML algorithm for the early detection of HF events via multi-parametric sensor data. AI/ML algorithms can help improve the workflow and outcomes of patients with HF, especially time series data collected via remote monitoring.[33]

In conclusion, integrating AI in telemedicine and remote patient monitoring opens up new frontiers in healthcare. It enhances accessibility, accuracy, and efficiency of care by allowing healthcare professionals to monitor and manage patients' health conditions remotely. As AI technology continues to evolve, it holds the potential to transform healthcare delivery and improve patient outcomes by bringing healthcare closer to individuals in the comfort of their homes.

3.5 AI in surgical procedures and Rehabilitation

AI is revolutionising surgical procedures and Rehabilitation by enhancing precision, efficiency, and patient outcomes. From assisting surgeons during complex surgeries to personalised rehabilitation plans, AI technologies are transforming the landscape of healthcare in these domains.

In surgical procedures, AI is used to augment surgeons' skills, improving surgical precision and reducing risks. A systematic review showed that AI-assisted surgery is safer and more efficient, with minimal or no complications compared to conventional surgery. A study found significant differences in operating time, docking time,

---

[33] Nitesh Gautam et al., 'Artificial Intelligence, Wearables and Remote Monitoring for Heart Failure: Current and Future Applications', *Diagnostics* 12, no. 12 (December 2022): 2964, https://doi.org/10.3390/diagnostics12122964.

staging time, and estimated blood loss but no significant difference in length of hospital stay, recovery time, and lymph nodes harvested. The practical implications of this paper are that AI-assisted surgery can improve patient outcomes and reduce the risk of complications.[34]

The da Vinci Surgical System is a prime example of AI-assisted surgery. This robotic system incorporates AI algorithms, allowing surgeons to perform minimally invasive procedures with enhanced agility and visualisation. The system translates the surgeon's movements into precise automatic actions that reduce the invasiveness of surgeries, minimise scarring, and promote faster recovery times. In a paper on the use of AI in colorectal cancer, the authors discussed how computer-aided detection systems can improve the polyp and adenoma detection rate, as well as how machine learning and bioinformatics analysis can help screen and identify more cancer biomarkers along with improving the readability of medical images. They showed how robotic surgery systems can be used to treat patients with colorectal cancer and how AI can be used in neoadjuvant chemoradiotherapy to improve treatment and efficacy evaluation.[35]

Furthermore, AI algorithms can analyse medical images, such as CT or MRI scans, to assist in surgical planning and guidance.[36] It can support brain tumour surgery by assisting surgeons in real-time decision-making, such as identifying tumour boundaries and avoiding critical structures. AI can also help monitor the patient's

---

[34] Ephraim Nwoye et al., 'Artificial Intelligence for Emerging Technology in Surgery: Systematic Review and Validation', *IEEE Reviews in Biomedical Engineering* 16 (2023): 241–59, https://doi.org/10.1109/RBME.2022.3183852.
[35] Zugang Yin et al., 'Application of Artificial Intelligence in Diagnosis and Treatment of Colorectal Cancer: A Novel Prospect', *Frontiers in Medicine* 10 (8 March 2023): 1128084, https://doi.org/10.3389/fmed.2023.1128084.
[36] Brian Fiani et al., 'Current Uses, Emerging Applications, and Clinical Integration of Artificial Intelligence in Neuroradiology', *Reviews in the Neurosciences* 33, no. 4 (27 June 2022): 383–95, https://doi.org/10.1515/revneuro-2021-0101.

vital signs and detect potential complications during the operation. This can result in safer and more effective surgeries.[37]

AI plays a transformative role in rehabilitation medicine by revolutionising how patients recover from injuries, disabilities, and neurological conditions. By leveraging AI technologies, rehabilitation medicine is becoming more personalised, precise, and effective.

One area where AI is making significant advancements is in the development of intelligent rehabilitation devices, including biomedical materials. The potential of 4D printing involves pre-programming smart materials to manufacture structures that dynamically respond to external stimuli. This technology can address some drawbacks of traditional 3D printing, such as inert materials and a possible mismatch between the printed part and the target surface. The emergence of AI can push these technologies forward, allowing for the selection of promising smart materials with desired architecture, properties, and functions. Time to manufacturing is expected to reduce and enable in-situ printing on target surfaces directly to achieve high-fidelity of human body micro-structures. 4D printing is a tool for designing advanced smart materials, and recent progress in AI-empowered 3D and 4D printing allows for a progressive future technique. The potential of 4D printing and AI in the biomedical sector for tissue and organ fabrication, patient-specific orthoses, drug delivery, and surgical planning provides a roadmap for future research.[38]

---

[37] Simon Williams et al., 'Artificial Intelligence in Brain Tumour Surgery—An Emerging Paradigm', *Cancers* 13, no. 19 (7 October 2021): 5010, https://doi.org/10.3390/cancers13195010.

[38] Raffaele Pugliese and Stefano Regondi, 'Artificial Intelligence-Empowered 3D and 4D Printing Technologies toward Smarter Biomedical Materials and Approaches', *Polymers* 14, no. 14 (January 2022): 2794, https://doi.org/10.3390/polym14142794.

These devices, such as exoskeletons and prosthetics, utilise AI algorithms to interpret signals from the user's muscles or brain and translate them into movements. Design, actuation, and control of robotic joints in prostheses and exoskeletons are crucial for optimal function. The significance of replicating the natural functioning of human joints in bionics requires the development of lightweight and efficient prosthetics and exoskeletons. Furthermore, employing compliant actuators that can adapt to the specific dynamics of robotic joints is important to enabling the prosthetics and exoskeletons which possess improved task adaptability across different movement conditions. There is a need for accurate joint motion detection and human intention recognition to achieve effective common control. By integrating these capabilities, prosthetics and exoskeletons can closely align with human motion intentions, thus resulting in more efficient and responsive devices.[39] This enables individuals with limb impairments to regain mobility and independence. AI-powered devices can adapt to the individual's needs, providing customised support and enhancing motor control.

Moreover, AI algorithms are utilised to create personalised rehabilitation programs tailored to each patient's needs. These algorithms can analyse vast amounts of patient data, including medical history, functional capabilities, and response to therapy, to design individualised treatment plans. This will allow for a more targeted and efficient rehabilitation process which optimises patient outcomes.[40]

---

[39] Yuanxi Sun, Long Bai, and Dianbiao Dong, 'Editorial: Lighter and More Efficient Robotic Joints in Prostheses and Exoskeletons: Design, Actuation and Control', *Frontiers in Robotics and AI* 10 (7 March 2023): 1063712, https://doi.org/10.3389/frobt.2023.1063712.

[40] Yuexing Gu et al., 'A Review of Hand Function Rehabilitation Systems Based on Hand Motion Recognition Devices and Artificial Intelligence', *Brain Sciences* 12, no. 8 (August 2022): 1079, https://doi.org/10.3390/brainsci12081079.

AI-powered motion-tracking systems and virtual reality (VR) technology are also transforming Rehabilitation. These technologies monitor and analyse patients' movements and responses during therapy sessions. AI algorithms can assess the patient's performance, provide real-time feedback, and adapt the therapy to maximise effectiveness. Combined with AI, VR simulations create immersive and interactive environments that increase patient engagement and motivation during rehabilitative exercises.[41]

Additionally, AI is being utilised to develop intelligent assessment tools for evaluating patients' progress and functional outcomes. These tools can analyse data from wearable sensors or motion-capture systems to objectively measure a patient's movement quality, strength, balance, and coordination.[42] AI algorithms can then provide reports to clinicians, assisting them in monitoring progress and adjusting treatment plans accordingly. There are emerging intelligent rehabilitation techniques that provide objective and accurate functional assessment for patients who suffered a stroke to promote the improvement of clinical guidelines for treatment. The methods include brain-computer interfaces, virtual reality, neural circuit-magnetic stimulation, and robot-assisted therapy. They can encourage the development of motor function rehabilitation in terms of informatisation, standardisation, and intelligence.[43]

AI transforms rehabilitation medicine by enabling personalised treatment plans, developing intelligent rehabilitation devices, and

---

[41] Kate E. Laver et al., 'Virtual Reality for Stroke Rehabilitation', *The Cochrane Database of Systematic Reviews* 11, no. 11 (20 November 2017): CD008349, https://doi.org/10.1002/14651858.CD008349.pub4.

[42] Hélène De Cannière et al., 'Wearable Monitoring and Interpretable Machine Learning Can Objectively Track Progression in Patients during Cardiac Rehabilitation', *Sensors (Basel, Switzerland)* 20, no. 12 (26 June 2020): 3601, https://doi.org/10.3390/s20123601. De Cannière et al.

[43] Cong-Cong Huo et al., 'Prospects for Intelligent Rehabilitation Techniques to Treat Motor Dysfunction', *Neural Regeneration Research* 16, no. 2 (24 August 2020): 264–69, https://doi.org/10.4103/1673-5374.290884.

enhancing patient engagement. Its integration into rehabilitation practice has the potential to optimise therapy outcomes, improve patient experiences, and revolutionise the field of rehabilitation medicine.

However, while AI brings promising advancements to surgical procedures and rehabilitation, addressing concerns such as data security, algorithmic bias, and regulatory oversight is essential. Safety, transparency, and ethical considerations remain critical as AI shapes these fields.

AI's integration into surgical procedures and rehabilitation is transforming the healthcare landscape. Surgeons benefit from AI-assisted precision, while patients experience improved outcomes and personalised rehabilitation plans. As technology advances and ethical guidelines evolve, the future holds great promise for AI in optimising surgical interventions and empowering individuals on their journey towards recovery.

Chapter 4 AI in Healthcare Education and Teaching

The advent of artificial intelligence has had a profound impact on healthcare education and teaching. The traditional model of medical education, often constrained by physical boundaries and rigid curricula, is being disrupted by the application of AI, which ushered in an era of personalised, adaptive, and accessible learning. Healthcare curricula should focus on knowledge management, effective use of AI, improved communication, and empathy cultivation. Integrating basic medical information with the teaching of probability (confidence rating of diagnostic and therapeutic recommendations), communication, and empathetic skills can capitalise on AI. There is a need to overhaul their curricula to prepare future healthcare professionals for AI's increasing role in healthcare and equip them with the necessary skills to manage information overload and communicate effectively with patients.[44]

In the digital transformation of health professional education, several core elements are integral to its successful implementation. Firstly, the learner lies at the heart of this transformation. Each learner may be represented by a 'Digital Twin'—a virtual representation that mirrors the learner's knowledge, skills, and learning progress. This Digital Twin concept allows for individualised tracking of learning trajectories, thereby enabling tailored instruction and feedback.

Subject matter experts (SMEs), often faculty members, play an invaluable role in this digital education landscape. Their deep understanding of the content ensures that the information

---

[44] Steven A. Wartman and C. Donald Combs, 'Reimagining Medical Education in the Age of AI', *AMA Journal of Ethics* 21, no. 2 (1 February 2019): 146–52, https://doi.org/10.1001/amajethics.2019.146.

delivered is accurate, up-to-date, and contextually relevant. Furthermore, their pedagogical expertise guides the development and implementation effective digital learning strategies.

Next, the role of the teacher in a digital learning environment undergoes a significant transformation. While they continue to guide and facilitate learning, their role becomes more of a mentor or coach, supporting learners as they navigate their personalised learning paths. Teachers also play a key role in humanising the digital learning experience by fostering community and engagement among learners.

Finally, the digital interfaces that serve as the platform for this transformation are crucial. These interfaces, ranging from learning management systems to AI-powered tutoring platforms, must be user-friendly, accessible, and engaging. They should support a wide range of learning activities, provide insightful analytics, and ensure the privacy and security of learners' data.

Each of these core elements uniquely creates a digital learning environment that is personalised, engaging, and effective for health professional education.

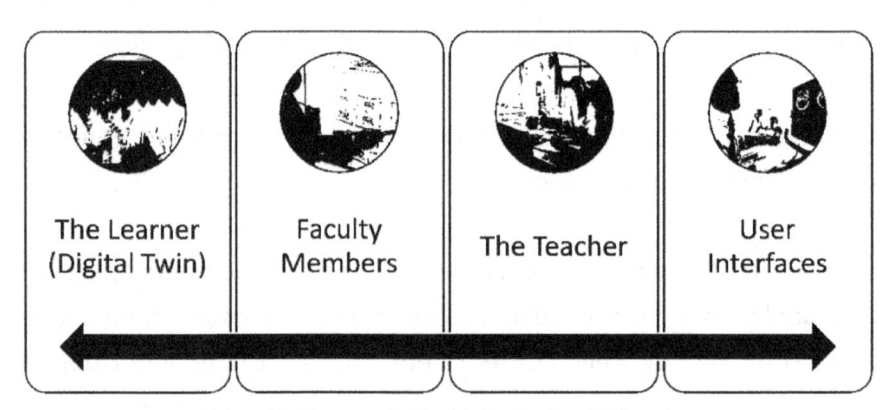

Figure 14. Elements in Health Professional Education

AI's transformative potential is evident in the sphere of simulation-based medical education. With virtual reality and AI-powered simulation tools, learners can practise complex procedures in a risk-free environment. For example, Touch Surgery, an AI-driven mobile surgical simulator, allows medical students and professionals to practice surgical procedures in a safe virtual environment, improving their proficiency and readiness for real-world situations.[45]

AI also has a pivotal role in creating personalised learning platforms. By analysing a learner's progress, these platforms can adapt in real-time to meet the learner's needs, therefore ensuring a more efficient and effective learning experience via customised learning paths. In a commentary, Mese posited that AI-driven content curation enhances radiology education by efficiently compiling and presenting up-to-date and pertinent learning resources. This streamlines resource development, enabling educators to concentrate on teaching and mentoring. AI analytics can track learner performance and identify areas needing further support. Mese highlighted the practical implications of AI, which can greatly enhance radiology education's efficiency and effectiveness, particularly in remote learning during the pandemic.[46] However, the primary use of AI in medical education was for learning support, mainly due to its ability to provide individualised feedback. Due to the lack of digitalisation and the sensitive nature of examinations, little emphasis was placed on curriculum review and Assessment of students' learning. Big data manipulation also warrants the need to ensure data integrity. Methodological improvements are required to increase AI adoption by addressing the technical difficulties of creating an AI application and using novel methods to assess the effectiveness of AI. To better integrate

---

[45] Medhat Alaker, Greg R. Wynn, and Tan Arulampalam, 'Virtual Reality Training in Laparoscopic Surgery: A Systematic Review & Meta-Analysis', *International Journal of Surgery* 29 (1 May 2016): 85–94, https://doi.org/10.1016/j.ijsu.2016.03.034.

[46] Ismail Mese, 'The Impact of Artificial Intelligence on Radiology Education in the Wake of Coronavirus Disease 2019', *Korean Journal of Radiology* 24, no. 5 (1 May 2023): 478–79, https://doi.org/10.3348/kjr.2023.0278.

AI into the medical profession, measures should be taken to introduce AI into the medical school curriculum for medical professionals to understand AI algorithms better and maximise its use.[47]

Additionally, AI is facilitating a new dimension in curriculum design. It can help assess students' needs and learning patterns, leading to more effective curriculum planning. AI can identify gaps in a student's understanding and recommend specific topics for study, thus facilitating a more comprehensive and balanced learning experience.

4.1 AI Use in healthcare education

Several key components play integral roles in enhancing the learning experience. *Automating administrative tasks* significantly increase efficiency, leaving educators more time to focus on the core aspects of teaching and learning. This includes formative evaluation, a continuous assessment method that monitors student learning to provide ongoing feedback. A major benefit of this digital transformation is the ability to perform automatic grading, which reduces the workload for educators and provides timely feedback to learners.

Another essential component is *smart content*, which is dynamic and adapts based on a learner's behaviour. This results in a more relevant and personalised learning experience, with the content adjusting to meet each student's unique needs and learning styles. This adaptive learning environment provides a personalised path through the material, helping students master the content more effectively.

---

[47] Kai Siang Chan and Nabil Zary, 'Applications and Challenges of Implementing Artificial Intelligence in Medical Education: Integrative Review', *JMIR Medical Education* 5, no. 1 (14 June 2019): e13930, https://doi.org/10.2196/13930.

The *Intelligent Tutoring System (ITS)* is a critical feature of this digital learning landscape. Utilising Natural Language Processing (NLP) and intelligent algorithms, the ITS provides customised, immediate, and automated instruction and feedback. This mimics the interaction between a student and a tutor, which allows for immediate correction of misconceptions and reinforcement of accurate understanding. In this system, the roles of the student, tutor, and subject matter expert are intricately intertwined, creating a personal and interactive learning environment.

These key components work together to create an ideal learning environment that is efficient and engaging and personalised to each learner's unique needs and learning styles. Through the automation of administrative tasks, the provision of smart content, and the implementation of an Intelligent Tutoring System, digital transformation is redefining health professional education.

The role of big data in healthcare education is multi-faceted, transforming how learners, teachers, course developers, and administrators approach their respective responsibilities.
Big data can provide unique insights for learners to identify and predict their learning status. Algorithms analyse student engagement, performance data, and learning styles to tailor personalised learning pathways. Big data also plays a role in recommending specific learning resources and activities which enable students to optimise their study time. Moreover, gathering and analysing data from multiple learners can enhance shared learning experiences and lead to collaborative problem-solving and peer learning.

Teachers, on the other hand, can benefit immensely from the feedback provided by big data. By examining learners' learning and behaviour patterns, they can identify those who require additional support, fostering a more inclusive and individualised learning environment. Furthermore, data analysis can pinpoint common errors, allowing educators to focus on improving the effectiveness of specific activities or areas of instruction.

Course developers can utilise big data to evaluate the structure of their courses and their impact on learning. This includes assessing the effectiveness of course materials and using data mining techniques to identify patterns and trends that can guide the development of new learning modules.

Administrators often tasked with organising resources and overseeing educational programs can also greatly benefit from big data. Analysing data on course enrolments, student performance, and teacher effectiveness can inform decisions about resource allocation, curriculum design, and teacher development programs. Furthermore, as big data can provide administrators with the tools to assess the effectiveness of both teachers and curricula, these institutions can continue delivering high-quality education.

In essence, big data brings a transformative potential to healthcare education, driving personalised learning experiences, informed instructional strategies, effective course development, and efficient administration.

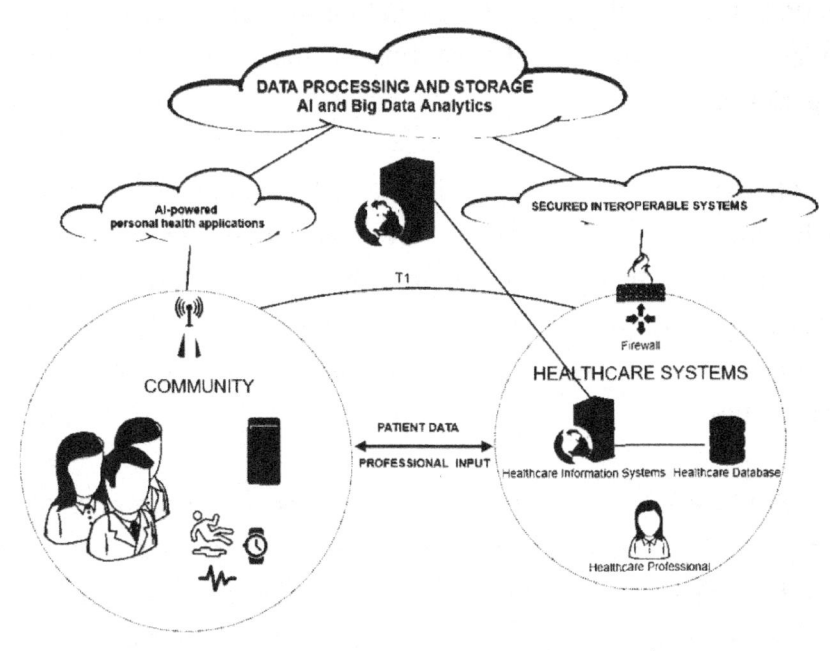

Figure 15. Digital Health and AI in Health Professional Education

There is a gradual shift in how technology is integrated, impacting the learning process in health professional education. Its progression can be viewed through the Substitution, Augmentation, Modification, and Redefinition (SAMR) model.

Substitution represents the first level, where technology replaces traditional methods with no significant functional change. For instance, a digital textbook replaces a printed one, but the learning process remains unchanged.

At the **Augmentation** level, technology still substitutes traditional methods but provides functional improvements. An example is an interactive e-book that enhances the reading experience with embedded links, multimedia, or interactive quizzes.

The **Modification** level involves a substantial transformation of the task due to technology. For instance, collaborative document editing allows students to work together in real-time, encouraging cooperative learning and fostering a more dynamic learning experience.

Redefinition, the highest level in the SAMR model, involves using technology to create entirely new tasks that were previously inconceivable. An example can be global collaboration projects, where students from different countries can work together on a common project, interacting and learning from each other's cultural perspectives.

This SAMR model presents a framework for educators to analyse and plan their technology integration into the learning process. The goal is to progress towards Redefinition, where technology is not just an add-on but transforms and enriches the learning experience. The role of faculty in healthcare education is multifaceted, extending far beyond traditional lecture-based instruction. Today, they are deeply involved in several areas that enhance the learning experience.

Curriculum design is key to the faculty's role, where they aim to develop precise, personalised, and remedial curricula. Precision and personalisation involve customising the curriculum to meet each student's unique needs and learning styles to enhance their understanding and mastery of the material. The remedial design focuses on addressing learning gaps and strengthening foundational knowledge, thus ensuring all students can progress effectively.

The faculty also plays a pivotal role in creating smart content, which includes developing digital resources and interactive activities. These are designed to increase engagement, stimulate interest, and facilitate active learning. This smart content, dynamic and responsive, delivers a learning experience that is more relevant and individualised.

In tutoring, faculty members serve as mentors and coaches to offer valuable feedback to students. This role often extends into guiding the application of intelligent algorithms in learning systems, ensuring the technology enhances, rather than inhibits, the learning process.

Finally, the faculty plays a vital role in the assessment process. AI automates and personalises assessments for efficiency and relevance and designs them to stimulate higher-order learning and promote self-regulated learning. This focus on cognitive complexity and learner independence prepares students to become proficient practitioners in the healthcare field.

By embracing these diverse roles, faculty members are integral to transforming healthcare education, making it more personalised, effective, and relevant in the digital age.

Curriculum Design	Smart Content Creation	Tutoring	Assessment
Precise	Digital Resources	Feedback	Automate & Personalise
Personalised	Interactive activities	Mentoring	Higher order learning
Remedial	Engagement	Intelligent algorithms	Self regulated learning

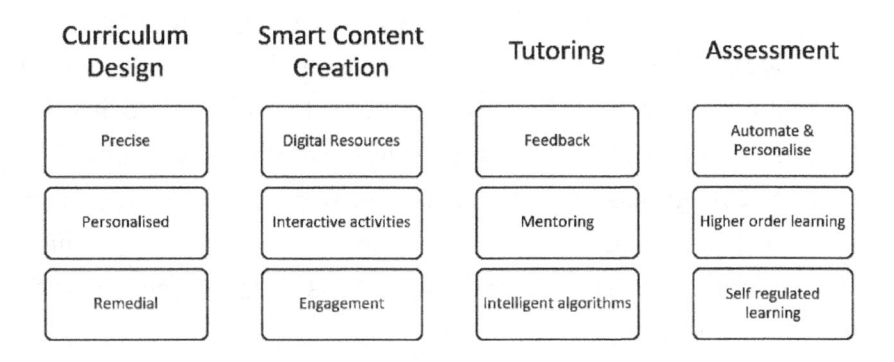

Figure 16. Role of Faculty in healthcare education

AI's ability to offer personalised, adaptable, and immersive learning experiences is revolutionising how we train the next generation of healthcare professionals. The opportunities are vast, and the potential for impact is immense. It is a brave new world of learning powered by AI. The usage of AI in health professional education is as follows:

1. **Personalised Learning Paths**: AI algorithms can analyse each learner's performance and learning style to tailor content, pace, and teaching methods according to their needs. This ensures a more personalised and effective learning experience.
2. **Simulated Learning Environments**: AI can power virtual or augmented reality simulations that provide students with a realistic, hands-on learning experience. For example, surgery simulations can allow medical students to practise procedures in a risk-free environment and improve their skills before working with real patients.
3. **Chatbots and Virtual Tutors**: AI-powered and virtual tutors can provide on-demand, personalised tutoring, answering questions and explaining as needed. They can adapt to the learner's pace and even simulate human-like interactions.
4. **Predictive Analytics**: AI can analyse students' performance data to identify patterns, predict learning outcomes, and suggest interventions when necessary. For example, the AI can suggest additional resources or learning strategies if a student consistently struggles with a particular concept.
5. **AI-Driven Assessment**: AI can provide real-time feedback during simulations and assessments to help learners understand where they have gone wrong and how to improve.
6. **Continual Learning and Updates**: In healthcare, where new information and research are continuously emerging, AI can help keep educational content up-to-date and ensure learners have the most recent and relevant information.

7. **Facilitating Collaborative Learning**: AI can help in creating online collaborative environments where healthcare professionals can interact, discuss cases, as well as share knowledge and experiences, which can be especially valuable in a vocational learning model.

In the evolving landscape of digital healthcare education, the role of the learner extends beyond the passive absorption of information. The learner now actively participates in various aspects of their education journey.

Accessing information and resources is a critical part of the learning process. With the advent of digital technologies, learners can now access a wealth of resources online and expand their learning beyond the confines of the classroom.

The interface with which learners interact is also crucial. With the development of Natural Language Processing (NLP) and Heads-Up Display (HUD) technologies, interfaces have become more user-friendly and immersive, thus facilitating a more engaging learning experience.

Feedback is another important aspect of learning. Learners can benefit from Just-In-Time (JIT) coaching, where feedback and guidance are provided in real-time, allowing immediate correction and reinforcement of understanding. This timely response greatly enhances the learning process.

Assessments play a vital role in a learner's education. They come in various forms, including diagnostic, formative, and summative, each serving different purposes. Diagnostic assessments help identify a learner's strengths and weaknesses, formative assessments provide ongoing feedback to improve learning, and summative evaluations evaluate a learner's mastery of the material at the end of a learning period.

Peer support is another essential aspect in encouraging collaboration and shared learning. Through peer interactions, learners can gain different perspectives, clarify doubts, and reinforce their understanding of the material.

Lastly, maintaining a portfolio allows learners to track their progress, showcase their work, and reflect on their learning journey. This self-evaluation tool helps learners become more aware of their learning processes and progress, fostering self-regulated learning.

These elements demonstrate the active and dynamic role of the learner in the modern healthcare education environment. It is a shift from being mere information consumers to being active participants in their learning journey.

Figure 17. Usage of AI in health professional education

4.2 Example of AI use

Consider an example using an AI algorithm for personalising learning paths for medical students studying cardiology. For this case, we will use a recommendation system, a subtype of information filtering system often used to predict a user's interest or ratings for a particular item.

Here is a simplified outline of how such a system can work:

1. **Data Collection**: The AI system collects student data, such as their learning style, pace, previous performance, preferences, strengths, and weaknesses. This can be done through quizzes, surveys, and monitoring students' interaction with the learning platform.
2. **Profile Building**: The AI builds a learner profile for each student based on the collected data.
3. **Content Analysis**: The AI algorithm also analyses the content available for learning. For example, some videos are better for visual learners, while text-based resources may better suit those who learn through reading.
4. **Matching and Recommendation**: The AI uses a recommendation algorithm, which can be based on techniques such as collaborative filtering, content-based filtering, or hybrid methods, to match the student's profile with appropriate content. For example, for a visual learner who is studying heart diseases and has shown a particular interest in hands-on experience, the AI may recommend an interactive 3D heart model or a virtual reality simulation.
5. **Feedback and Adjustment**: As students interact with the recommended content, the AI collects input, either through direct ratings or indirectly, by assessing factors such as the amount of time spent on the content or how well the student performed on subsequent assessments related to the content. The AI uses this feedback to adjust its future

recommendations, thereby continually improving the personalisation of the learning path.

6. **Evaluation and Continual Learning**: The AI evaluates the student's progress, updating the learner profile and adjusting the recommendations as needed. For instance, if a student initially struggled with an electrocardiogram (ECG) interpretation but has since demonstrated mastery through assessments, the AI will update the learner profile and content recommendations accordingly.

A flowchart for the above AI algorithm example may be:

1. **Start**: All processes begin from a Start node.
2. **Input Student Profile & Content List**: The first operation is to input the student's profile and a list of available learning content.
3. **Initialize Recommendations**: Create an empty list to hold the content recommendations.
4. **Loop through Content**: Go to the next step for each content in the content list.
5. **Calculate Matching Score**: Use the student's profile and the content attributes to calculate a matching score.
6. **Score Greater than Threshold?** This is a decision node. If the score exceeds a pre-set threshold, add the content to the recommendations list (return to step 4 to loop through the following content). If not, skip adding to the recommendations list and return to step 4.
7. **End Loop**: Once all content has been evaluated, exit the loop, and proceed to the next step.
8. **Sort Recommendations**: Sort the list of recommendations based on the calculated matching scores.
9. **Select Top N Recommendations**: Select the top 'N' items from the sorted recommendations list, where 'N' is the desired number of recommendations.

10. **End**: The process ends with the final recommendations for the student.

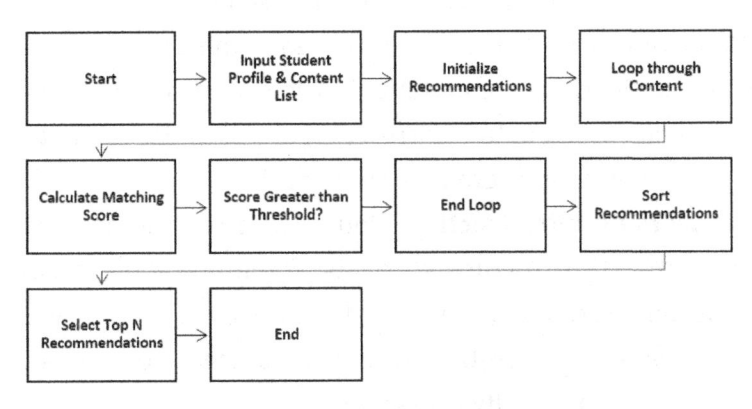

Figure 18. Process for AI in learning example

Remember, this is a simplified example, and the actual implementation of AI for personalised learning will likely involve more sophisticated and complex algorithms. But it provides a sense of how AI can help personalise education by dynamically adapting to each student's needs and progress.

4.3 Infrastructure and Architecture for AI in healthcare education

The infrastructure and architecture required for implementing an AI-powered personalised learning system, such as the one described in the above example, will consist of several components:

1. **Data Storage**: This is where all the data, such as student information, learning materials, and interaction logs, are stored. This can be in relational databases, NoSQL databases, or data warehouses hosted on-premises or in the cloud. You may also need big data technologies like Hadoop or Spark, depending on the data size.

2. **Computational Resources**: You need servers to run your AI algorithms. This can range from traditional Central Processing Unit (CPU) -based servers to more specialised hardware like Graphical Processing Units (GPUs) or Tensor Processing Units (TPUs), which can significantly speed up machine learning computations. The servers can be physical machines in a data centre, virtual machines in a cloud environment, or a combination of both.
3. **Networking Infrastructure**: You need a reliable and secure network infrastructure to allow communication between different system components, to connect to the internet (if your system is web-based), and to protect your data and services from security threats.
4. **AI Software Stack**: This includes the programming languages (like Python or Java), machine learning frameworks (like TensorFlow or PyTorch), and other software tools needed to develop and run AI algorithms.
5. **User Interface**: This can be a web-based or mobile-based application where students interact with the system. The user interface must be intuitive and responsive to ensure a good user experience.
6. **Security Measures**: Security measures such as encryption, secure access controls, and regular security audits are imperative to protect sensitive student data.
7. **Data Privacy Compliance**: The system should be designed to comply with data privacy regulations such as GDPR or HIPAA, including features like consent management, data anonymisation, and the right to be forgotten.

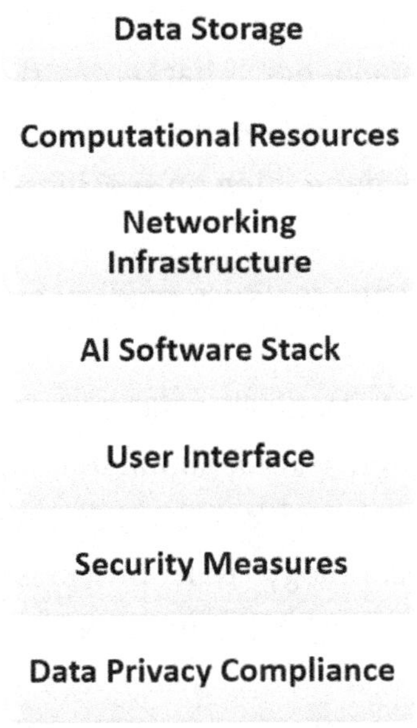

Data Storage

Computational Resources

Networking Infrastructure

AI Software Stack

User Interface

Security Measures

Data Privacy Compliance

Figure 19. Fundamental Components for AI in healthcare education

The system architecture will include the following:

1. The **User Interface** communicates via Application Programming Interfaces (APIs) with the backend servers.
2. The **APIs** interact with the AI engine, which retrieves necessary data from the data storage, runs the AI algorithms, and returns the results.
3. The **AI Engine** consists of machine learning models for user profiling, content analysis, recommendation, and feedback processing tasks. These models are regularly trained and updated based on the latest data.
4. A **Data Pipeline** is set up to collect, clean, transform, and store data from various sources. This pipeline feeds into the AI engine, providing it with the data it needs to make recommendations.

Designing and implementing such a system requires a multidisciplinary team, including data scientists, machine learning engineers, data engineers, backend developers, front-end developers, and cybersecurity experts. The exact requirements and architecture may vary depending on specific needs and constraints.

4.4 Simulation and virtual reality in medical education

The dynamic field of medical education has been significantly impacted by the introduction of simulation and virtual reality (VR). The conventional practice of 'see one, do one, teach one' is being augmented with technology that provides a risk-free training environment, enhancing the learning experience and, ultimately, patient safety.

Simulation-based medical education allows healthcare professionals to acquire new skills and practise complex procedures in a safe, controlled environment. It enables students to make and learn from their mistakes without real-world consequences. High-fidelity mannequins are commonly used in medical schools, providing a realistic representation of various clinical scenarios, ranging from basic Cardiopulmonary Resuscitation (CPR) to complex surgical procedures. In challenging situations, it has been demonstrated that simulation-based training can increase students' confidence, increase the rates of correct clinical diagnoses, and improve retention of skills and knowledge when compared with traditional teaching methods.[48] Ruberto proposed a platform which utilises machine learning to detect and classify a participant's cognitive load in real time by monitoring their cognitive functioning through ECG and Galvanic Skin Response (GSR) signals. The algorithm adjusts the simulated environment based on the

---

[48] Shereen Ajab et al., 'An Alternative to Traditional Bedside Teaching During COVID-19: High-Fidelity Simulation-Based Study', *JMIR Medical Education* 8, no. 2 (9 May 2022): e33565, https://doi.org/10.2196/33565.

participant's mental state by altering the Augmented Reality (AR) patient's respiratory symptoms. This approach has significant implications for simulation design, as it ensures that the simulation's difficulty aligns with the participant's abilities, thus leading to improved learning outcomes.[49]

Scenario: Nursing Simulation Training

Nursing students often use simulation training as a safe and controlled environment to learn and practise skills before applying them in real clinical settings. AI can be used to personalise this simulation training based on each student's unique learning needs and progress.

AI-Powered Personalised Learning System can be used in this case with the following steps:

1. **User Profiling**: When nursing students log into the learning system, they fill out a profile that captures their preferred learning styles (visual, auditory, kinaesthetic, etc.), interests, and previous experience or knowledge in various areas of nursing.
2. **Content Delivery**: The AI system delivers educational content that matches the student's preferred learning style. For instance, if a student chooses kinaesthetic learning, the system can prioritise interactive simulation exercises. In contrast, for another student who is a more visual learner, the system can provide more infographics, videos, or visual aids.

---

[49] Aaron J. Ruberto et al., 'The Future of Simulation-Based Medical Education: Adaptive Simulation Utilising a Deep Multitask Neural Network', *AEM Education and Training* 5, no. 3 (2021): e10605, https://doi.org/10.1002/aet2.10605.

3. **Learning Path Adaptation**: The AI keeps track of their performance as the student interacts with the system. For example, the system identifies if the student struggles with a particular nursing skill in the simulation, such as wound care. It provides additional resources and exercises for the student to improve in this area.
4. **Feedback and Assessment**: After each simulation, the AI provides personalised feedback based on the student's performance by highlighting areas of strength and areas for improvement. The system can also assess the student's progress and adjust the learning path as necessary.
5. **Peer Collaboration and Interaction**: The AI system can facilitate collaborative learning by connecting students with similar skills or topics. This can be done through discussion forums, virtual study groups, or shared projects.
6. **Expert Intervention**: If the system detects that a student is consistently struggling despite personalised content and additional practice, it can flag this up to a human tutor or mentor for further intervention.

In this way, an AI-powered personalised learning system can provide nursing students with a learning experience tailored to their unique needs and help them to gain proficiency in nursing skills more efficiently and effectively.

Virtual reality (VR) takes simulation further by immersing the learner in a 3D environment. With VR, medical students can experience scenarios that may be difficult to recreate in a traditional setting, such as complex surgical procedures or rare clinical situations.

Scenario: Emergency Care Training

Virtual Reality (VR) offers immersive, realistic experiences that can enhance learning and skill development, particularly in fields like nursing, where hands-on practice is crucial. Here is an example of how VR can be used in nursing education. Emergency care requires quick decision-making and precise actions under high-pressure situations. A VR system can simulate such scenarios, providing students with a safe learning and practice environment.

AI-Powered VR Training System

Simulation Selection: A student nurse puts on a VR headset and selects an emergency care scenario from a menu. For instance, a chosen method can be where a patient arrives with stroke symptoms.

Immersive Experience: The VR system provides an immersive 3D environment miming a real-world emergency room. The student nurse can interact with the patient, medical equipment, and other healthcare professionals.

Guided Learning: As the student nurse interacts with the VR environment, an AI assistant guides them through the steps they should take, such as checking the patient's vital signs, asking about symptoms, or administering a drug to address the blood clot. The AI assistant provides this guidance based on the student's learning needs and progress and becomes less intrusive as the student becomes more competent.

Real-time Feedback and Assessment: The AI monitors the student's actions and decisions throughout the simulation. It provides real-time feedback and offers pointers or corrections when the student makes a mistake. For example, if the student forgets to check the patient's blood pressure, the AI will remind them to do so.

Debrief and Review: After the simulation, the AI comprehensively reviews the student's performance. It highlights areas where the student did well and areas they must work on. The student can rewatch their simulation from different angles to better understand their actions and the AI's feedback.

Personalised Progression: Based on the student's performance and improvement over time, the AI adjusts the complexity of future simulations. For example, it may introduce more complex cases or unexpected complications.

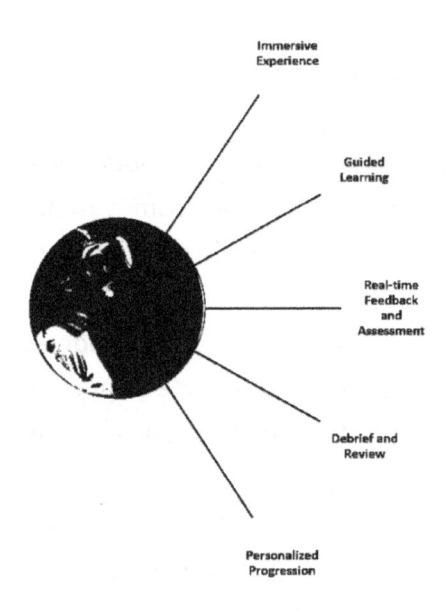

Figure 20. VR in healthcare education

Nursing students can use AI with VR to learn, practice, and improve their skills in a realistic, safe, and supportive environment. This training method can help students prepare for real-life scenarios and improve patient outcomes.

Implementing an AI-powered VR system for nursing education requires integrating several vital components. Appropriate VR hardware, including VR headsets, controllers, and potentially additional accessories for full-body tracking or haptic feedback, is necessary to create an immersive learning environment. This also necessitates high-performance computers with powerful graphics capabilities to ensure a smooth and engaging virtual experience.

At the heart of this immersive system lies AI-powered virtual reality (VR) software, which weaves together intricate simulations, AI-guided instruction, and personalized feedback to create a truly transformative learning experience. To ensure the utmost integrity, this software is designed to adhere to rigorous privacy and security standards, safeguarding the sensitive data of learners.

Moreover, the VR software must have access to accurate and up-to-date medical and educational content, which is used to guide simulations and furnish relevant feedback. This information should be derived from reliable sources and subjected to review by experts in medical and nursing education.

For the AI capabilities to be developed and refined, there must be access to relevant training data. This can include data gathered from past simulations, anonymised real-world medical cases, or synthetic data created specifically for this purpose.

Regarding physical infrastructure, depending on the scale of implementation, a dedicated VR lab with ample space for safe movement may be necessary. Additionally, undertaking such an ambitious project requires substantial training and support. Both students and educators will need guidance on effectively utilising the VR system, and ongoing technical support is necessary to resolve any potential hardware or software issues.

Ethical considerations must also be diligently attended to. This involves careful deliberation on the privacy, consent, data security, and possible psychological implications of utilising realistic VR simulations in an educational context.

Finally, a robust evaluation system is crucial to ensure the ongoing efficacy and improvement of the VR training system. Regular feedback from students and educators, thorough analysis of performance data from the AI system, and periodic updates to the VR simulations based on the latest medical research and best practices in nursing education will all contribute to this innovative educational approach's continuous evolution and improvement.

Evidence suggests that virtual reality (VR) is an effective tool for educating health professionals and enhancing their knowledge and cognitive skills. VR interventions have shown slight improvement in post-intervention knowledge scores compared to traditional learning methods or other digital education formats. Additionally, VR has demonstrated the ability to enhance health professionals' cognitive skills compared to traditional learning approaches. However, findings regarding attitudes and satisfaction were varied and inconclusive. A systematic review recommends future research to assess the effectiveness of more immersive and interactive forms of VR across different settings, which consider outcomes such as attitude, satisfaction, potential adverse effects, cost-effectiveness, and changes in clinical practice or behaviour.[50]

One of the significant advantages of VR is its capability to offer personalised and interactive learning experiences. AI, VR, and deep learning (DL) technologies hold promise in enhancing surgeons' capabilities through decision support, technical skill assessment, and the semi-autonomous execution of various surgical tasks. The growing interest in AI's role in surgery has resulted in a significant volume of literature, generating excitement and concerns regarding

---

[50] Phone Myint Kyaw et al., 'Virtual Reality for Health Professions Education: Systematic Review and Meta-Analysis by the Digital Health Education Collaboration', *Journal of Medical Internet Research* 21, no. 1 (22 January 2019): e12959, https://doi.org/10.2196/12959.

its safety and effectiveness. Surgeons and surgical data scientists must stay informed about the current advancements, identify areas that require further knowledge and technological development, and critically assess the literature flooding the field.[51]

Simulation and VR also play an important role in team training, allowing healthcare professionals to practise their teamwork and communication skills in a high-stress environment under simulation. Studies have shown that this can improve team dynamics and patient outcomes. Shah and co-workers have demonstrated the importance of inter-professional team training in Otorhinolaryngology surgery and in the broader context of patient safety in the operating room. Simulation-based education (SBE) can enhance patient safety and outcomes by offering a controlled environment for healthcare professionals to practise and improve their skills. Additionally, SBE promotes teamwork and communication among healthcare providers, improving patient care.[52]

Simulation and VR represent an exciting frontier in medical education. These technologies offer unique opportunities for healthcare professionals to develop their skills, enhance their understanding, and prepare for the challenges with the delivery of patient care. As these technologies continue to evolve, their impact on medical education is set to increase further, ushering in a new era of innovative, immersive, and effective learning.

---

[51] Michael P. Rogers et al., 'The Future Surgical Training Paradigm: Virtual Reality and Machine Learning in Surgical Education', *Surgery* 169, no. 5 (1 May 2021): 1250–52, https://doi.org/10.1016/j.surg.2020.09.040.

[52] Anjan Shah et al., 'Simulation-Based Education and Team Training', *Otolaryngologic Clinics of North America* 52, no. 6 (1 December 2019): 995–1003, https://doi.org/10.1016/j.otc.2019.08.002.

4.5 Personalised Learning with AI-driven education platforms

Personalised learning with AI-driven education platforms has emerged as a transformative approach to education across various fields, including healthcare. These platforms leverage the power of artificial intelligence to tailor the learning experience to each learner's individual needs, preferences, and abilities.

One of the key advantages of AI-driven personalised learning is its ability to adapt and customise the content and instructional methods according to the learner's specific requirements. Through continuous data collection and analysis, AI algorithms can gather insights about the learner's strengths, weaknesses, learning styles, and progress. This information is then used to create personalised learning paths, selecting appropriate resources, activities, and assessments that align with the learner's unique needs.

For healthcare professionals, personalised learning with AI-driven platforms offers numerous benefits. It enables them to efficiently acquire and update their knowledge and skills in a way that is tailored to their specific practice areas and interests. For example, a surgeon specialising in Orthopaedics may receive learning materials and case studies related to Orthopaedic procedures, while a paediatrician may focus on topics relevant to their speciality. This personalised approach ensures that healthcare professionals receive targeted education directly applicable to their practice.

AI-driven education platforms can also provide adaptive learning experiences. As the learner progresses, the AI algorithm adjusts the difficulty level of the content and activities to match their proficiency. This ensures that learners are consistently challenged and feel energised and energised. By customising the learning experience to an individual's capabilities, personalised learning helps optimise engagement and motivation, leading to more effective learning outcomes. In a study examining the usage of the adaptive learning platform Osmosis among medical students in the United States, the authors showed educational data mining techniques. Valuable insights include enhancing the implementation of adaptive learning platforms in medical education and proposing further exploration in this field.[53]

Moreover, AI-driven platforms can offer real-time Assessment and feedback to learners. Through analysing learners' performance, AI algorithms can identify areas of improvement and provide timely feedback, thus guiding learners towards mastery. This immediate feedback loop helps learners understand their strengths and weaknesses, allowing them to focus on areas that require further attention. This paper investigates the feasibility of using the web-based platform Kahoot! as a low-cost system for studying and evaluating medical students in Pathology. The study developed modules covering different tumour types and incorporated text-based questions on histo-morphology. Kahoot! was implemented before and after traditional medical education, and student feedback was collected. It showed that Kahoot! was a simple and cost-effective tool that improved learning outcomes in pathomorphological topics and was well-received by students. This paper contributes by assessing the feasibility and effectiveness of Kahoot! as a learning and teaching tool in Pathology, especially highlighting its simplicity, low cost, and high acceptance among students.[54]

---

[53] Ashwin Menon et al., 'Using "Big Data" to Guide Implementation of a Web and Mobile Adaptive Learning Platform for Medical Students', *Medical Teacher* 39, no. 9 (September 2017): 975–80, https://doi.org/10.1080/0142159X.2017.1324949.
[54] Daniel Neureiter et al., 'Feasibility of Kahoot! As a Real-Time Assessment Tool in (Histo-)Pathology Classroom Teaching', *Advances in Medical Education and Practice* 11 (2020): 695–705, https://doi.org/10.2147/AMEP.S264821.

Integrating AI-driven education platforms into healthcare training and professional development holds great potential for advancing the field. As these platforms evolve and improve, healthcare professionals can benefit from more efficient, effective, and tailored learning experiences. The combination of personalised learning with AI-driven platforms has the potential to enhance healthcare education, support lifelong learning, and ultimately improve patient care.

Just-In-Time (JIT) learning is an approach that provides the necessary information exactly when it is needed instead of overwhelming learners with the information they may not use immediately. It is particularly useful in healthcare settings where professionals must constantly update their knowledge and skills. Smart devices such as smartphones, tablets, or wearable technology can facilitate JIT learning by providing easy access to information right at the point of care.

Here is an example of how AI can be used to provide JIT learning for a nurse using a smart device at the workplace:

Scenario: Administering a New Medication

Let us take a nurse about to administer a new medication to a patient. This is the first time they have used this medication, and they need quick information about its dosage, side effects, and contraindications.

AI-Powered JIT Learning Application
1. **Prompt**: The nurse opens a JIT learning application on their smart device and enters or speaks the name of the medication.
2. **Information Retrieval**: The AI, trained in medical databases and textbooks, instantly retrieves relevant information

about the medication. It briefly details the medication's usage, dosage, potential side effects, and contraindications.
3. **Personalised Content Delivery**: Knowing the nurse's learning style from their user profile, the AI delivers this information to suit them best. For example, if the nurse is a visual learner, it may provide an infographic or a short video.
4. **Interactive Question & Answer (Q&A)**: The AI application can offer an interactive Q&A feature. The nurse may ask further questions (e.g., "Can this medication be administered alongside drug X?"), and the AI will answer in real-time.
5. **Follow-up Learning**: Based on this interaction, the AI can recognise that the nurse may benefit from more learning about pharmacology. It recommends related resources or mini courses the nurse can access during their break.
6. **Feedback and Improvement**: The AI can also ask for quick feedback after the interaction – whether the nurse found the information provided helpful. Any unanswered questions? This feedback helps the AI improve future recommendations and interactions.

By leveraging AI and smart devices, JIT learning can support healthcare professionals in their daily tasks, improve patient care, and enhance continuous learning in the workplace.

4.6 AI-assisted curriculum Design and Assessment

AI-assisted curriculum Design and Assessment is an innovative approach that utilises artificial intelligence (AI) technologies to enhance the development and evaluation of educational curricula. With the growing availability of big data and advancements in machine learning algorithms, AI has the potential to revolutionise the way curricula are designed, implemented, and assessed across various educational domains, including medical education.

AI can assist in the initial stages of curriculum design by analysing large sets of educational data. Through machine learning algorithms, AI can detect patterns and trends in student performance, engagement, and learning preferences. These insights can then be used to identify areas where the current curriculum may need to be adapted to better suit the needs of students.

Once the curriculum framework is established, AI can assist in personalising the curriculum for individual learners. Using predictive algorithms, AI can estimate a learner's ability level and preferred learning style based on past performance and interaction patterns. This allows for developing a tailored curriculum that adjusts content, pacing, and difficulty based on the learner's unique needs.

During the implementation phase, AI can provide real-time analytics on how the curriculum is being interacted with. This includes data on areas in which students excel, where they struggle, and how engaged they are with different materials. Such information can be invaluable in identifying gaps in the curriculum and making necessary adjustments.

Finally, AI can assist in the continual refinement and evolution of the curriculum. By consistently tracking and analysing student performance and feedback, AI can identify which aspects of the curriculum are most effective and require improvement. This allows for a curriculum that is dynamic and responsive, which is continually adapting and improving to meet the needs of learners.

Similarly, AI can assist in creating a more personalised, effective, and responsive curriculum that enhances the learning experience for students.

One of the key advantages of AI-assisted curriculum design is its ability to analyse large datasets of student performance and learning outcomes. By mining this data, AI algorithms can identify patterns, trends, and correlations that may not be readily apparent to human educators. This information can inform the development of more targeted and effective curricula tailored to student's specific requirements and learning styles. AI can analyse data from multiple sources, including assessments, learning management systems, and online platforms, to gain insights into student progress and identify areas for improvement.

Furthermore, AI can assist in the adaptive design of curricula, allowing for personalised learning experiences. AI algorithms can dynamically adjust the curriculum content, pacing, and instructional methods to optimise individual learning trajectories by collecting real-time data on student performance and preferences. This personalised approach ensures that each student receives tailored instruction, which enhances engagement, motivation, and learning outcomes.

AI can also play a significant role in assessing student progress and competency. Machine learning algorithms can analyse assessment data, including examinations, quizzes, and assignments, to provide automated and immediate student feedback. AI algorithms can identify areas of strengths and weaknesses, highlight misconceptions, and offer targeted recommendations for improvement. This formative assessment approach facilitates continuous learning and allows for timely interventions to address learning gaps.

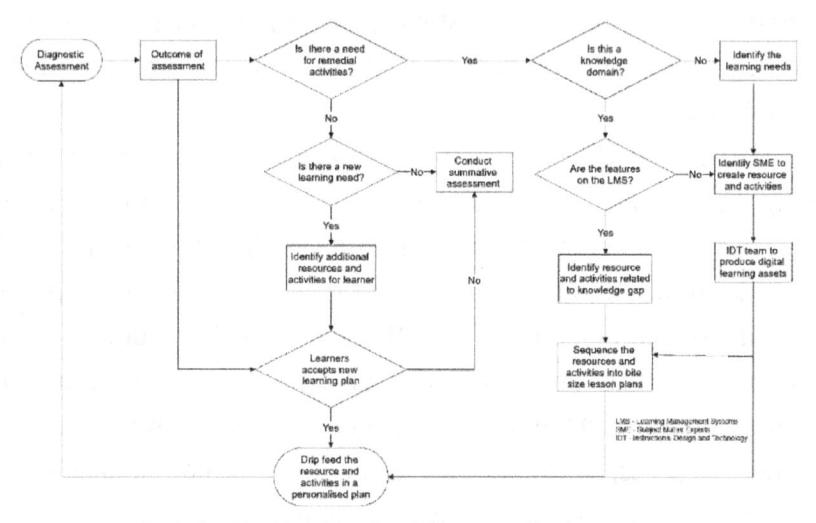

Figure 21. The Algorithm for AI in Personalised Assessment

Moreover, AI can contribute to developing intelligent tutoring systems that provide personalised support and guidance to students. These systems can employ natural language processing and machine learning techniques to interact with students, answer questions, and provide explanations, fostering independent learning and critical thinking skills.

However, it is important to note that while AI-assisted curriculum design and Assessment offer great potential, they should be implemented with caution and human oversight. Ethical considerations, such as data privacy and algorithmic bias, must be carefully addressed to ensure fair and equitable educational practices.

In summary, AI-assisted curriculum design and Assessment hold promise in enhancing educational experiences by leveraging the power of AI to analyse data, personalise instruction, provide timely feedback, and support students' individual needs. By incorporating AI into curriculum development and assessment practices, educational institutions can optimise learning outcomes and better prepare students for the challenges of a rapidly evolving world.

In health professional education, the current approach to teaching and learning follows a well-structured process. Initially, students engage with the presented material, absorbing and processing the complex concepts and information integral to their field of study. This learning process is then measured through diagnostic assessments, often as multiple-choice questions (MCQs). These provide an efficient and objective means to gauge each student's understanding and retention of the course content.

Following the Assessment, constructive feedback is provided. This vital step serves not just as a tool to reinforce correct understanding or rectify misconceptions but also as a means to promote reflection and self-directed learning amongst the students. A remediation process is initiated if a student's performance falls below a certain threshold in the diagnostic Assessment. This may involve supplementary instruction, targeted practice, or other interventions designed to address the identified areas of difficulty.

Ultimately, the goal of this process is to facilitate progression. As students grasp the foundational knowledge and refine their skills, they are prepared to advance towards more complex levels of study. This cyclical learning, Assessment, feedback, remediation, and progression process forms the backbone of health professional education today.

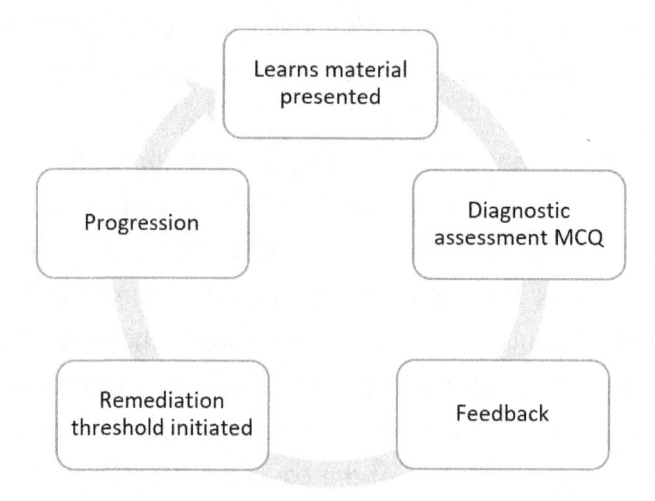

Figure 22. The current process in healthcare education

AI technologies are transforming the landscape of health professional education, leading to a more personalised and efficient learning experience. This new approach starts with presenting personalised material tailored to each student's unique learning needs and styles. The material is adapted based on a student's prior knowledge, strengths, and areas for improvement, hence fostering an environment that supports individual learning trajectories.

Assessment becomes a continuous and integrated part of the learning process, with formal and informal evaluations facilitated by natural language processing (NLP) algorithms. These algorithms can analyse written and spoken responses, providing a more comprehensive understanding of students' learning progress.

Next, automated personalised feedback is provided through an Intelligent Tutor System (ITS). These AI-based systems can provide real-time, targeted feedback that mirrors a human tutor's guidance by helping students identify and correct misconceptions, understand complex concepts, and build critical thinking skills.

An AI-guided remediation curriculum is initiated if a learner struggles with specific concepts or skills. This involves providing additional learning resources and exercises designed to target the learner's particular areas of weakness.

As students master new knowledge and skills, their achievements are recognised and rewarded, often through digital badges or similar credentials. This recognition can boost motivation and engagement, supporting ongoing learning.

Finally, AI technology can also facilitate peer assessment. Creating a platform where learners can review and provide feedback on each other's work encourages collaborative learning and critical thinking. Peer assessment can also provide valuable perspectives and insights that enhance learning.

This AI-driven approach to health professional education personalises learning at every stage, enhancing engagement, optimising Assessment and feedback, and supporting remediation and progression tailored to individual learners' needs.

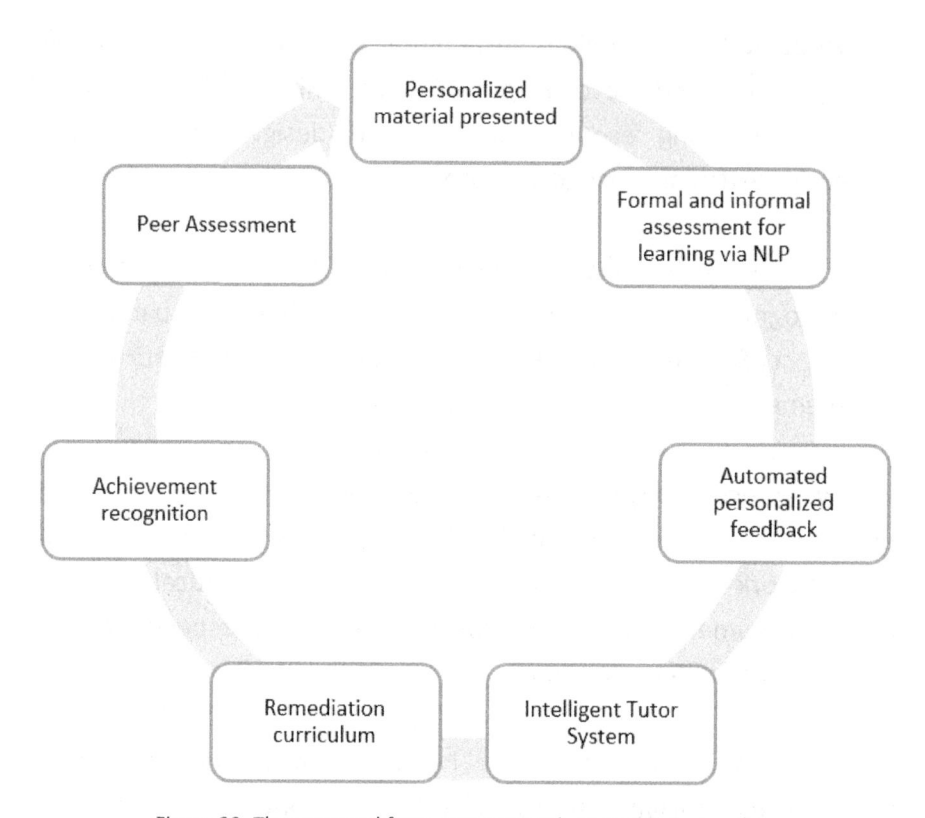

Figure 23. The proposed future process with AI-enabled education.

4.7 AI in continuing professional development.

AI in continuing professional development (CPD) is a promising application that can revolutionise how professionals acquire and maintain knowledge and skills throughout their careers. By leveraging AI technologies, CPD programs can be enhanced in several ways.

One significant benefit of AI in CPD is its ability to personalise learning experiences. AI algorithms can analyse individual professionals' learning preferences, performance data, and career goals to provide tailored recommendations for CPD activities. This personalisation ensures that professionals engage in relevant, meaningful learning experiences that address their needs and interests. AI can suggest relevant courses, webinars, articles, and other resources that align with their areas of expertise and areas for growth.

Moreover, AI can facilitate adaptive learning in CPD. By continuously monitoring professionals' progress and performance, AI algorithms can dynamically adjust the learning content and delivery to optimise their learning outcomes. Adaptive learning systems can identify areas where professionals require additional support or challenge and provide targeted resources or activities accordingly. This adaptability ensures that CPD programs remain relevant, engaging, and effective.

AI can also play a role in assessing professionals' competency and tracking their progress. Machine learning algorithms can analyse data from assessments, practice simulations, or real-world performance to evaluate professionals' skills and knowledge. AI can provide feedback, identify areas for improvement, and suggest targeted learning activities to bridge any identified gaps. This data-driven approach to competency assessment can provide professionals with a clear understanding of their strengths and areas for development, thus enabling them to take proactive steps to enhance their professional competence.

Additionally, AI can enhance the accessibility and flexibility of CPD programs. Through AI-powered platforms, professionals can access learning materials and resources anytime and anywhere by eliminating barriers related to time and location. AI technologies, such as natural language processing and chatbots, can also provide on-demand support and guidance, allowing professionals to receive immediate answers to their questions or access relevant information at their convenience.

Scenario for AI in Continuing Professional Development for Radiologists

Meet Dr Chua, a radiologist working in a large hospital. As part of her Continuing Professional Development (CPD), she needs to stay updated with the latest advancements in Radiology, including Artificial Intelligence (AI) in imaging diagnostics. However, finding time for CPD amidst her busy schedule is a constant challenge.

Recognising this issue, the hospital implemented an AI-driven CPD platform specifically designed to cater to the needs of busy healthcare professionals like Dr Chua. Here is how it helped her:

1. **Personalised Learning Plans:** The AI system analysed Dr Chua's past learning records, her speciality within Radiology, and her performance metrics to identify areas where she needed to update her knowledge. It then created a personalised learning plan focused on the latest advancements in radiological imaging and the use of AI in diagnostics.
2. **Intelligent Tutoring System:** Dr Chua could interact with the AI tutoring system whenever she had doubts or required clarifications. The plan provided immediate, accurate answers to her queries, thus making her learning process more efficient and effective.
3. **Simulations and Virtual Reality:** Dr Chua was provided access to AI-driven simulations that allowed her to see the practical application of AI in Radiology. These realistic simulations provided a safe environment to understand and practise new techniques before applying them in real-world scenarios.
4. **Just-in-Time Learning:** The AI system would push short, digestible learning content to Dr Chua in between her work

schedules. This allowed her to learn at her own pace without disrupting her work.
5. **Performance Tracking:** The AI system automatically tracked Dr Chua's progress and adjusted her learning plan based on her performance, ensuring she focused on the most relevant and beneficial learning content.
6. **Learning Communities:** The AI system connected Dr Chua with other radiologists using the platform, which has fostered an online learning community. Here, they discussed challenging cases and shared best practices which enhanced their collective knowledge.

Through the AI-driven CPD platform, Dr Chua could keep up with the latest advancements efficiently and effectively, making her more confident and competent in her role. The case of Dr Chua exemplifies the transformative potential of AI in Continuing Professional Development in healthcare.

However, it is important to note that the integration of AI in CPD should be done thoughtfully and ethically. Safeguarding data privacy and ensuring algorithmic transparency and fairness are crucial considerations. AI should enhance human expertise and decision-making rather than replace human professionals entirely.

In summary, AI in Continuing Professional Development has immense potential to revolutionise how professionals learn, grow, and maintain competence throughout their careers. By personalising learning experiences, enabling adaptive learning, assessing competency, and improving accessibility, AI can enhance the effectiveness and impact of CPD programs, ultimately benefiting professionals and the industries they serve.

Chapter 5: AI in Healthcare Research

The era of artificial intelligence has ushered in a transformative phase in healthcare research. The ability to process massive amounts of data assemblages and derive insightful patterns from them is revolutionising how researchers gather to explore complex data sets, discern patterns, and predict outcomes with unprecedented accuracy and speed.

Machine learning is at the heart of this revolution, a subset of AI that enables computers to learn from data without being explicitly programmed. Machine learning algorithms have been employed to analyse large datasets, such as genomics, clinical trials, and patient records, enabling researchers to draw meaningful insights and make significant strides in personalised medicine, predictive analytics, and disease modelling.

AI has also made significant contributions to drug discovery and development. It has accelerated the process by identifying potential drug candidates, predicting their effectiveness and possible side effects, thereby reducing the time and cost of bringing new therapies to market.

In imaging and diagnostics, AI has shown remarkable capabilities. Advanced algorithms have been developed to detect abnormalities in medical images, such as plain radiographs (X-rays), Computed Tomography (CT) or Magnetic Resonance Imaging (MRI) scans, often matching or surpassing the accuracy of human experts. This has profound implications for early diagnosis and treatment of various conditions, including cancer and neurological disorders.

Despite these advancements, we are still in the early days of AI's transformative impact on healthcare research. The future of AI in this realm is promising and holds exciting prospects. AI's potential to integrate and interpret multidimensional data can lead to the developing of predictive models for complex diseases, thus enhancing prevention and early intervention strategies.

AI is also set to revolutionise the design and execution of clinical trials. It can help identify suitable participants, monitor their progress in real-time, and rapidly analyse results, leading to more efficient and reliable trials.

Furthermore, the rise of quantum computing and its integration with AI can open up new frontiers in healthcare research by enabling the analysis of immensely complex biological systems and the modelling of molecular interactions at an unprecedented scale.

However, realising the full potential of AI in healthcare research also requires navigating significant challenges, such as ethical considerations, data privacy and security, algorithmic bias, and regulatory frameworks. As we progress, it will be crucial to address these issues while harnessing AI's potential to transform healthcare research.

In conclusion, AI has been instrumental in advancing healthcare research and promises to drive further innovations and discoveries in the future. Its integration into healthcare is a continuous learning and adaptation journey characterised by immense opportunities and profound challenges. Nevertheless, the trajectory points towards an end where AI is integral in unravelling the complexities of human health and disease, fundamentally transforming how we understand and approach healthcare.

AI also redefines data analysis and predictive modelling, offering more precise and sophisticated statistical analysis methods.

Machine learning models can identify complex patterns and predict future trends based on historical data, which is particularly useful in disease prediction and health outcomes. An example is Google's DeepMind, which is utilised for medical imaging or radiological scans and can predict diseases like age-related macular degeneration or diabetic retinopathy more accurately than human experts.[55]

Machine Learning (ML) techniques are instrumental in accelerating drug discovery, offering notable benefits in predicting binding affinities and optimising drug design. For instance, the AutoDock Vina tool, which uses ML, has been utilised to predict the binding affinity of small molecules to the SARS-CoV-2 main protease, a potential drug target for COVID-19. This allows for fast-tracking possible treatments in the battle against the pandemic. Furthermore, ML techniques have been employed to refine drugs like the Autotaxin inhibitor GLPG1690, a clinical agent against pulmonary fibrosis. By optimising its structure and reducing side effects, ML has enhanced the safety and effectiveness of this treatment, demonstrating the substantial potential of AI in the realm of drug discovery and design.[56]

AI further facilitates the coordination of research collaboration and communication. Tools such as Slack, integrated with AI, can enhance productivity and teamwork by automating administrative tasks and facilitating easier file sharing and communication.

In summary, this chapter will take a deep dive into these fascinating domains, shedding light on the groundbreaking applications of AI in healthcare research. Through compelling real-world examples, we

---

[55] De Fauw et al., 'Clinically Applicable Deep Learning for Diagnosis and Referral in Retinal Disease'.
[56] Suresh Dara et al., 'Machine Learning in Drug Discovery: A Review', *Artificial Intelligence Review* 55, no. 3 (1 March 2022): 1947–99, https://doi.org/10.1007/s10462-021-10058-4.

will unveil the immense potential and intricate challenges that lie within this dynamic field.

5.1 AI-powered literature reviews and evidence synthesis

One of the significant shifts driven by AI has been in how literature reviews and evidence synthesis are done. Now, researchers have tools such as AI-powered text analysis algorithms and machine learning models to scan copious amounts of data, identify relevant studies, and summarise key findings. For example, Rayyan, a free web and epistemological application used to expedite the initial stages of the systematic review, leverages AI to reduce the time required to perform literature reviews drastically.

The traditional process of literature reviews and evidence synthesis, which involves manually sifting through thousands of articles and extracting relevant information, has been time-consuming and labour-intensive. With the advent of AI, these processes have been revolutionised, enabling researchers to access and analyse vast amounts of data more quickly and accurately.

AI-powered tools employ natural language processing (NLP) and machine learning techniques to search and evaluate scientific articles, identify key themes and trends, and synthesise data from multiple sources. These tools can assist researchers in streamlining the literature review process, reducing the possibility of errors and biases while ensuring a comprehensive analysis of the available literature. They are increasingly gaining popularity due to their ability to quickly analyse enormous amounts of information, potentially saving researchers significant time and effort.

One example of an AI-powered literature review tool is Iris.ai, which uses NLP algorithms to scan documents and create concept maps. It identifies connections between research areas and enables more targeted and relevant search results. The review process is expedited by reducing the number of articles that needs to be read by the researcher. AI technology can be used to improve the efficiency and accuracy of literature searches in the medical field, but it may not necessarily increase the number of relevant results.[57]

DistillerSR is a widely recognised tool used in the healthcare and scientific research community for managing data during systematic reviews, health technology assessments, and clinical guideline development. This cloud-based software employs AI to streamline the literature review process, making it more efficient and comprehensive.

DistillerSR facilitates the entire review process, from project management, study screening and selection, to data extraction, quality assessment, and report generation. Key features of DistillerSR include the de-duplication of studies, customisable screening and data extraction forms, workflow management, inter-rater reliability calculation, and visual analytics.

A significant advantage of DistillerSR is its AI-driven prioritisation feature. The tool uses a proprietary algorithm to learn from screening decisions made by reviewers and then ranks remaining studies according to their likelihood of being relevant. This allows researchers to focus on the most promising studies, saving time and resources.

---

[57] Dominik Schoeb et al., 'Use of Artificial Intelligence for Medical Literature Search: Randomized Controlled Trial Using the Hackathon Format', *Interactive Journal of Medical Research* 9, no. 1 (30 March 2020): e16606, https://doi.org/10.2196/16606.

For example, DistillerSR has been used in various published research. In a systematic review of treatments for acute pain, a second investigator, who utilised the artificial intelligence function in Distiller SR (DistillerSR AI), provided another independent review to address the benefits and harms of opioid, non-opioid pharmacological, and non-pharmacological treatments for specific types of acute pain.[58]

Covidence is a popular tool for researchers conducting systematic reviews. Its features are designed to streamline the study selection process, data extraction, and quality assessment.
One example of a study that employed Covidence is "Parental and Family Factors for Anxiety Disorders in Youth: A Systematic Review and Meta-analysis," published in the Journal of Affective Disorders in 2020. In this research, the authors examined the association of parental and family factors with anxiety disorders in youths. The researchers screened over 14,000 studies and ultimately included 86 in their analysis.[59]

This study used confidence in multiple stages of the systematic review. After importing references from bibliographic databases into Covidence, duplicates were automatically removed. Then, two independent researchers used the platform to screen titles and abstracts for relevance based on predefined criteria. The full texts of potentially relevant studies were uploaded into Covidence for further screening. The tool was also used for data extraction and risk of bias assessment. Discrepancies at any stage were resolved via discussion or the involvement of a third researcher.

---

[58] Roger Chou et al., 'Literature Update Period: 22 January, 2022, through 6 May, 202', 2020.
[59] Marie Bee Hui Yap et al., 'Parental Factors Associated with Depression and Anxiety in Young People: A Systematic Review and Meta-Analysis', *Journal of Affective Disorders* 156 (March 2014): 8–23, https://doi.org/10.1016/j.jad.2013.11.007.

Overall, Covidence played an instrumental role in the systematic review process by enhancing the efficiency of study selection, data extraction, and quality assessment. It also fostered collaboration among the research team through its easy-to-use interface and transparent workflow, which facilitated resolving discrepancies and tracking the review's progress.

It is important to mention that while Covidence helps streamline and automate parts of the systematic review process, it still needs to replace the intellectual and interpretative work researchers undertake when conducting a systematic review. Researchers must still use their judgement and expertise to decide which studies to include, what data to extract, and how to interpret the findings. Similarly, while tools such as DistillerSR can make the literature review process more efficient, they do not replace the need for scrutiny and interpretation by expert researchers. The device is a facilitator, assisting in managing and organising data, but the intellectual analysis remains a human task.

In summary, AI-powered literature reviews and evidence synthesis tools can potentially transform how healthcare researchers approach their work. By automating manual processes and providing more sophisticated data analysis, these tools can enhance the efficiency, accuracy, and comprehensiveness of literature reviews, ultimately leading to better-informed decisions and advancements in healthcare.

5.2 AI in data analysis and predictive modelling

The realm of healthcare research has been forever transformed by the advent of artificial intelligence (AI), specifically through the power of machine learning and deep learning. These groundbreaking methodologies have ushered in a new era of data analysis and predictive modeling, enabling researchers to navigate vast, intricate datasets with ease. Uncovering hidden relationships and generating precise predictions, AI empowers researchers to make informed decisions that ultimately enhance patient outcomes.

The steps involved in the data analysis and predictive modelling include the following:

1. **Problem Definition:** Before anything else, it is important to understand and define the problem that needs to be solved. What is the objective of the predictive model? What kind of data is available? What will the predictions from the model be used for?
2. **Data Collection:** Relevant data needs to be collected depending on the problem at hand. This data can be collected from various sources, such as databases, sensors, and social media platforms.
3. **Data Cleaning and Pre-processing:** The collected data is often raw and cannot be used directly for modelling. It may contain missing values, inconsistencies, or noise that can negatively impact the predictive model's performance. Hence, it is important to pre-process the data, which can involve handling missing values, dealing with outliers, feature scaling, and encoding categorical variables.
4. **Feature Selection:** Not all collected data is necessarily useful for prediction. Feature selection involves choosing the most relevant variables contributing to the prediction task. This can be done based on domain knowledge or machine learning techniques such as correlation analysis, mutual information, or wrapper methods.

5. **Model Selection:** Depending on the problem, appropriate AI or machine learning models are chosen. For instance, for a binary classification problem, logistic regression, decision trees, random forests, or neural networks may be suitable.
6. **Training the Model:** The selected model is then trained on the pre-processed data. This involves adjusting parameters in the model to capture best the relationship between the variables and the target prediction.
7. **Validation and Tuning:** The trained model's performance needs to be validated. This is usually done by splitting the original data into a training set and a validation set, typically in the 80-20 ratio. The model is trained on the training set, and its performance is evaluated on the validation set. The model's hyperparameters may be tuned at this stage to improve its performance.
8. **Evaluation:** Once the model is trained and validated, its performance is evaluated on a test set of data it hasn't seen before. Metrics such as accuracy, precision, recall, F1 score, or Area Under Curve (AUC) of the Receiver Operating Characteristic (ROC) Curve (AUC-ROC) may be used, depending on the problem.
9. **Deployment:** If the model's performance on the test set is satisfactory, it can be deployed in the real-world system, where it will receive new, live data and make predictions in real time.
10. **Monitoring and Maintenance:** The deployed model must be regularly monitored and maintained. If the model's performance drops over time, it may need to be retrained or replaced.

One of the most prominent applications of AI in data analysis is using supervised and unsupervised machine learning algorithms to identify patterns and associations in healthcare data. For instance, clustering algorithms such as K-means and hierarchical clustering can be used to group patients based on similarities in their medical histories, thus enabling tailored treatment strategies and interventions. Below are a couple of examples:

Supervised Learning - Predicting Diabetes Mellitus:
A real-world example of supervised machine learning in healthcare is the prediction of diabetes mellitus. A systematic review of the applications of machine learning and data mining techniques in diabetes mellitus (DM) research. The study focuses on four categories: Prediction and Diagnosis, Diabetic Complications, Genetic Background and Environment, and Health Care and Management. The paper highlights the usefulness of extracting valuable knowledge, leading to new hypotheses targeting deeper understanding and further investigation in DM. The study found that supervised learning approaches were more commonly used than unsupervised ones, and Support Vector Machines (SVM) were the most successful and widely used algorithms. Clinical datasets were mainly used in the selected articles. The paper contributes to the field of DM research by providing insights into the applications of machine learning and data mining techniques in this condition and by highlighting the potential of these techniques in generating valuable knowledge for further investigation.[60]

Unsupervised Learning - Patient Segmentation:
Unsupervised machine learning, particularly clustering algorithms, has been used extensively in healthcare for patient segmentation. This is useful in identifying patient subgroups that share similar characteristics, which can aid in providing more personalised care.

---

[60] Ioannis Kavakiotis et al., 'Machine Learning and Data Mining Methods in Diabetes Research', *Computational and Structural Biotechnology Journal* 15 (1 January 2017): 104–16, https://doi.org/10.1016/j.csbj.2016.12.005.

A study compared the performance of Multiple Linear Regression (MLR) and eight machine learning techniques for pharmaco-genetic algorithm-based prediction of tacrolimus stable dose (TSD) in a large Chinese cohort. MLR, Artificial Neural Network (ANN), Regression Tree (RT), Multivariate Adaptive Regression Splines (MARS), Boosted Regression Tree (BRT), Support Vector Regression (SVR), Random Forest Regression (RFR), Lasso Regression (LAR) and Bayesian Additive Regression Trees (BART) were applied. Their performances were compared in this work.

Regression Tree (RT) performed best in derivation and validation cohorts among all the machine learning models. Of 1,045 renal transplant patients recruited, 80% were randomly selected as the "derivation cohort" to develop a dose-prediction algorithm. In contrast, the remaining 20% constituted the "validation cohort" to test the final algorithm chosen. The study is the first to use machine learning models to predict TSD, which will further facilitate future personalised medicine in tacrolimus administration.[61]

Through these compelling illustrations, we witness the remarkable potential of both supervised and unsupervised machine learning in unravelling patterns and making accurate predictions within the intricate realm of healthcare data. This transformative capability sets the stage for a future where patient care becomes increasingly personalised and efficient, revolutionising the way healthcare is delivered.

Additionally, AI-driven predictive modelling has significantly improved patient outcomes, disease progression, and resource utilisation forecasting. Techniques such as Artificial Neural Networks, Decision Trees, and Support Vector Machines can

---

[61] Jie Tang et al., 'Application of Machine-Learning Models to Predict Tacrolimus Stable Dose in Renal Transplant Recipients', *Scientific Reports* 7, no. 1 (8 February 2017): 42192, https://doi.org/10.1038/srep42192.

analyse vast amounts of clinical data and generate predictions about the likelihood of specific events or conditions. For example, a study was performed on developing different types of machine learning models for predicting the readmission risk of Chronic Obstructive Pulmonary Disease (COPD) patients. The study was conducted on a real-world database containing the medical claims of 111,992 patients from the Geisinger Health System from January 2004 to September 2015. The patient features used to build the machine learning models include both knowledge-driven ones, extracted according to clinical knowledge potentially related to COPD readmission, and data-driven features removed from the patient data. The analysis showed that the prediction performance regarding the area Under the receiver operating characteristic (ROC) Curve (AUC) could be improved from around 0.60 using knowledge-driven features to 0.653 by combining both knowledge-driven and data-driven elements, based on the one-year claims history before discharge. Moreover, the study also demonstrates that the complex deep learning models, in this case, cannot improve the prediction performance, with the best AUC around 0.65.[62]

AI has also demonstrated remarkable potential in precision medicine, combining genetic, environmental, and lifestyle data to create personalised treatment plans. Machine learning models can analyse genomic data to identify biomarkers associated with disease susceptibility or response to specific treatments. This information can be used to develop targeted therapies, ultimately enhancing treatment efficacy and reducing adverse side effects.[63]

---

[62] Xu Min, Bin Yu, and Fei Wang, 'Predictive Modeling of the Hospital Readmission Risk from Patients' Claims Data Using Machine Learning: A Case Study on COPD', *Scientific Reports* 9, no. 1 (20 February 2019): 2362, https://doi.org/10.1038/s41598-019-39071-y.
[63] Kexin Huang et al., 'Machine Learning Applications for Therapeutic Tasks with Genomics Data', *Patterns* 2, no. 10 (9 August 2021): 100328, https://doi.org/10.1016/j.patter.2021.100328.

Moreover, AI-driven data analysis has been applied to electronic health records (EHRs) to uncover previously unrecognised patterns and associations. Natural language processing algorithms can extract and analyse unstructured data from EHRs, such as clinical notes, to generate actionable insights for healthcare providers.[64]

In summary, the use of AI in data analysis and predictive modelling is revolutionising healthcare research by facilitating the discovery of novel patterns and relationships, improving the accuracy of predictions, and enabling the development of personalised treatment strategies. As these technologies advance, researchers and healthcare providers will be better equipped to optimise patient care and achieve better outcomes.

5.3 AI in drug discovery and clinical trial design

The traditional drug discovery and development process is a lengthy and expensive endeavour, often taking more than a decade and costing billions of dollars. Artificial intelligence has emerged as a game-changer in this field, significantly expediting the process and improving success rates. AI's impact on clinical trial design has also been transformative by enhancing patient selection, trial efficiency, and data analysis.

In drug discovery, AI algorithms analyse large chemical compound databases and predict their interactions with biological targets. Machine learning models, such as deep learning and reinforcement learning, can recognise patterns and relationships between molecular structures and their therapeutic effects, guiding the

---

[64] Braja G Patra et al., 'Extracting Social Determinants of Health from Electronic Health Records Using Natural Language Processing: A Systematic Review', *Journal of the American Medical Informatics Association* 28, no. 12 (1 December 2021): 2716–27, https://doi.org/10.1093/jamia/ocab170.

design of novel drug candidates.[65]. A notable example is the discovery of a new antibiotic, Halicin, by Massachusetts Institute of Technology (MIT) researchers using an AI-driven platform. This discovery showcased the potential of AI in identifying new drugs with unique properties.[66]

In addition to discovering new molecules, AI is employed to repurpose existing drugs, which is a more cost-effective and time-saving approach. By analysing the known properties of approved drugs and their potential targets, AI algorithms can identify new therapeutic indications, leading to faster and more efficient drug development.[67]

AI has made a considerable impact on clinical trial design as well. For example, AI-driven patient selection tools can analyse electronic health records, genomics data, and other medical information to identify potential participants matching specific clinical trial inclusion criteria. This approach streamlines patient recruitment, reduces enrolment time, and increases the likelihood of successful trial outcomes. A software tool called Trial Pathfinder uses real-world clinical data of people with cancer to optimise the inclusiveness and safety of eligibility criteria for clinical trials. The device can run clinical-trial emulations and learn how to optimise trial-inclusion eligibility criteria while maintaining patient safety.[68] The practical implications of this are:

---

[65] Jessica Vamathevan et al., 'Applications of Machine Learning in Drug Discovery and Development', *Nature Reviews. Drug Discovery* 18, no. 6 (June 2019): 463–77, https://doi.org/10.1038/s41573-019-0024-5.
[66] Jonathan M. Stokes et al., 'A Deep Learning Approach to Antibiotic Discovery', *Cell* 180, no. 4 (20 February 2020): 688-702.e13, https://doi.org/10.1016/j.cell.2020.01.021.
[67] Sudeep Pushpakom et al., 'Drug Repurposing: Progress, Challenges and Recommendations', *Nature Reviews Drug Discovery* 18, no. 1 (January 2019): 41–58, https://doi.org/10.1038/nrd.2018.168.
[68] Chunhua Weng and James R. Rogers, 'AI Uses Patient Data to Optimise Selection of Eligibility Criteria for Clinical Trials', *Nature* 592, no. 7855 (April 2021): 512–13,

- The tool can help improve the clinical trial design by optimising the eligibility criteria for patient enrolment.
- The tool can increase the inclusiveness of clinical trials by learning from real-world clinical data of people with cancer.
- The tool can maintain patient safety while optimising the eligibility criteria for clinical trials.

Furthermore, AI-powered adaptive trial designs can optimise clinical trials by allowing for modifications to the trial structure based on interim results. Machine learning algorithms can evaluate patient outcomes in real time and recommend adjustments, such as sample size changes or treatment arm alterations, to increase the trial's efficiency and success rate.[69]

Lastly, AI can enhance the analysis of clinical trial data by detecting previously unrecognised patterns or trends, leading to more robust and generalisable results. For instance, AI techniques such as natural language processing can extract valuable information from unstructured data, like adverse event reports or clinical notes, to better understand treatment outcomes and safety profiles.[70]

In summary, AI's integration into drug discovery and clinical trial design holds immense promise for revolutionising how new drugs are developed and tested. By accelerating drug discovery, optimising patient selection, and improving trial design and data analysis, AI can bring safer, more effective therapies to patients faster.

---

https://doi.org/10.1038/d41586-021-00845-y.
[69] N. Stallard et al., 'Efficient Adaptive Designs for Clinical Trials of Interventions for COVID-19', *Statistics in Biopharmaceutical Research* 12, no. 4 (1 October 2020): 483–97.
[70] Seyedmostafa Sheikhalishahi et al., 'Natural Language Processing of Clinical Notes on Chronic Diseases: Systematic Review', *JMIR Medical Informatics* 7, no. 2 (27 April 2019): e12239, https://doi.org/10.2196/12239.

AI-driven research collaboration and communication

AI-driven research collaboration and communication have emerged as a transformative force in healthcare. With the rapid advancement of artificial intelligence (AI) technologies, healthcare professionals can now access powerful tools to enhance their ability to collaborate, share knowledge, and drive research forward.

One of the key benefits of AI-driven research collaboration is its ability to facilitate interdisciplinary collaboration among healthcare professionals. Traditionally, healthcare research has been siloed within specific disciplines, which makes it challenging to bridge the gap between different areas of expertise. However, AI technologies offer the potential to break down these barriers by enabling professionals from diverse backgrounds to collaborate on complex research projects. Through AI-powered platforms and tools, healthcare professionals can connect with experts from various fields, hence leveraging their collective knowledge and skills to tackle complex healthcare challenges.

Furthermore, AI-driven research collaboration platforms can streamline the process of data sharing and analysis. Healthcare professionals generate vast amounts of data through various sources, including electronic health records, medical imaging, and genomic sequencing. However, analysing and interpreting this data can be time-consuming and resource intensive. AI algorithms can automate data processing tasks, thus enabling researchers to extract meaningful insights more efficiently. By leveraging AI tools, healthcare professionals can collaborate on data-driven research projects, sharing and analysing large datasets securely and standardised.

These enable and enhance the following:

1. **Streamlining Research Process**: These platforms can help organise and manage research activities, which are traditionally scattered across various tools and platforms. They can enable real-time collaboration, version control, data management, and other functions that make the research process more efficient.
2. **Facilitating Collaboration**: These platforms can provide a shared space where researchers can collaborate in real-time, regardless of geographical location. This can lead to more diverse and multidisciplinary collaborations.
3. **Increasing Accessibility**: By making research data and results accessible to a wider audience, these platforms can democratise the research process. They can also facilitate open science practices like preprints and available data.
4. **Automating Routine Tasks**: Several routine tasks in the research process, such as literature review, data analysis, or manuscript formatting, can be automated using AI, freeing up researchers' time to focus on more complex aspects of their work.
5. **Enhancing Discovery and Innovation**: AI-driven platforms can also help researchers find relevant literature, data, or other researchers more effectively. These platforms can use machine learning algorithms to provide personalised recommendations based on a researcher's interests or previous work.

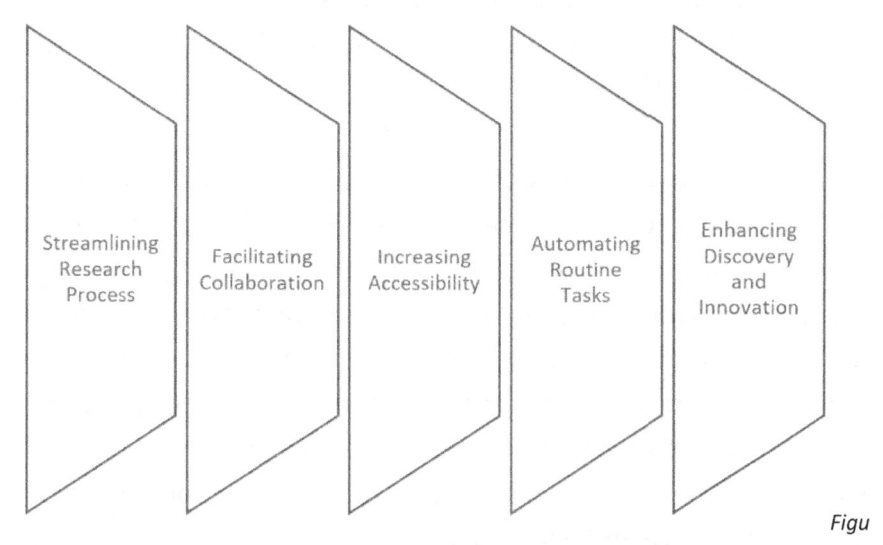

Figure 24. The benefits of AI-driven research platforms

Some examples of AI-driven research collaboration platforms include:

1. **IRIS.AI**: This tool uses AI to help researchers conduct literature reviews. It can read and understand scientific text and provide relevant articles based on a researcher's project description.
2. **Labii ELN & LIMS**: This Electronic Laboratory Notebook (ELN) and Laboratory Information Management System (LIMS) uses AI to help researchers manage and analyse laboratory data. It can automate tasks such as data entry and calculation, making laboratory management more efficient.
3. **Semantic Scholar**: Developed by the Allen Institute for AI, this tool uses AI to help researchers find relevant literature. It can understand the content and context of scientific papers and provide a list of the most relevant articles based on a researcher's search query.
4. **Scite**: This platform uses AI to provide insight into the context of research citations, helping researchers

understand how a scientific paper has been cited (for example, whether it has been supported or contradicted by later research).

AI-driven communication tools also play a crucial role in enhancing collaboration among healthcare professionals. These tools utilise natural language processing and machine learning algorithms to facilitate efficient and effective communication. For instance, AI-powered chatbots can assist healthcare professionals by providing relevant research articles and clinical guidelines or answering frequently asked questions. These chatbots can save valuable time and improve productivity, allowing professionals to focus more on direct patient care and research activities.

Moreover, AI-driven communication platforms can enable real-time collaboration and knowledge sharing among healthcare professionals, irrespective of their geographical locations. Researchers can connect with colleagues and experts worldwide through video conferencing, instant messaging, and virtual meeting platforms. This global collaboration promotes the exchange of ideas, accelerates research progress, and fosters innovation in healthcare.

Typeset.io is an online tool designed to simplify the process of writing, collaborating, and publishing academic papers. The platform combines AI technology and features specifically for scholarly writing to make the research writing and publishing process more efficient. Here is how it works:
1. **Writing**: Typeset.io provides an online writing editor that formats your paper as you write. You can choose from over 40,000 journal formats to ensure that your paper adheres to the specific requirements of your target journal. This can save considerable time that may otherwise be spent on formatting.

2. **Collaboration**: You can invite co-authors to collaborate on your paper in real time. Each contributor can work on the document simultaneously, saving changes automatically.
3. **Reference Management**: Typeset.io integrates with popular reference management software like Mendeley, Zotero, and EndNote, allowing you to import and format your citations easily. The platform also has a built-in feature to search and add PubMed, CrossRef, and Google Scholar sources.
4. **Auto-Formatting**: With Typeset.io, you do not need to worry about the intricacies of formatting standards for different journals. The platform automatically formats your paper according to your chosen journal's guidelines.
5. **Plagiarism Check**: Typeset.io provides an integrated plagiarism checker. This ensures that all text is original before submission to a journal, thereby minimising the risk of rejection.
6. **Proofreading**: The platform uses AI to provide proofreading services. It checks your document for grammatical errors and provides suggestions for improving your writing.
7. **Publishing**: Once your paper is ready, you can submit it directly to various academic journals through the Typeset.io platform.

By streamlining the academic writing process, Typeset.io allows researchers to focus on their research rather than formatting and technical details, ultimately making the publication process more efficient and less stressful.

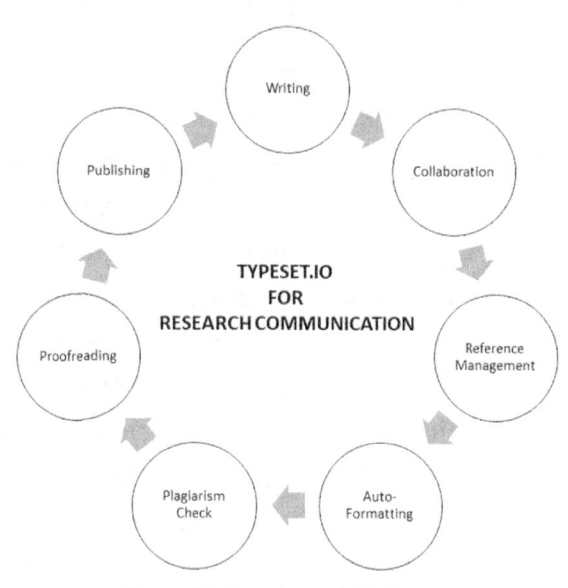

Figure 25. Functions of TYPESET.IO

The Copilot AI assistant by Typeset.io is a valuable tool for researchers in various fields, including healthcare. Copilot utilises the power of (Generative Pre-trained Transformer 4) GPT-4, a fourth- generation machine-learning model, to assist researchers in understanding research papers and providing contextual information. While the search results do not provide specific details about Copilot's application in healthcare research, it can be inferred that Copilot can be utilised to explain healthcare-related research papers and answer queries related to such documents.

To complement Copilot, Typeset.io offers SciSpace, an end-to-end purpose-built workspace for researchers, publishers, and institutions. SciSpace enables efficient collaboration, automates repetitive tasks, and facilitates quick information discovery. Researchers working in healthcare can benefit from SciSpace's collaborative features, which allow them to work together seamlessly on healthcare research projects.

Furthermore, Typeset.io itself provides an authoring and collaboration solution for researchers. It includes an editor designed specifically for research writing, simplifying version control and collaboration, automating formatting, and enabling instant publication in multiple formats. This solution can be particularly useful for healthcare researchers by allowing them to focus more on their research and less on the technical aspects of writing and formatting their work.

Typeset.io's comprehensive suite of tools and solutions, including Copilot, SciSpace, and their authoring and collaboration solutions, can be valuable resources for healthcare researchers. These tools aid in understanding research papers, streamlining research workflows, and enhancing cooperation, ultimately contributing to more efficient and productive healthcare research endeavours.

However, while AI-driven research collaboration and communication offer numerous benefits, challenges exist. Privacy and Security of sensitive patient data are paramount when utilizing AI technologies. Healthcare professionals must ensure proper safeguards are in place to protect patient confidentiality and comply with regulatory requirements.

In conclusion, AI-driven research collaboration and communication have the potential to revolutionize healthcare. These technologies empower healthcare professionals to collaborate across disciplines, leverage vast amounts of data, and improve the efficiency and effectiveness of research endeavours. By embracing AI tools and platforms, healthcare professionals can unlock new possibilities for advancing medical knowledge, improving patient outcomes and shaping the future of healthcare.

Chapter 6 Ethical, Legal, and Social Implications of AI in Healthcare

As artificial intelligence (AI) continues to advance and permeate numerous sectors, its impact on healthcare has been both promising and profound. Integrating AI technologies in healthcare settings holds tremendous potential for improving diagnosis, treatment, and patient outcomes. However, alongside these transformative capabilities, it is crucial to critically examine the ethical, legal, and social implications (ELSI) that arise from the implementation of AI in healthcare. This chapter aims to delve into the multifaceted dimensions of ELSI in the context of AI-driven healthcare by exploring the ethical considerations, legal frameworks, and social implications accompanying the use of AI technologies in medical practice.

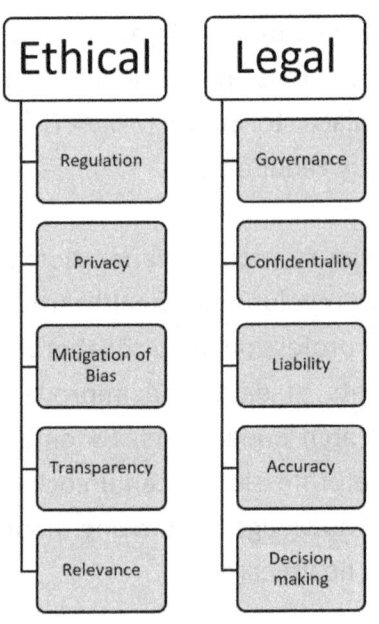

Ethical
- Regulation
- Privacy
- Mitigation of Bias
- Transparency
- Relevance

Legal
- Governance
- Confidentiality
- Liability
- Accuracy
- Decision making

Figure 26. Legal and Ethical Considerations in AI in Healthcare

Biomedical Ethics

Ethical considerations are at the forefront when discussing AI in healthcare. The four foundational principles of medical ethics - beneficence, non-maleficence, autonomy, and social justice - play a significant role in directing healthcare decision-making processes and facilitating the ethical evolution of health technology. Beneficence is about acting in the patient's best interest, translating to the technological sphere the development and deployment of technologies that enhance patients' health and the quality of their lives. Non-maleficence, encapsulating the 'do no harm' principle, entails averting harm to patients, which in the context of healthcare technology, will ensure patient data privacy and security.

On the other hand, autonomy is about respecting patients' rights to make informed decisions concerning their healthcare. In a technology-infused healthcare setting, this principle will infer that patients should have ultimate control over their health data and be able to determine who can access it and how it is used. Social justice, the final pillar, speaks to healthcare resources' fair and equitable distribution. This principle advocates that access to beneficial and innovative health technologies should not be restricted to certain groups based on socioeconomic status or geographical location, thereby helping to diminish disparities in healthcare access and outcomes. These principles are not just ideals that healthcare professionals strive to uphold in their practice; they also serve as guiding light in developing and deploying healthcare technology.

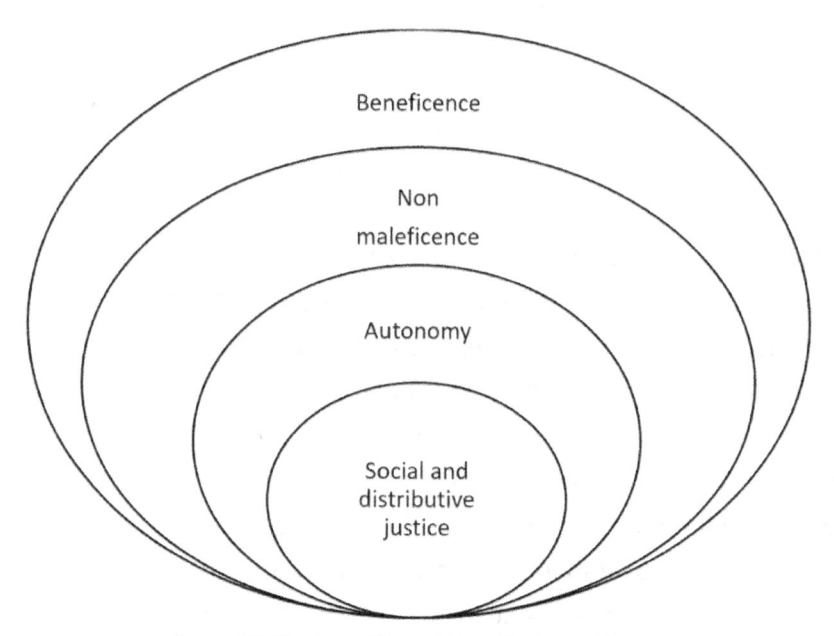

Figure 27. The four pillars of bioethics in healthcare

Michael Cheng's exploration of the influence of artificial intelligence (AI) on human society leads him to propose a unique set of principles for AI bioethics. Recognizing AI's profound industrial, social, and economic shifts in the 21st century, Cheng contends that new AI bioethics principles must be established. These principles will guide AI technologies, ensuring their evolution continues to benefit humanity. Cheng posits that the field of technology bioethics must be transcendental to compensate for AI's innate inability to empathize. This limitation cannot be overcome merely through computation but requires a process of conscientization. By steadfastly prioritizing the principles of beneficence, non-maleficence, autonomy, and social justice, we can strive for a future where technology is harnessed to improve health outcomes and enhance care quality universally.[71]

---

[71] Michael Cheng-Tek Tai, 'The Impact of Artificial Intelligence on Human Society and Bioethics,' *Tzu-Chi Medical Journal* 32, no. 4 (14 August 2020): 339–43, https://doi.org/10.4103/tcmj.tcmj_71_20.

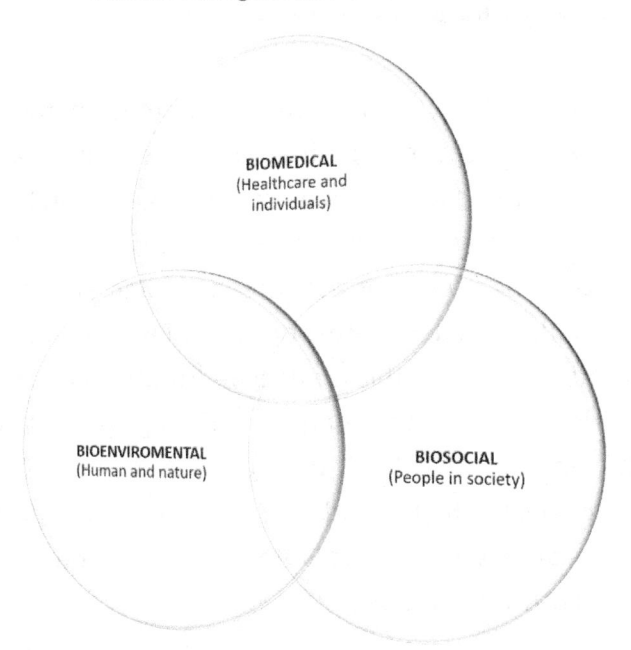

Figure 28. The various domains of bioethics in society adapted from Tai, M. C.-T. (2020). The impact of artificial intelligence on human society and bioethics. Tzu-Chi Medical Journal, 32(4), 339–343. https://doi.org/10.4103/tcmj.tcmj_71_20

Questions arise regarding patient autonomy, informed consent, and the potential bias and discrimination embedded in AI algorithms. For instance, AI-powered diagnostic systems may rely on biased data that disproportionately affect marginalized communities, leading to disparities in healthcare outcomes. Additionally, using AI in decision-making processes raises questions about accountability and the potential delegation of responsibility from human healthcare professionals to algorithms. These ethical dilemmas require careful examination and robust ethical frameworks to ensure AI technologies' fair and just implementation. [72].

---

[72] Brent Daniel Mittelstadt et al., 'The Ethics of Algorithms: Mapping the Debate,' *Big Data & Society* 3, no. 2 (1 December 2016): 2053951716679679, https://doi.org/10.1177/2053951716679679.

Ethical Framework for AI in Healthcare

A firm ethical foundation is indispensable for meaningful healthcare decision-making, necessitating an earnest and holistic assessment of patient needs in specific circumstances. A cornerstone of this process is the trust established between the clinician, the patient, and the data being used. This assessment should embrace medical evidence and the broader context of the patient's environment and personal situation. Key to this is effective communication grounded on the principles of participation and engagement from the individuals making the final decisions. It is incumbent upon clinicians to ensure that healthcare technology integrates these ethical considerations to facilitate a shared decision-making process, as illustrated in Figure 3[73].

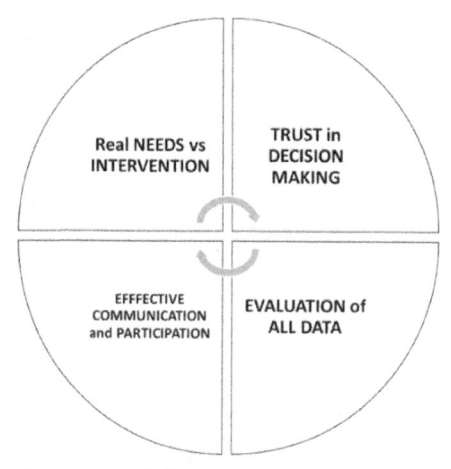

Figure 29. Process for shared ethical decision-making in healthcare (Gundersen & Bærøe, 2022)

Gundersen and Bærøe critically explore four alternative models of AI's design and application in patient care: the ordinary evidence model, the ethical design model, the collaborative model, and the

---

[73] Torbjørn Gundersen and Kristine Bærøe, 'The Future Ethics of Artificial Intelligence in Medicine: Making Sense of Collaborative Models', *Science and Engineering Ethics* 28, no. 2 (1 April 2022): 17, https://doi.org/10.1007/s11948-022-00369-2.

public deliberation model. They argue that the collaborative model holds the most potential for a wide range of AI technologies. In contrast, the public deliberation model becomes necessary when the technology fundamentally alters the conditions for ethical shared decision-making. To illustrate their argument, they present this framework shown in Table 1.

Table 1. From: Gundersen, T., & Bærøe, K. (2022). The Future Ethics of Artificial Intelligence in Medicine: Making Sense of Collaborative Models. Science and Engineering Ethics, 28(2), 17(p5). https://doi.org/10.1007/s11948-022-00369-2

Short description of the components of shared decision-making	Expanded descriptions of the features of what is required of doctors in shared decision-making (These can be perceived as minimum standards)	How AI can undermine the conditions for shared decision-making
(a) Understanding the patient's condition	Doctors must understand the connection between patients' conditions and the need for potential interventions on a general, technical, and normative level and translate them into individual patients' particular contexts.	Suppose the clinical outcome of AI is beyond what doctors can understand themselves. In that case, their clinical competence is undermined, and by that, a crucial presupposition for why the patients have reason to trust them in the first place.[74]
(b) Trust in evidence	Doctors must base their decision on sources of evidence they trust to ensure the information is relevant and adequate.	If doctors suggest treatments based on AI sources for the information they cannot fully account for, they force patients to place blind trust in their recommendations. This is just another version of paternalism.
(c) Due assessment of benefits and risks	Doctors must understand all relevant information of benefits and risks and trade-offs between them.	If doctors need help understanding how and why AI has reached an outcome, such as the classification of a radiograph, uncertainty regarding assessments of risks, benefits and trade-offs will follow. This, in turn, undermines patients' reasons to have confidence in the medical judgments from their role as experts in the relationship.
(d) Accommodating	Doctors must convey	If AI systems make it hard for

Short description of the components of shared decision-making	Expanded descriptions of the features of what is required of doctors in shared decision-making (These can be perceived as minimum standards)	How AI can undermine the conditions for shared decision-making
patient's understanding, communication, and deliberation	an assessment of risks and benefits to patients in a clear and accessible manner, ensure they have understood the information, and invite them to share their thoughts and deliberate together on the matter.	doctors to understand how and why they reach their outcomes, they cannot facilitate patients' understanding. Instead, they will have to paternalistically require that the patient accept that the AI 'knows best.'

Reddy and his team (2020) stressed the importance of implementing a governance framework to tackle the complexities of technology use in healthcare. Advocating for a model rooted in fairness, transparency, trustworthiness, and accountability, they delineate this governance framework's shape (refer to Figure 30). Integral to this framework is the relentless monitoring and evaluation of AI systems in use, by consistently assessing their ethical impacts, ideally through integration with a transdisciplinary clinical governance committee. Beyond this, Reddy et al. underscore the significance of increasing awareness and extending education to all parties involved regarding AI's ethical implications in healthcare. They also advise fostering collaborative relationships with academic institutions and healthcare providers to guarantee a holistic approach to governance in this swiftly advancing field.[75]

---

[75] Reddy et al., 'A Governance Model for the Application of AI in Health Care.'

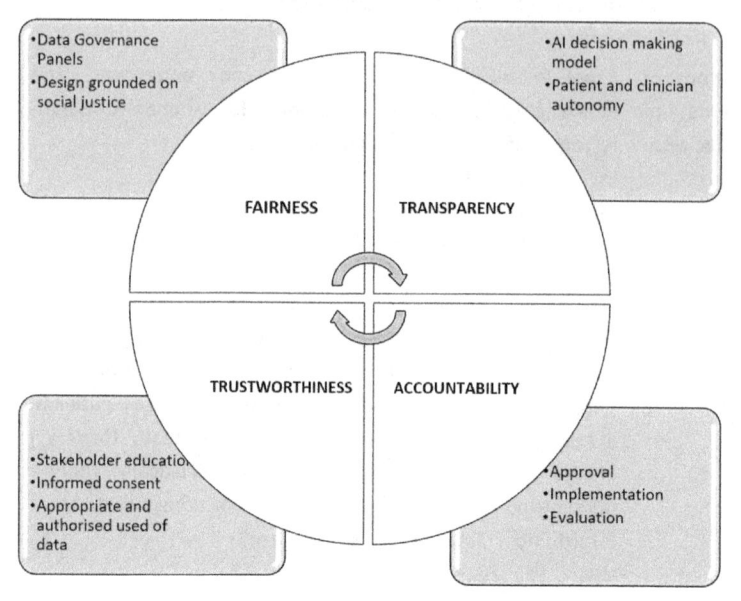

Figure 30. Governance model for AI in Healthcare (Adapted from Reddy, S., Allan, S., Coghlan, S., & Cooper, P. (2020). A governance model for the application of AI in healthcare. Journal of the American Medical Informatics Association, 27(3), p 493

From a legal standpoint, AI's rapid development and adoption in healthcare have prompted the need for regulatory frameworks that can effectively govern its use. Various legal considerations come into play, such as privacy and data protection, intellectual property rights, liability, and the responsibility of healthcare professionals when utilizing AI systems. Striking the right balance between fostering innovation and safeguarding patient rights and safety is essential. Legal frameworks must evolve to keep pace with AI advancements, thus ensuring that the deployment of AI technologies in healthcare adheres to established legal standards and protects the rights and well-being of patients.[76]

Furthermore, the introduction of AI in healthcare carries significant social implications that extend beyond the realms of ethics and law. The integration of AI technologies may impact the dynamics

---

[76] I. Glenn Cohen et al., 'The Legal and Ethical Concerns That Arise from Using Complex Predictive Analytics in Health Care,' *Health Affairs (Project Hope)* 33, no. 7 (July 2014): 1139–47, https://doi.org/10.1377/hlthaff.2014.0048.

between healthcare professionals and patients, the distribution of resources, and the accessibility of healthcare services. For example, AI-powered telemedicine platforms can improve access to care for remote and underserved populations. Still, they may also exacerbate healthcare disparities for individuals without access to technology or reliable internet connections. Societal factors such as trust, transparency, and equity play a crucial role in shaping the acceptance and implementation of AI in healthcare.

The Intersection of Society and AI and Healthcare

The ethics of digital health in a sociotechnical context covers a broad spectrum of factors, from individual health-related habits and interpersonal dynamics to organizational protocols and government regulations. This complex area demands a thorough and holistic understanding of the intricate interplay between technology and society, particularly within the healthcare sphere.

The social implications of adopting medical AI during the COVID-19 pandemic were investigated in a representative study of two European countries (Denmark and France). In this study, people's trust in medical AI and, to a lesser extent, open-mindedness were key predictors of medical AI adoption. However, the study also revealed that mistrust and perceived uniqueness neglect from human physicians, as well as a lack of social belonging, significantly increased people's medical AI adoption. These results suggested that for medical AI to be widely adopted, people might need to express less confidence in human physicians and even feel disconnected from humanity. The study proposed that successful medical AI adoption policy should focus on trust-building measures without eroding trust in human physicians.[77]

---

[77] Darius-Aurel Frank et al., 'Drivers and Social Implications of Artificial Intelligence

De Cremer and Kasparov (2022) spotlighted the double-edged nature of healthcare technology by accentuating its capacity to empower and segregate. They offered several suggestions to navigate the sociotechnical ethics of digital health. Foremost, they encouraged collaboration among technology pioneers, industry stakeholders, and regulatory bodies to craft an ethical framework aligned with societal and regulatory norms. Subsequently, they underscored the role of responsible leadership, which should focus on outcomes and the ethical processes that lead to these outcomes. Integrating ethical considerations into organizational structures was proposed to include leadership teams and boards while encouraging an ongoing moral consciousness and education within the corporate environment. Finally, they stressed the imperative of social justice and early access to AI, highlighting the need for inclusivity and ensuring that technological advancements be made universally accessible, thereby not marginalizing any demographic groups.[78]

The successful implementation and endorsement of digital health technologies hinge upon stakeholders' capacity to address these challenges proactively, systematically, and ethically. This involves creating ethical guidelines and regulations but, equally importantly, cultivating an ethos of responsibility in the design, development, deployment, and usage of digital health technologies. Shaw and Donia illustrated the sociotechnical system created by adopting digital health technologies in healthcare settings, where they recommended an exhaustive ethical evaluation of digital health technologies that incorporated social justice considerations, thereby fostering a sociotechnical perspective in ethical analysis.[79]

Adoption in Healthcare during the COVID-19 Pandemic', *PLOS ONE* 16, no. 11 (22 November 2021): e0259928, https://doi.org/10.1371/journal.pone.0259928.
[78] David De Cremer and Garry Kasparov, 'The Ethics of Technology Innovation: A Double-Edged Sword?', *AI and Ethics* 2, no. 3 (1 August 2022): 533–37, https://doi.org/10.1007/s43681-021-00103-x.

The insights garnered from this review significantly impact various stakeholders across the healthcare sector. Integrating technology, particularly AI, into healthcare mandates the creation of transparent and interpretable models to establish accountability and instil trust. Ethical concerns regarding data privacy and Security underscore the criticality of implementing stringent cybersecurity protocols and data governance frameworks.

Moreover, the sociotechnical ethics of digital health accentuate the demand for fairness and inclusivity regarding access to health technologies. This reiterates the necessity for ethical leadership of the highest order, along with effective government regulation, to protect the interests of society. These conclusions have merged into the proposed ethical framework presented in Figure 31, which seeks to guide the adoption and assimilation of technology in healthcare.

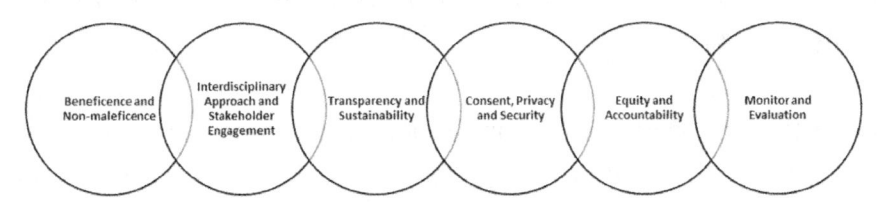

Figure 31. An optimal framework for the ethical consideration of Technology in Healthcare

Interdisciplinary collaboration is essential to address these complex ethical, legal, and social implications (ELSI) challenges. Healthcare professionals, ethicists, legal experts, policymakers, and patients must work together to develop comprehensive guidelines, ethical frameworks, and legal regulations promoting responsible and equitable use of AI technologies in healthcare. By addressing the

---

[79] James A. Shaw and Joseph Donia, 'The Sociotechnical Ethics of Digital Health: A Critique and Extension of Approaches From Bioethics,' *Frontiers in Digital Health* 3 (2021), https://www.frontiersin.org/articles/10.3389/fdgth.2021.725088.

ELSI head-on, we can ensure that AI-driven healthcare aligns with the values of fairness.

The automation capabilities of AI may render some tasks traditionally performed by human staff obsolete. For example, AI-powered systems can take over responsibilities such as appointment scheduling, handling prescription renewals, or managing patient records, typically assigned to administrative personnel.

These technological advancements can potentially lead to significant changes in the healthcare job market. As AI takes over mundane tasks, healthcare workers may find their roles evolving or, in some cases, diminishing. However, it is crucial to consider that while certain studies may be automated, the human element in healthcare remains irreplaceable. Compassionate care, complex decision-making, and patient interactions are aspects where human healthcare professionals excel, and these areas are less likely to be usurped by AI.

Nevertheless, the concern about job displacement is valid and needs to be addressed with thoughtful planning and implementation. It is essential to ensure that as AI is integrated more fully into healthcare, there are opportunities for upskilling and retraining existing staff to work in tandem with these new technologies. By doing so, we can ensure that the transition to AI-driven healthcare is as smooth and beneficial as possible for all involved.

If access to AI-driven healthcare tools becomes largely dependent on financial means or the availability of high-quality internet services, this can inadvertently widen existing health disparities. For example, whether telehealth services or AI-powered health applications, AI-driven health technologies require access to stable and high-speed internet connections for effective use. However, not all populations have equal access to such services. Rural areas and socio-economically disadvantaged regions may face infrastructural challenges, resulting in limited or inconsistent internet access, which can hinder using these advanced tools.

Moreover, the cost of AI-driven healthcare services or devices may be beyond the reach of many, particularly those in low-income brackets. As such, if AI-driven healthcare becomes a significant part of standard care, it can inadvertently create a system where high-quality care is only accessible to those who can afford these advanced tools.

Therefore, while the integration of AI in healthcare holds great promise, it is crucial to consider and address the potential for a digital divide. Policymakers, healthcare providers, and technology developers should collaborate to ensure equitable access to these technologies. Strategies can include making AI-powered tools more affordable, improving internet infrastructure in underserved areas, and implementing policies that ensure equitable access to these advanced healthcare tools. By doing so, we can work towards a future where AI in healthcare serves as a tool for reducing health disparities, not exacerbating them.

6.1 Data Privacy and Security

Data privacy and Security are paramount considerations when harnessing the power of artificial intelligence (AI) in healthcare. The use of AI technologies necessitates collecting, storing, and analysing vast amounts of sensitive patient data, including medical records, genomic information, and diagnostic images. While these data are valuable for improving healthcare outcomes, they pose significant risks if not adequately protected. Therefore, robust measures must be implemented to safeguard data privacy and ensure the Security of patient information.

Data privacy concerns arise due to the potential for unauthorized access, misuse, or disclosure of personal health information. To protect patient confidentiality and privacy rights, healthcare organizations must adhere to strict regulatory frameworks, such as the Health Insurance Portability and Accountability Act (HIPAA) in the United States or the General Data Protection Regulation (GDPR) in the European Union. These regulations outline data collection, storage, sharing, and informed consent guidelines, aiming to ensure that patient data is handled ethically and responsibly.[80]

AI technologies also introduce unique challenges to data security. Machine learning algorithms rely on large datasets to train and improve their performance. However, this reliance on data poses risks such as breaches or malicious attacks targeting healthcare systems. Adversarial attacks, where AI models are manipulated or fooled, can compromise the integrity and reliability of AI-driven healthcare applications. Moreover, integrating AI with cloud computing introduces additional security concerns, as data may be transmitted and stored on external servers.

Encryption techniques, access controls, and secure authentication protocols can safeguard data during transmission and storage. Regular security audits and vulnerability assessments are essential to identify and address potential weaknesses in the system. Additionally, implementing strict user access policies and training healthcare professionals on data security best practices can minimize the risk of internal breaches.

---

[80] W. Nicholson Price and I. Glenn Cohen, 'Privacy in the Age of Medical Big Data,' *Nature Medicine* 25, no. 1 (January 2019): 37–43, https://doi.org/10.1038/s41591-018-0272-7.

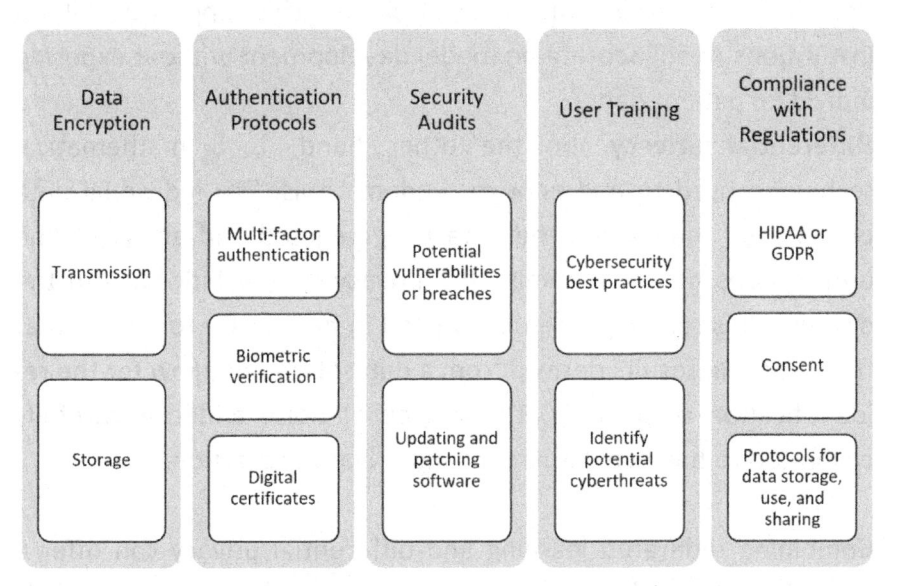

Figure 32. Mitigation for healthcare data privacy and Security

Furthermore, advancements in privacy-preserving AI techniques offer promising solutions to balance data utility and privacy. Techniques like federated learning and differential privacy allow healthcare institutions to collaborate and derive insights from shared datasets without directly exchanging sensitive patient information. By aggregating and analysing data locally, the privacy of individual patients is preserved while still benefiting from the collective intelligence of the data.

Federated Learning is a machine learning approach that enables multiple institutions to build a common, robust machine learning model without sharing raw data. Instead of transferring raw data to a central location, the learning process is distributed across multiple nodes (in this case, healthcare institutions). Each institution trains a local model on its dataset and sends only the model updates (parameters or gradients), not the raw data, to a central server. The server aggregates these updates to form a global model, which is then sent back to each institution for another round of local updates. This iterative process continues until the model is sufficiently trained. This approach allows institutions to collaborate on model development without exposing individual patient data.[81]

Differential privacy, on the other hand, is a mathematical technique used to add enough random "noise" to individual data points such that, when the data is aggregated and analysed, the output does not compromise the privacy of any individual in the dataset. This technique can be applied in healthcare to ensure that the statistical results derived from a dataset do not allow for the re-identification of patients. The degree of noise added is carefully calibrated to balance data utility and privacy protection.

Combining federated learning and differential privacy can offer a powerful approach to collaborative healthcare research and AI model development that protects patient privacy. For instance, federated learning can collectively train an AI model across multiple hospitals. At the same time, differential privacy ensures that the individual patient data used for local model updates does not leak sensitive information.

These techniques, while promising, are challenging. The quality of federated learning models can be influenced by the number and diversity of participating institutions, and differential privacy requires careful tuning to ensure that data utility is not overly compromised. Nevertheless, with ongoing research and development, these techniques are poised to play a crucial role in enabling privacy-preserving AI applications in healthcare.

Collaboration between healthcare professionals, data scientists, and privacy experts is crucial in addressing data privacy and security challenges in AI-driven healthcare. Striking the right balance

---

[81] Liron S. Duraku et al., 'Collaborative Hand Surgery Clinical Research without Sharing Individual Patient Data; Proof of Principle Study,' *Journal of Plastic, Reconstructive & Aesthetic Surgery*, 2022.

between data accessibility for research and innovation while protecting patient privacy requires ongoing dialogue and the development of ethical frameworks. Adhering to legal requirements and industry standards is essential, but a proactive approach beyond compliance is necessary to anticipate and mitigate emerging privacy and security threats.[82]

In conclusion, data privacy and Security are critical considerations in AI-driven healthcare. Protecting sensitive patient information and ensuring healthcare data's confidentiality, integrity, and availability are paramount. Adhering to regulatory frameworks, implementing robust security measures, and leveraging privacy-preserving techniques are key steps to safeguard data privacy and mitigate security risks. By prioritizing data privacy and Security, healthcare organizations can foster trust, promote responsible data sharing, and harness the full potential of AI technologies to revolutionize healthcare delivery and improve patient outcomes.

6.2 Bias and Fairness in AI Algorithms

Bias and fairness in AI algorithms have emerged as significant concerns in implementing artificial intelligence (AI) in healthcare. While AI technologies have the potential to revolutionize healthcare by enhancing diagnostics, treatment decisions, and patient outcomes, the presence of bias in algorithms can lead to inequitable healthcare delivery and exacerbate existing disparities. Addressing prejudice and promoting fairness in AI algorithms is essential to ensure equitable and just healthcare for all individuals.

---

[82] Hun-Sung Kim, In Ho Kwon, and Won Chul Cha, 'Future and Development Direction of Digital Healthcare,' *Healthcare Informatics Research* 27, no. 2 (April 2021): 95–101, https://doi.org/10.4258/hir.2021.27.2.95.

One area where bias can manifest in AI algorithms is the training data used to develop and refine the models. If the training data is skewed or not representative of the diverse patient population, the algorithms may inadvertently learn and perpetuate biases present in the data. For example, if historical healthcare data primarily represents certain demographic groups or geographic regions, AI algorithms trained on such data may not generalize well to diverse patient populations, leading to inaccurate diagnoses or treatments for under-represented groups.

To illustrate this, a study by Obermeyer et al. (2019) examined an algorithm to determine which patients would benefit from additional healthcare resources. The study found that the algorithm was less likely to refer Black patients than White patients with similar medical needs. This bias stemmed from historical data that reflected racial disparities in healthcare access and resource allocation. The study highlighted the importance of addressing discrimination in AI algorithms to prevent unfair treatment and mitigate inequities in healthcare delivery.[83]

Various approaches have been proposed to mitigate bias and promote fairness in AI algorithms. One method involves carefully curating training datasets to ensure representation and diversity. This includes collecting data from a wide range of sources and ensuring that under-represented groups are adequately represented in the data. Additionally, algorithms can be designed to explicitly account for fairness by using techniques such as "fairness-aware" training or incorporating fairness constraints during the learning process.

---

[83] Ziad Obermeyer et al., 'Dissecting Racial Bias in an Algorithm Used to Manage the Health of Populations, *Science (New York, N.Y.)* 366, no. 6464 (25 October 2019): 447–53, https://doi.org/10.1126/science.aax2342.

Another approach involves conducting regular audits and evaluations of AI algorithms to identify and mitigate bias. This includes analysing the performance of algorithms across different demographic groups to detect and address disparities. External organizations, such as regulatory bodies or independent review boards, can play a role in auditing AI algorithms for fairness and ensuring accountability.

Moreover, transparency and interpretability of AI algorithms are crucial for addressing bias and fairness concerns. Healthcare professionals and stakeholders should have access to clear explanations of how AI algorithms make decisions. By understanding the underlying factors and variables that influence algorithmic outputs, biases can be detected, challenged, and corrected more effectively.

Efforts to address bias and fairness in AI algorithms are ongoing. For instance, the "AI Fairness 360" toolkit developed by International Business Machines (IBM) Research provides a comprehensive set of open-source tools and algorithms to help developers detect and mitigate bias in AI models across various domains, including healthcare.[84]

In conclusion, bias and fairness in AI algorithms are critical considerations in healthcare. Ensuring that AI algorithms are free from bias and promote fairness is crucial for equitable healthcare delivery. By carefully curating data, incorporating fairness constraints, conducting regular audits, and promoting transparency, healthcare professionals can work towards

---

[84] Rachel Bellamy et al., 'AI Fairness 360: An Extensible Toolkit for Detecting and Mitigating Algorithmic Bias', *IBM Journal of Research and Development*, 1 July 2019, 3, https://doi.org/10.1147/JRD.2019.2942287.

developing AI algorithms that provide fair and unbiased healthcare outcomes for all individuals.

6.3 Liability and accountability in AI-driven decision-making

Liability and accountability in AI-driven decision-making have become crucial topics in artificial intelligence (AI) integration in healthcare. As AI algorithms play an increasingly prominent role in supporting clinical decision-making, examining the allocation of liability and establishing accountability frameworks to ensure patient safety, ethical standards, and legal compliance is essential. The most prevalent issues identified in the literature were patient safety, algorithmic transparency, lack of proper regulation, liability & accountability, impact on the patient-physician relationship, and governance of AI-empowered healthcare.[85]

One aspect of liability and accountability in AI-driven decision-making is determining responsibility when errors or adverse outcomes occur. Traditionally, healthcare professionals have been held accountable for their actions and decisions. However, with AI technologies, the lines of responsibility can become blurred. Suppose an AI algorithm contributes to a faulty diagnosis or treatment decision. In that case, questions arise regarding who should bear the liability—the healthcare professional, the organization implementing the AI system, or the algorithm's developers.

A notable example highlighting the complexities of liability and accountability in AI-driven decision-making is the case of diagnostic errors. When an AI algorithm provides a diagnosis that turns out to

---

[85] Anto Čartolovni, Ana Tomičić, and Elvira Lazić Mosler, 'Ethical, Legal, and Social Considerations of AI-Based Medical Decision-Support Tools: A Scoping Review,' *International Journal of Medical Informatics* 161 (1 May 2022): 104738, https://doi.org/10.1016/j.ijmedinf.2022.104738.

be incorrect, determining the responsibility becomes challenging. If the healthcare professional unthinkingly relies on the algorithm's output without critically evaluating it, questions may arise about their professional judgment and the adequacy of their supervision over the AI system. On the other hand, if the algorithm itself is flawed or biased, responsibility may fall on the developers or the organization for implementing an algorithm without proper validation and quality control measures.

To address these challenges, frameworks for liability and accountability in AI-driven decision-making are being developed. These frameworks aim to clarify the roles and responsibilities of different stakeholders involved in creating, deploying, and using AI systems in healthcare. For example, legal guidelines may be established to outline the obligations of healthcare professionals, organizations, and algorithm developers in ensuring the safety, accuracy, and transparency of AI-driven decision-making processes.

The features of accountability can be dissected into seven components that explain its functionality.[86]

1. The first is 'Context,' which pertains to the specific fields or domains in which an accountability relationship is established. This can range from healthcare to education or any other area where there is a need to hold someone or something accountable for their actions or decisions.
2. The second feature is 'Range.' It delineates the tasks, actions, decisions, services, or assessments for which the agent is held accountable. It sets the boundaries or scope of what is covered under accountability.

---

[86] Claudio Novelli, Mariarosaria Taddeo, and Luciano Floridi, 'Accountability in Artificial Intelligence: What It Is and How It Works,' *AI & SOCIETY*, 7 February 2023, 1–12, https://doi.org/10.1007/s00146-023-01635-y.

3. 'Agent' refers to the entity or person exercising delegated powers or tasks. The agent is responsible for the functions and agrees to be praised or blamed based on the outcomes of these tasks.
4. 'Forum' refers to the entity that engages in questioning or supervision. This can also be the entity whose interests are served through the delegation of tasks. The forum is the principal entity that oversees the agent's actions or decisions.
5. 'Standard' involves the principles, rules, and benchmarks against which the accountable agent's conduct is assessed. These standards set the criteria for what is acceptable or expected from the agent.
6. The 'Process' outlines the procedures for holding the agent accountable. This can include regular check-ins, reviews, audits, or other methods of ensuring the agent is fulfilling their responsibilities correctly and effectively.
7. Finally, 'Implications' refer to the consequences or outcomes triggered by the accountability assessment. These can be formal, such as disciplinary action or rewards, or informal, such as reputation damage or praise.

These features provide a comprehensive overview of accountability functions, helping us understand their importance and impact on various tasks and fields.

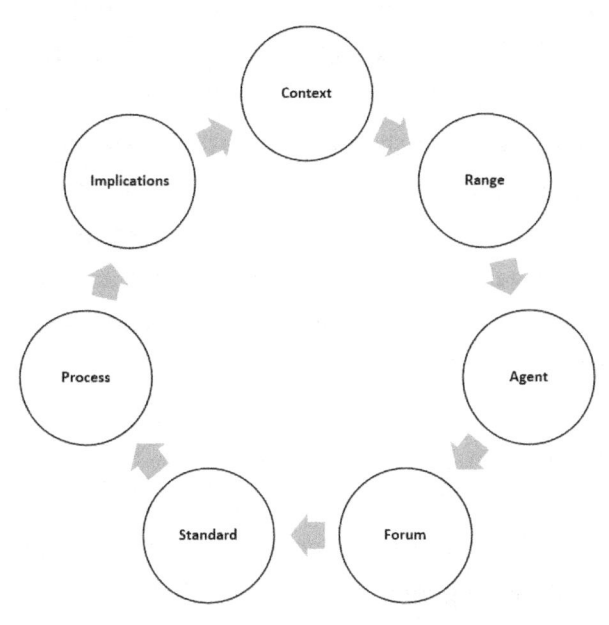

Figure 33. The seven components of accountability

Additionally, liability insurance and risk management strategies can play a role in managing the potential risks associated with AI-driven decision-making. Healthcare organizations may need to reassess their insurance coverage to account for possible errors or adverse outcomes of AI technologies. Similarly, developers of AI algorithms may need to consider liability and indemnity clauses when licensing their technologies to healthcare institutions.

Moreover, establishing regulatory frameworks is vital in defining the standards and requirements for AI-driven decision-making in healthcare. Regulatory bodies can play a significant role in overseeing AI systems' safety, efficacy, and ethical considerations. For instance, the US Food and Drug Administration (FDA) has issued guidelines for regulating AI-based medical devices, outlining the need for transparency, explainability, and ongoing monitoring of these technologies.

In conclusion, liability and accountability in AI-driven decision-making present complex challenges in healthcare. Clear frameworks for determining responsibility, liability insurance, and regulatory guidelines must address these challenges and ensure patient safety, ethical practice, and legal compliance. By establishing robust accountability mechanisms, healthcare professionals, organizations, and AI developers can work together to foster responsible and reliable AI-driven decision-making processes in healthcare.

6.4 Informed consent and transparency

Informed consent and transparency are critical considerations in using artificial intelligence (AI) in healthcare. These principles ensure that patients and individuals understand the implications, risks, and benefits associated with the use of AI technologies in their healthcare journey. Promoting informed consent and transparency respects patients' autonomy and fosters trust, accountability, and ethical practice in AI-driven healthcare.

Informed consent involves providing patients with comprehensive information about AI-driven interventions' purpose, nature, and potential consequences. Patients should clearly understand how AI technologies will be used in their care, including the data collection, analysis, and decision-making processes involved. They should be made aware of any potential limitations or uncertainties associated with AI algorithms and alternative options available to them. Informed consent ensures that patients actively participate in their healthcare decisions, enabling them to make well-informed choices based on their values and preferences.

Transparency plays a crucial role in promoting trust and accountability in AI-driven healthcare. It involves providing clear explanations and justifications for using AI algorithms and their impact on decision-making. Transparency encompasses several aspects, including algorithmic clarity, data, and organizational transparency.

Algorithmic transparency refers to the understandability and explainability of AI algorithms. Patients and healthcare professionals should be able to comprehend how the algorithms arrive at their recommendations or decisions. Explainable AI techniques, such as model interpretability and visualizations, can aid in understanding the underlying factors and variables contributing to AI-driven outputs. Transparent algorithms enable healthcare professionals to assess the reliability and appropriateness of AI-driven recommendations while allowing patients to participate meaningfully in shared decision-making.

Data transparency involves openness about the data sources, collection methods, and data management practices utilized in AI-driven healthcare. Patients should be informed about the types of data being collected, how their data will be used, and the measures in place to protect their privacy and confidentiality. Additionally, transparency in data usage includes informing patients if their data is being shared with third parties for research or other purposes and offering options for opting out or controlling their data usage.

Organizational transparency ensures that healthcare institutions and AI developers are open about their policies, procedures, and guidelines regarding the use of AI technologies. This includes disclosing any conflicts of interest, financial relationships, or biases that may influence the deployment or outcomes of AI algorithms. Transparent organizational practices instil confidence in patients and stakeholders, as they can assess the integrity and reliability of AI-driven healthcare systems.

An example of promoting informed consent and transparency in AI-driven healthcare is using decision-support tools. For instance, if an AI algorithm is utilized to provide treatment recommendations for a particular medical condition, patients should be informed about the underlying data used to train the algorithm, the validation studies conducted, and the level of confidence or uncertainty associated with the algorithm's predictions. This information lets patients make informed decisions regarding their treatment options and actively engage in shared decision-making with healthcare professionals.

The successful integration of AI in healthcare relies heavily on a robust bioethical framework grounded in the principles of medical ethics: beneficence, non-maleficence, autonomy, and social justice. These principles are paramount to informing the design and deployment of AI technologies in healthcare to ensure patient welfare, privacy, freedom, and equitable access to care. Another critical ethical consideration pertains to data privacy and Security, emphasizing the necessity for robust cybersecurity measures and stringent data governance frameworks. Techniques such as federated learning and differential privacy are instrumental in securing data handling while allowing an essential understanding of shared datasets.

Additionally, it is of utmost importance that AI algorithms are engineered and applied in a way that diminishes bias and guarantees fairness. This requires a commitment to transparency in algorithm design, meticulous bias testing, and the regular update of algorithms to align with changing demographics and medical knowledge. Moreover, the challenge of liability and accountability in AI-driven decision-making must be addressed. In scenarios where

AI leads to incorrect or harmful decisions, it becomes crucial to have clear rules of responsibility and liability. Establishing stringent oversight mechanisms is essential to these rules to ensure accountability is enforced effectively. Informed consent and transparency form the cornerstone of ethical AI in healthcare. Patients must be provided comprehensive information about the AI technologies used in their care, including data collection, analysis, and decision-making processes. Transparency in AI algorithms, data handling practices, and organizational policies is pivotal for fostering trust and accountability.

As we cast our gaze towards the future, the ethical, legal, and social implications of AI in healthcare emerge as a topic of profound significance. With AI technologies increasingly integrated into healthcare, ethical considerations such as privacy, fairness, accountability, and transparency take centre stage. It is imperative to forge comprehensive bioethical frameworks, establish robust data governance models, foster fair and transparent AI algorithms, and promote accountable decision-making mechanisms. The trajectory of AI in healthcare hinges not only on technological advancements but also on the ethical fortitude of its implementation. This exhilarating and complex journey necessitates continued attention, open discussion, and innovative solutions from all stakeholders involved.

Chapter 7 Overcoming Barriers to AI Adoption in Healthcare

Integrating artificial intelligence (AI) in healthcare holds immense potential to transform patient care, clinical decision-making, and healthcare delivery. However, the adoption of AI technologies in healthcare faces numerous barriers that must be surmounted to harness its benefits fully. This chapter explores the challenges and strategies for overcoming these barriers to facilitate the widespread adoption of AI in healthcare settings.

Challenges and Barriers

One significant barrier to AI adoption in healthcare is the need for interoperability and standardization of healthcare systems and data. Healthcare institutions often have fragmented data systems that make it difficult to aggregate and analyse data across different sources. This hamper developing and deploying AI algorithms that rely on comprehensive and diverse datasets. For example, integrating electronic health records (EHRs) from other healthcare providers can be challenging due to variations in data formats and coding systems. Overcoming this barrier requires the establishment of standardized protocols, data exchange formats, and interoperability frameworks that enable seamless data sharing and integration.

Another barrier is the resistance to change and the need for AI literacy among healthcare professionals. Scepticism and concerns about AI technologies' reliability, accuracy, and ethical implications can hinder their adoption. Healthcare professionals may need to understand their capabilities and limitations to embrace AI-driven tools and decision support systems. Therefore, initiatives are required to enhance AI education and training for healthcare professionals, fostering their understanding of AI algorithms, their applications, and their integration into clinical workflows. Demonstrating successful use cases and highlighting the benefits of AI adoption can also alleviate concerns and drive acceptance among healthcare professionals.

Financial considerations and resource constraints pose additional barriers to AI adoption in healthcare. Implementing AI technologies often requires significant investments in infrastructure, hardware, software, and human resources. Small healthcare organizations or those with limited budgets may need help to allocate resources for AI initiatives. However, emerging cloud-based AI solutions and collaborations with technology partners can help mitigate these barriers by reducing upfront costs and providing access to AI capabilities without extensive infrastructure requirements. Additionally, policymakers and funding agencies can play a role in supporting AI adoption through funding programs, grants, and incentives for healthcare organizations.

Ethical and regulatory considerations also present barriers to AI adoption in healthcare. Ensuring patient privacy, data security, transparency, and accountability are critical factors that must be addressed. For instance, regulations such as the General Data Protection Regulation (GDPR) in Europe and the Health Insurance Portability and Accountability Act (HIPAA) in the United States impose strict requirements for data privacy and security. Compliance with these regulations and establishing ethical guidelines for AI-driven healthcare are essential to building trust among patients, healthcare professionals, and regulatory authorities.

In Ophthalmology, the challenges and barriers to real-world AI adoption in ophthalmic practices include:
- Lack of standardization in data collection and analysis
- Limited access to high-quality data
- Difficulty in integrating AI technology with existing clinical workflows.
- Ethical and liability considerations
- Patient Acceptance and Trust in AI Technology[87]

A study analysed several real-world examples of AI applications in healthcare and found that major hospitals use AI-enabled systems to augment medical staff in patient diagnosis and treatment activities for various diseases. AI systems are also impacting and improving the efficiency of nursing and managerial activities of hospitals. The paper discusses the opportunities and challenges in applying AI-based technologies and possible ways to prepare for the expanded application of advanced digital technologies in the healthcare industry. The practical implications of this paper are that rapid advances in AI and related technologies will help care providers create new value for their patients and improve the efficiency of their operational processes. Nevertheless, effective applications of AI will require effective planning and strategies to transform the complete care service and operations to reap the benefits of what technologies offer.

The paper also discusses several challenges in applying AI-based technologies in the healthcare industry. One of the major challenges is the need for more standardization of data and the need for interoperability between different systems. Another challenge is the ethical and legal issues surrounding the use of AI in healthcare, such as data privacy and security concerns. Additionally,

---

[87] Rishi P. Singh et al., 'Current Challenges and Barriers to Real-World Artificial Intelligence Adoption for the Healthcare System, Provider, and the Patient,' *Translational Vision Science & Technology* 9, no. 2 (11 August 2020): 45, https://doi.org/10.1167/tvst.9.2.45.

there is a need for healthcare professionals to be trained in the use of AI-based technologies. To overcome these challenges, this paper suggests that there is a need for collaboration between different stakeholders, including healthcare providers, technology companies, and policymakers. Data standardization and interoperability between other systems can be achieved by developing common data standards and protocols. Ethical and legal issues can be addressed by developing guidelines and regulations. Healthcare professionals can be trained in the use of AI-based technologies through the development of training programs and educational resources.[88]

Mitigating Barriers

Collaboration and partnerships between healthcare organizations, technology developers, researchers, and regulatory bodies are crucial to overcoming these barriers. Multidisciplinary teams can work together to develop interoperability standards, educate healthcare professionals, address ethical concerns, and create supportive policy frameworks. Furthermore, establishing clear governance structures, evaluating the effectiveness of AI interventions, and disseminating best practices and guidelines for AI adoption can facilitate the integration of AI technologies into routine healthcare practices.

Artificial Intelligence (AI) adoption in healthcare has been slow, despite its significant potential, primarily due to liability concerns. However, a well-structured AI liability insurance can help address these challenges, simultaneously aligning with the interests of key

---

[88] DonHee Lee and Seong No Yoon, 'Application of Artificial Intelligence-Based Technologies in the Healthcare Industry: Opportunities and Challenges,' *International Journal of Environmental Research and Public Health* 18, no. 1 (January 2021): 271, https://doi.org/10.3390/ijerph18010271.

healthcare stakeholders, including patients, physicians, and healthcare organization leadership. Notably, a market for AI insurance will favour high-quality, safe, and effective AI products, as these are the ones insurers will be most willing to underwrite. Thus, effectively designed AI insurance products can reduce liability-related uncertainties for developers and clinicians, fostering innovation, competition, adoption, and trust in beneficial AI technologies in healthcare. Introducing AI liability insurance in the market can also serve as a quality control mechanism, as insurers will naturally be more inclined to underwrite AI products that are safe, effective, and high-quality. This selective underwriting process can stimulate competition among AI developers by encouraging them to adhere to stringent safety and effectiveness standards.

Furthermore, an AI insurance product can significantly reduce the uncertainty associated with liability risks. For manufacturers, including those developing software as a medical device, this means more clarity regarding their products' financial and legal implications. For clinicians, it eases concerns about the potential legal consequences of using AI in their practice.

Implementing AI insurance policies is likely to result in increased trust in AI technologies in healthcare, hence promoting further innovation and fostering competition. Therefore, AI liability insurance can play a crucial role in encouraging the integration of AI into mainstream healthcare practices, benefiting patients, clinicians, and healthcare organizations alike.[89]

Overcoming barriers to AI adoption is essential to realize AI's potential in healthcare fully. By addressing challenges related to interoperability, AI literacy, financial constraints, and ethical

---

[89] Ariel Dora Stern et al., 'AI Insurance: How Liability Insurance Can Drive the Responsible Adoption of Artificial Intelligence in Health Care,' *NEJM Catalyst* 3, no. 4 (16 March 2022): CAT.21.0242, https://doi.org/10.1056/CAT.21.0242.

considerations, healthcare organizations can embrace AI technologies and unlock their transformative benefits. The barriers to AI adoption can be surmounted through collaboration, education, policy support, and a patient-centred approach, leading to improved healthcare outcomes, enhanced clinical decision-making, and more efficient and effective healthcare delivery.

Identifying and addressing organizational barriers is crucial for successfully adopting and integrating artificial intelligence (AI) in healthcare. Organizations often need help with various challenges that can hinder the implementation of AI technologies, including cultural resistance, lack of leadership support, resource constraints, and inadequate infrastructure. Overcoming these barriers requires a comprehensive understanding of the organizational landscape and targeted strategies to promote AI adoption.

Cultural resistance is a common barrier encountered when introducing AI in healthcare organizations. Resistance to change, fear of job displacement, and scepticism about the reliability and accuracy of AI technologies can create a culture that is resistant to embracing innovation. To address this, organizations should prioritize building a culture of innovation, fostering an environment that encourages experimentation, learning, and open communication. Involving key stakeholders, including healthcare professionals, in decision-making and providing training and education on AI technologies can help alleviate concerns and build confidence in AI-driven initiatives.

Lack of leadership support and vision can hinder the adoption of AI in healthcare organizations. Without leadership buy-in and a clear vision for AI integration, initiatives may lack direction and fail to receive the necessary resources and support. Leadership should champion the benefits of AI technologies and communicate a strategic vision that aligns with the organization's goals and values. Engaging leaders in AI education and providing them with opportunities to understand the potential impact of AI on healthcare outcomes can help garner support and commitment.

Resource constraints, including financial limitations and insufficient human resources, can pose significant challenges to AI adoption. Implementing AI technologies often requires substantial investments in infrastructure, data management, talent acquisition, and ongoing maintenance. Healthcare organizations must carefully assess their resources and explore partnerships, collaborations, or cloud-based solutions that can help alleviate financial burdens and provide access to AI capabilities. Leveraging external expertise through collaborations with technology vendors or academic institutions can supplement in-house resources and accelerate AI implementation.

Inadequate infrastructure and data governance pose additional barriers to AI adoption. Legacy systems, fragmented data sources, and interoperability challenges can impede the integration of AI technologies. Organizations must prioritize data governance and establish data management frameworks that ensure data quality, security, and interoperability. Investing in robust infrastructure, such as high-performance computing and storage systems and implementing data standards and interoperability protocols can enable seamless integration of AI algorithms into existing workflows.

An example of addressing organizational barriers is the successful implementation of AI-powered chatbots in healthcare organizations. Initially, there may be resistance to using chatbots for patient interactions due to concerns about their effectiveness and potential impact on the patient-provider relationship.[90] To overcome this, organizations can conduct pilot projects to demonstrate the benefits and value of chatbots in enhancing patient engagement and improving access to healthcare information. Organizations can address concerns and gain organizational acceptance for AI-driven chatbot initiatives through effective communication, involving stakeholders in the development process, and monitoring outcomes.

Identifying and addressing organizational barriers is crucial for the effective adoption of AI in healthcare. By fostering a culture of innovation, gaining leadership support, addressing resource constraints, and ensuring robust infrastructure and data governance, organizations can overcome barriers and pave the way for successful AI integration. Embracing AI technologies can lead to improved healthcare outcomes, enhanced efficiency, and transformative advancements in patient care.

Cultivating a culture of innovation and collaboration

Cultivating a culture of innovation and collaboration is vital for successfully adopting and integrating artificial intelligence (AI) in healthcare. A culture that encourages innovation fosters creativity, and values collaboration can drive the development and implementation of AI technologies, leading to transformative advancements in healthcare delivery and patient outcomes.

Example of Innovation in service design

---

[90] Yang Cheng and Hua Jiang, 'AI-Powered Mental Health Chatbots: Examining Users' Motivations, Active Communicative Action and Engagement after Mass-Shooting Disasters,' *Journal of Contingencies and Crisis Management* 28, no. 3 (2020): 339–54, https://doi.org/10.1111/1468-5973.12319.

Patricio et al. explored the role of service design in transforming health service systems towards more people-centric, integrated, and technologically equipped care. Their goal was establishing research blueprint that harnesses Service Design research to facilitate healthcare transformation. They probed into how Service Design, anchored in human-centred principles, can maximize technology's potential to reorient healthcare systems toward more personalized care. It further discusses the transformative impact of Service Design in not just elucidating healthcare phenomena but also designing innovative solutions to drive change and enhance well-being. By taking a Service Systems viewpoint, stakeholders can navigate healthcare systems' intricacies, facilitating integrated care. This paper offers practical insights by outlining a framework for Service Design research in healthcare, highlighting key areas for future exploration, and proposing avenues to enhance Service Design in healthcare through interdisciplinary collaborations, methodological evolution, and solid theoretical foundations.[91]

One example of cultivating a culture of innovation and collaboration is the implementation of innovation programs or initiatives within healthcare organizations. These programs provide a platform for employees to propose and develop innovative ideas that leverage AI technologies to address healthcare challenges. By encouraging employees to contribute their ideas and providing resources and support for innovation projects, organizations can create an environment that nurtures innovation and fosters a sense of ownership and engagement among staff.

Furthermore, fostering collaboration across multidisciplinary teams is essential for AI adoption in healthcare. AI technologies require

---

[91] Lia Patrício et al., 'Leveraging Service Design for Healthcare Transformation: Toward People-Centered, Integrated, and Technology-Enabled Healthcare Systems,' *Journal of Service Management* 31, no. 5 (1 January 2020): 889–909, https://doi.org/10.1108/JOSM-11-2019-0332.

input and expertise from various stakeholders, including healthcare professionals, data scientists, engineers, and administrators. Collaboration enables diverse perspectives to come together, facilitating the design, development, and implementation of AI solutions that align with the needs of healthcare providers and patients. For instance, joint projects between clinicians and data scientists can enhance the development of AI algorithms customized to specific clinical scenarios, leading to more accurate diagnoses or personalized treatment recommendations.

Example of collaboration

The development of an information-sharing system to support multi-professional collaboration in the community-based integrated healthcare system was explored by Kanai and Kumazawa. The design aimed to provide appropriate health, medical, and welfare services to older adults living at home. The field test of the system in three districts of Nomi City, Ishikawa Prefecture, Japan, showed that the system effectively reduced the burden on professionals such as care managers and improved efficiency. Active information sharing by professionals promoted activities of confirming and inputting messages for elderly family members. Also, older people were aware that the stakeholders watched over them carefully. The awareness had the effect of making their daily life regular.

Collaboration was encouraged by the development of a supporting system for sharing information about older people at home. The plan was designed to be used by several stakeholders involved in the community's comprehensive healthcare system, including health, medical, and welfare staff and neighbours. This field test in Nomi City showed that the system effectively promoted collaboration among professionals and improved the quality of care for older people.[92]

Establishing collaborative partnerships with external entities, such as academic institutions, technology vendors, and start-ups, can promote innovation and accelerate AI adoption. Collaborations provide access to cutting-edge research, expertise, and resources that may not be available within the organization. For example, healthcare organizations can collaborate with technology vendors to co-develop AI-powered solutions that address specific healthcare challenges by leveraging the vendor's expertise in AI algorithms and the organization's domain knowledge and clinical data.

In addition to examples, several studies have highlighted the importance of cultivating a culture of innovation and collaboration in healthcare organizations. Sayuri et al. explored the perceptions of tri-sectoral associations in the healthcare sector, focusing on diabetes care in England. The study highlighted potential challenges to tri-sectoral alliances and the government's knowledge translation policy due to preconceived notions and a lack of understanding of other sectors. The results suggested that mechanisms to facilitate trust-building and collaboration are necessary. The practical implications of this paper are that policymakers and healthcare professionals need to actively work towards improving collaborative relationships between academia, industry, and healthcare sectors to facilitate innovation adoption and improve patient outcomes.[93]

---

[92] Hideaki Kanai and Akinori Kumazawa, 'An Information Sharing System for Multi-Professional Collaboration in the Community-Based Integrated Healthcare System,' *International Journal of Informatics, Information System and Computer Engineering (INJIISCOM)* 2, no. 1 (26 June 2021): 1–14, https://doi.org/10.34010/injiiscom.v2i1.4862.

[93] Suzanne Sayuri Ii et al., 'Knowledge Translation in Tri-Sectoral Collaborations: An Exploration of Perceptions of Academia, Industry and Healthcare Collaborations in Innovation Adoption,' *Health Policy* 122, no. 2 (1 February 2018): 175–83, https://doi.org/10.1016/j.healthpol.2017.11.010.

AI workforce development and training

AI workforce development and training are critical in preparing healthcare professionals and organizations to adopt and integrate artificial intelligence (AI) technologies successfully. As AI continues to advance and permeate various healthcare domains, it is essential to equip the workforce with the necessary knowledge, skills, and competencies to effectively utilize AI tools, leverage AI-driven insights, and navigate AI's ethical and practical implications in healthcare.

One example of AI workforce development is the provision of targeted training programs and educational initiatives. These programs aim to familiarize healthcare professionals with the fundamentals of AI, including machine learning, natural language processing, and computer vision. Training can encompass various formats, such as workshops, online courses, or hands-on experiential learning. By providing healthcare professionals with a solid foundation in AI concepts, they can understand the potential applications, limitations, and ethical considerations associated with AI technologies in healthcare.

The critical need for enhancing healthcare systems and workforce capabilities amid crises through the ethical use of digital health technologies, including AI, in professional education and healthcare delivery is a pivotal step towards health system strengthening. In the paper by Sarbadhikari and Pradhan, they discuss the importance of utilizing digital health technologies, including Artificial Intelligence (AI), in enhancing healthcare professional education and delivery capacity.[94] It emphasizes the need for an

---

[94] Suptendra N. Sarbadhikari and Keerti B. Pradhan, 'The Need for Developing Technology-Enabled, Safe, and Ethical Workforce for Healthcare Delivery,' *Safety and Health at Work* 11, no. 4 (1 December 2020): 533–36, https://doi.org/10.1016/j.shaw.2020.08.003.

ethical and safe approach to developing and utilizing digital health technology, and ethically appropriate training is imparted to enhance the capacity of human resources for health, thereby strengthening the overall health system. The practical implications of this paper are:

- Strengthening the health system is a safety imperative, especially in a crisis.
- Utilizing digital health technologies, including AI, can enhance healthcare professional education and delivery capacity.
- An ethical and safe approach is necessary to develop and utilize digital health technology.
- Ethically appropriate training is required to enhance the capacity of the human resources for health, leading to an overall health system strengthening.

Moreover, specialized training can be provided to develop AI-specific skill sets within the healthcare workforce. This includes data analytics, data engineering, and AI algorithm development training. Healthcare professionals who possess these skills can actively contribute to the story, implementation, and customization of AI algorithms, thereby enabling the integration of AI technologies into clinical workflows. For example, radiologists can undergo training in AI-assisted radiology to effectively interpret AI-generated findings and collaborate with AI algorithms for more accurate diagnoses. This highlights the urgent need for educators to integrate artificial intelligence training across health professions, as failing to do so can leave the healthcare workforce ill-equipped to harness the benefits of AI or manage its potential risks. The unified efforts of educators are essential in maximizing AI's potential and mitigating any unintended fallout. This perspective significantly appeals to the health professional education community by emphasizing the critical role of equipping the healthcare workforce to navigate the evolving landscape of healthcare under the influence of AI.

Collaboration between academia and healthcare organizations can facilitate AI workforce development. Academic institutions can offer specialized AI courses and degree programs that cater to the specific needs of healthcare professionals. These programs can cover topics such as AI ethics, data governance, and the societal implications of AI in healthcare. Collaboration with healthcare organizations allows for integrating real-world case studies and practical experiences into the curriculum, ensuring that healthcare professionals receive hands-on training aligned with industry requirements.

In addition to healthcare professionals, organizational leaders and administrators also require training to understand AI adoption's strategic implications and potential benefits. Executives and managers must develop a comprehensive understanding of AI technologies, their potential impact on workflows and resource allocation, and the organizational changes necessary to support AI initiatives. This training can empower leaders to make informed decisions, allocate resources effectively, and drive the cultural shift needed for successful AI integration within the organization.

Continuous learning and upskilling are key components of AI workforce development. Given the rapid advancements in AI technologies, healthcare professionals need access to ongoing education and professional development opportunities. This can include participation in conferences, webinars, and workshops focused on AI in healthcare. Additionally, healthcare organizations can establish communities of practice or AI-centric forums where professionals can share knowledge, exchange best practices, and collaborate on AI-driven projects.

Several studies emphasize the importance of AI workforce development in healthcare. The growth of Artificial Intelligence (AI) adoption in healthcare has the potential to revolutionize patient care and reshape the roles of healthcare professionals. However, studies on how different AI applications may directly impact healthcare professionals' jobs still need more extensive. In an analysis using a framework to examine AI applications in healthcare, the authors scrutinized 80 publications from a grey-literature platform. They demonstrated that AI applications in diagnosis and treatment, patient engagement and empowerment, and administrative activities significantly influenced healthcare professionals' job design, including autonomy and control, skill variety and use, job feedback, social and relational factors, and job demands. While the impacts of AI applications are largely discussed in the context of doctors and patients, AI can also enhance patient engagement, adherence, and empowerment. However, these impacts can be influenced by various contextual factors, indicating the need for more international research exploring AI's implications on healthcare professionals' job design.[95]

The future of AI workforce development and healthcare training appears promising and challenging. As AI continues to develop and mature, it is becoming increasingly clear that integrating this technology into healthcare will require a well-prepared workforce equipped with the necessary skills to use and manage AI tools effectively. This suggests a future where education and training programs will evolve significantly.

---

[95] Aizhan Tursunbayeva and Maarten Renkema, 'Artificial Intelligence in Healthcare: Implications for the Job Design of Healthcare Professionals,' the *Asia Pacific Journal of Human Resources* n/a, no. n/a, accessed 21 May 2023, https://doi.org/10.1111/1744-7941.12325.

AI education will need to become an integral part of healthcare curricula across all levels of education - from undergraduate programs to professional training and continuing education courses. This will involve theoretical knowledge of AI and machine learning principles and practical skills such as interpreting AI outputs, understanding potential bias in AI algorithms, and effectively implementing AI tools in clinical settings.

The future will also likely see a more multidisciplinary approach to healthcare, as the implementation of AI will require collaboration between medical professionals, data scientists, bioethicists, and policymakers. Therefore, training programs should focus on fostering communication and collaboration skills alongside technical expertise.

In addition to this, the importance of ethical and responsible AI use will likely be a major focus in workforce training. As AI becomes more widely used in healthcare, professionals will need to understand how to use these tools ethically by respecting patients' rights to privacy and informed consent and understanding AI's social and ethical implications.

Lastly, the ongoing evolution of AI technology will necessitate continuous learning and adaptation. This suggests a future where healthcare professionals are engaged in lifelong learning, regularly updating their skills and knowledge to keep pace with AI developments.

However, the path toward this future is challenging. Existing barriers to AI adoption, such as resistance to change, lack of technical knowledge, and concerns about job displacement, will need to be addressed. A well-structured framework for AI education, paired with supportive policies and inclusive strategies, will be crucial to the successful development of the AI-ready healthcare workforce of the future.

Financial Considerations and Investment in AI Infrastructure

Financial considerations and investment in AI infrastructure are critical factors that influence the successful adoption and integration of Artificial Intelligence (AI) technologies in healthcare. Implementing AI systems requires significant financial resources to support infrastructure development, data management, hardware and software acquisition, talent recruitment, and ongoing maintenance. Adequate investment in AI infrastructure is necessary to unlock the full potential of AI in healthcare and achieve improved patient outcomes and operational efficiencies.

However, there needs to be more evidence on the cost of adopting AI in healthcare. A systematic review of the cost-effectiveness studies dedicated to AI in healthcare and to assess whether they meet the established quality criteria attempted to explore this. The authors defined quality criteria for economic impact studies based on established and adapted criteria schemes for cost impact assessments. They tried to identify relevant publications for an in-depth analysis of the economic impact assessment. The quality of the identified economic impact studies was evaluated based on the defined quality criteria for cost-effectiveness studies. The paper found that very few publications have thoroughly addressed the economic impact assessment, and the financial assessment quality of the reviewed journals on AI showed severe methodological deficits. None of the studies comprised a methodologically complete cost impact analysis. The paper identified two areas for improvement in future studies: including the initial investment and operational costs for the AI infrastructure and service and evaluating alternatives to achieve a similar impact to provide a comprehensive comparison.[96]

Pietris et al., in a paper to determine the health economic impact of implementing AI in Ophthalmology in Australia, conducted a systematic review. They analyzed a population of patients who have or are being evaluated for an ophthalmological diagnosis, using a health economic assessment system to assess the cost-effectiveness of AI. The results showed that despite the lack of Australia-specific data, foreign analyses overwhelmingly showed that AI was just as economically viable, if not more so, than traditional human screening programs while maintaining comparable clinical effectiveness. This evidence was largely in the setting of diabetic retinopathy screening. The practical implication of this review is that AI can be a cost-effective alternative to traditional human screening programs in Ophthalmology, particularly in diabetic retinopathy screening. However, primary Australian research is needed to accurately analyse the health and economic implications of implementing AI on a large scale, and further research is required to investigate the economic feasibility of adopting AI technology in other areas of Ophthalmology, such as glaucoma and cataract screening.[97]

One example of financial considerations and investment in AI infrastructure is the establishment of high-performance computing (HPC) systems. HPC systems provide the computational power required to efficiently process and analyse large volumes of

---

[96] Justus Wolff et al., 'The Economic Impact of Artificial Intelligence in Health Care: Systematic Review,' *Journal of Medical Internet Research* 22, no. 2 (20 February 2020): e16866, https://doi.org/10.2196/16866.

[97] James Pietris et al., 'Health Economic Implications of Artificial Intelligence Implementation for Ophthalmology in Australia: A Systematic Review,' *The Asia-Pacific Journal of Ophthalmology* 11, no. 6 (December 2022): 554, https://doi.org/10.1097/APO.0000000000000565.

healthcare data. Investing in HPC infrastructure allows healthcare organizations to handle complex AI algorithms and conduct resource-intensive tasks, such as deep learning and data mining, which are integral to AI-driven applications. With the increasing availability of cloud-based HPC solutions, healthcare organizations can access scalable and cost-effective computing resources, reducing the upfront capital expenditure required to build and maintain on-premises HPC infrastructure.

Data storage and management infrastructure also require financial investment for successful AI adoption. AI algorithms rely on vast amounts of data to train and learn patterns. Healthcare organizations need robust storage systems capable of handling the massive volumes of data generated by electronic health records, medical imaging, and other sources. Investment in scalable and secure data storage solutions, such as cloud-based or network-attached storage (NAS), enables efficient data management and access for AI applications. Additionally, organizations must invest in data governance frameworks to ensure data quality, privacy, and compliance with regulatory requirements.

Healthcare organizations also need to invest in acquiring AI-specific hardware and software tools. This includes procuring high-performance servers, graphics processing units (GPUs), and other specialized hardware to support AI workloads. In addition, software tools and platforms specifically designed for AI, such as machine learning frameworks and development environments, facilitate AI algorithms' development, deployment, and management. Investing in the right hardware and software infrastructure ensures healthcare organizations have the resources to support AI initiatives effectively.

Furthermore, talent acquisition and development investment are crucial for building AI capabilities within healthcare organizations.

Skilled AI professionals, including data scientists, machine learning engineers, and AI specialists, are essential for developing, implementing, and managing AI-driven initiatives. Healthcare organizations must allocate resources to attract and retain top AI talent through hiring or collaborations with academic institutions and research centres. Additionally, investing in training and upskilling existing staff in AI-related skills equips healthcare professionals with the knowledge and competencies to leverage AI technologies effectively.

The current funding schemes for AI in healthcare often lead to a misalignment of interests. Existing funding models, derived from experiences in the digital era, expect a quick return on investment (ROI) within a few years. However, AI in healthcare products is more akin to biotechnology products, which undergo complex development and rigorous regulatory requirements. The need to adapt biotechnology funding schemes to AI in the healthcare sector can be attributed to the limited exit options for biotechnology companies, mainly through Initial Public Offerings (IPOs) and Mergers and Acquisitions (M&A) with large biotechnology or pharmaceutical companies. Moreover, IPO activity has decreased outside of biotechnology, and few large acquiring companies for medical AI exist. As a result, investors need help to ensure a significant ROI on their investments in AI in healthcare. This challenge is often overlooked by founders who promote their products as equivalent to any other AI software, sometimes categorizing them as non-medical devices, leading to limitations in product capabilities or regulatory backlash.

The development of AI in healthcare faces the "valley of death" phase, where start-ups exist but struggle to generate revenue. This phase aligns with the Build + Launch phases in the framework.[98]

There is a need for a realistic assessment of the development roadmap for AI healthcare products, and early-stage funding should be aware of the true timelines and adjust expectations accordingly. Increased public funding schemes, such as the one initiated by the European Union in 2021 to target the Valley of Death, can help address this issue. As the sector matures, the hope is that large pharmaceutical and medical technology companies will increase their acquisition activities, thus providing a clearer pathway for product and company development.

While the industry response to the funding crisis has been to lobby for reduced regulations, this approach may not be sustainable. Although reducing regulatory barriers may expedite technological innovation, it can divert spending towards navigating shortcuts and paying for product-risk insurance rather than focusing on clinical validation and software engineering. A more mature approach to clinical validation, based on natural methods like the framework proposed, is preferable. Certification of AI platforms or manufacturers, where only new components or the manufacturer requires certification upon upgrades, can also be a viable alternative to traditional regulatory pathways.

The Technology or Innovation Lifecycle framework is a model that characterizes the stages of a technology's life from inception to obsolescence. The framework typically includes several steps: Conception/Idea Generation, Research and Development, Growth, Maturity, and Decline.
1. Conception/Idea Generation: This phase involves brainstorming, generating, and screening ideas for a new product or technology.

---

[98] Venkata K. K. Upadhyayula et al., 'Advancing Game Changing Academic Research Concepts to Commercialization: A Life Cycle Assessment (LCA) Based Sustainability Framework for Making Informed Decisions in Technology Valley of Death (TVD),' *Resources, Conservation and Recycling* 133 (1 June 2018): 404–16, https://doi.org/10.1016/j.resconrec.2017.12.029.

2. Research and Development: During this phase, the idea's feasibility is tested, prototypes are developed, and initial trials or pilot studies are conducted.
3. Build + Launch Phases (sometimes known as the commercialization or growth phase): This is the point at which the technology is introduced to the market. The product is refined and prepared for market launch during the Build phase. The product is made available to the public during the Launch phase, and initial marketing and sales efforts begin.

However, between the Research and Development and Build + Launch phases, start-ups often face the "valley of death." This is a difficult period for start-ups, often characterized by high cash outflows for product development and initial marketing, with little or no incoming revenue.

During the valley of death, many startups struggle to survive due to lack of funding, insufficient revenue, or difficulties getting the technology to work as expected or be accepted by the market. The challenge during this phase is to cross this valley by securing enough funding or generating enough revenue to sustain the business until the product can gain traction in the market.

4. Maturity: If the product successfully passes through the valley of death and is adopted by the market, it enters the maturity phase. Stable sales and revenue characterize this stage.
5. Decline: Eventually, most products reach a decline phase, where sales begin to fall. This could be due to market saturation, technological obsolescence, or competition from newer, more innovative products.

This framework underscores the importance of strategic planning, securing adequate funding, and effective marketing and sales strategies to navigate the challenging transition from development to commercial viability, particularly for emerging technologies such as AI in healthcare.

A thoughtful and sustainable approach to funding AI in healthcare is necessary, considering the complex nature of the products, their regulatory requirements, and the potential impact on patient health.[99]

The cost and investment required for AI in healthcare moving forward will depend on several factors, including the specific applications of AI, the scope of implementation, and the regulatory landscape. However, some general considerations can be summarized:

1. Research and Development: Significant investment is needed for research and development (R&D) related to AI in healthcare. This includes developing new algorithms, improving existing models, and conducting clinical trials and validation studies. R&D costs can vary depending on the complexity of the AI applications and the level of innovation involved.
2. Data Infrastructure and Integration: AI in healthcare relies on robust data infrastructure and integration with existing healthcare systems. Investments are required to ensure data interoperability, security, and seamless integration of AI algorithms into clinical workflows. This includes data collection, storage, management solutions, and the

---

[99] David Higgins and Vince I. Madai, 'From Bit to Bedside: A Practical Framework for Artificial Intelligence Product Development in Healthcare,' *Advanced Intelligent Systems* 2, no. 10 (2020): 2000052, https://doi.org/10.1002/aisy.202000052.

development of secure and scalable computing infrastructure.
3. Computing Resources: AI algorithms often require significant computing power to process and analyse large datasets. High-performance computing resources, such as cloud computing or dedicated hardware accelerators, may be necessary, and the associated costs should be considered.
4. Data Quality and Annotation: High-quality, annotated datasets are crucial for training and validating AI models. Investment is needed to ensure data quality, including cleaning, annotation, and curation. This may involve collaboration with healthcare providers, research institutions, and data annotation companies.
5. Regulatory Compliance: AI in healthcare is subject to regulatory compliance, particularly in data privacy, ethics, and medical device regulations. Compliance with these regulations requires investment in legal expertise, regulatory consultations, and adherence to standards and guidelines set by regulatory authorities.
6. Talent and Workforce: Building and maintaining an AI-focused workforce is essential. This includes hiring skilled data scientists, AI engineers, healthcare professionals with AI expertise, and other specialized personnel. Investment in training, professional development, and attracting top talent will be necessary.
7. Infrastructure and Maintenance: Ongoing investment is required to maintain and update AI systems, ensure data security, and address any technical issues that may arise. This includes regular algorithm updates, software patches, system monitoring, and cybersecurity measures.

8. **Clinical Validation and Adoption:** The adoption of AI in healthcare requires rigorous clinical validation to demonstrate its safety, efficacy, and utility. Clinical trials, real-world studies, and regulatory submissions incur costs related to study design, patient recruitment, monitoring, and analysis.

Estimating the comprehensive cost and investment required for AI in healthcare poses a challenge, given the diverse nature of projects and the ever-evolving landscape. Nonetheless, the integration of AI in healthcare necessitates significant investment, spanning crucial areas such as research and development, robust infrastructure, meticulous data management, compliance adherence, talent acquisition, and continuous maintenance. Effective resource allocation and successful integration of AI into healthcare systems depend on collaborative efforts among industry, academia, healthcare providers, and regulatory bodies.

Chapter 8 Practical Implications of AI for Healthcare Professionals

Introduction:

Artificial intelligence (AI) is revolutionizing how healthcare professionals practice, conduct research and educate the next generation of healthcare providers. The practical implications of AI for healthcare professionals are profound and far-reaching, promising to enhance clinical decision-making, improve patient outcomes, accelerate research discoveries, and transform educational methodologies. By harnessing the power of AI in their clinical practice, research endeavours, and teaching approaches, healthcare professionals can leverage innovative technologies that can streamline workflows, optimize treatment plans, and personalize patient care. However, healthcare professionals must understand and navigate the practical implications of AI effectively, ensuring its integration aligns with ethical considerations, regulatory requirements, and the needs of patients and providers alike. This chapter explores the practical implications of AI for healthcare professionals in their clinical practice, research, and teaching domains, shedding light on the transformative potential and key considerations that shape the effective utilization of AI technologies in healthcare settings.

8.1 AI in Clinical Practice

AI's ability to analyze vast amounts of data, recognize patterns and make informed decisions, AI is revolutionizing the way healthcare professionals diagnose, treat, and manage patients. The practical implications of AI in clinical practice are profound, promising to improve accuracy, efficiency, and patient outcomes. From diagnostics and decision support to personalized medicine and workflow optimization, AI is reshaping the landscape of healthcare delivery. This section delves into the practical applications of AI in clinical practice, explores real-world examples and discusses the benefits, challenges, and considerations that healthcare professionals need to navigate when integrating AI into their practice. By understanding the practical implications of AI in clinical settings, healthcare professionals can harness its power to enhance patient care, optimize workflows, and stay at the forefront of innovation in an increasingly AI-driven healthcare ecosystem.

AI in Diagnostics and Decision Support

AI has demonstrated remarkable potential in assisting healthcare professionals with accurate and timely diagnosis through advanced imaging analysis, pattern recognition, and predictive modelling. Real-world examples showcase the practical implications of AI in improving diagnostic accuracy and clinical decision-making.

In Radiology, AI algorithms have been developed to analyse medical imaging data and assist radiologists in detecting abnormalities. For instance, a study published in Nature Communications demonstrated an artificial intelligence system had been developed that achieves radiologist-level accuracy in identifying breast cancer in ultrasound images. The AI system achieved an area under the receiver operating characteristic curve (AUROC) of 0.976 on a test set of 44,755 exams. In a retrospective reader study, the AI achieved a higher AUROC than the average of ten board-certified breast radiologists (AUROC: 0.962 AI, 0.924 ± 0.02 radiologists).

With the help of AI, radiologists decreased their false positive rates by 37.3% and reduced requested biopsies by 27.8% while maintaining the same level of sensitivity. The system reduces false-positive findings and ordered biopsies while retaining the same level of sensitivity, highlighting the potential of AI in improving breast ultrasound diagnosis.[100]

AI algorithms can also support clinicians in decision-making processes by providing evidence-based recommendations. For example, IBM's Watson for Oncology is an AI-powered platform that analyses colossal amounts of patient data, medical literature, and treatment guidelines to assist oncologists in developing personalized treatment plans for cancer patients. By leveraging AI-driven decision support systems, clinicians can access comprehensive and up-to-date information by considering the latest evidence-based practices when making treatment decisions.[101]

Here are some practical steps for clinicians incorporating AI in diagnostics and decision support:

1. Stay informed: Stay updated with the latest advancements in AI technologies relevant to your specialty. Regularly explore research and developments in AI-assisted diagnostic tools and decision support systems to identify potential opportunities for integration into your clinical practice.
2. Validate and verify: While AI algorithms can be powerful tools, validating and verifying their results is crucial. Understand the limitations and potential biases of the AI algorithms you employ to ensure they align with the specific context of your patients and practice.
3. Collaborate with AI systems: Treat AI algorithms as tools to augment your clinical expertise rather than replace human

---

[100] Yiqiu Shen et al., 'Artificial Intelligence System Reduces False-Positive Findings in the Interpretation of Breast Ultrasound Exams,' *Nature Communications* 12, no. 1 (24 September 2021): 5645, https://doi.org/10.1038/s41467-021-26023-2.
[101] Na Zhou et al., 'Concordance Study Between IBM Watson for Oncology and Clinical Practice for Patients with Cancer in China,' *The Oncologist* 24, no. 6 (2019): 812–19, https://doi.org/10.1634/theoncologist.2018-0255.

judgment. Collaborate with AI systems by critically evaluating their recommendations and incorporating them into your decision-making process, considering patient preferences and individualized care.
4. Maintain open communication: Communicate with patients about using AI technologies in their diagnosis and treatment. Explain the role of AI as an additional tool in your decision-making process, fostering trust and transparency in the patient-clinician relationship.

By embracing AI-powered diagnostic tools and decision support systems, clinicians can enhance diagnostic accuracy, optimize treatment decisions, and improve patient outcomes. However, it is important to continuously evaluate and monitor the performance of AI algorithms to ensure their effectiveness and reliability in clinical practice.

ChatGPT in clinical practice

ChatGPT (Chat Generative Pre-trained Transformer), as an advanced language model, can be an asset in clinical practice by offering a range of applications to enhance patient care and support healthcare professionals.

Firstly, it can serve as an information retrieval tool, allowing clinicians to quickly access relevant medical information, such as guidelines, treatment protocols, or research findings, aiding in informed decision-making at the point of care.

Secondly, ChatGPT can provide decision support by offering insights and recommendations based on clinical guidelines and best practices. Healthcare professionals can interact with ChatGPT to discuss complex cases, explore treatment options, and seek suggestions for challenging diagnostic scenarios. Additionally,

ChatGPT can play a role in patient education and health literacy by providing understandable explanations of medical conditions, treatment plans, and procedures. It can address patient queries, reinforce key healthcare messages, and improve patient engagement and understanding. Furthermore, in remote monitoring and triage, ChatGPT can facilitate communication with patients by enabling them to report symptoms, receive personalized recommendations for self-care, and help identify urgent situations that require immediate attention. Lastly, ChatGPT's language capabilities can aid in overcoming language barriers between clinicians and patients, thereby ensuring effective communication and understanding.

When using ChatGPT in clinical practice, here are some advice to consider:

1. Verify Responses: While ChatGPT provides information, it is important to verify the accuracy and validity of the responses independently. Review trusted sources and consult with colleagues or reference materials to ensure the data aligns with current medical knowledge.
2. Exercise Clinical Judgment: Remember that ChatGPT is an AI tool and does not possess real-time patient data. Always rely on your clinical judgment and expertise when making decisions. Use ChatGPT as a supplementary resource rather than a substitute for professional judgment.
3. Maintain Patient Privacy: Ensure patient privacy and confidentiality are upheld when using ChatGPT. Be cautious when entering patient-specific information or discussing sensitive cases. Comply with applicable privacy regulations and follow institutional policies.

4. Continuously Update Knowledge: Keep current with medical research, guidelines, and best practices. Regularly seek professional development opportunities to stay informed about advancements in your field. ChatGPT's responses are based on pre-existing knowledge and may not reflect the most recent evidence.
5. Communicate Transparently with Patients: When incorporating ChatGPT into patient interactions, clearly communicate its role as an AI tool. Explain its limitations and that it is meant to support, not replace, the expertise and care provided by healthcare professionals. Encourage patients to ask questions and seek clarification if needed.
6. Evaluate Ethical Considerations: Consider ethical considerations when using AI tools in clinical practice. Ensure that patient autonomy, consent, and beneficence are prioritized. Evaluate the AI system's fairness, transparency, and accountability.
7. Continuous Monitoring and Improvement: Continuously monitor the performance and reliability of ChatGPT. Please report any inaccuracies, biases, or limitations encountered during its use to improve the system and contribute to its ongoing development.
8. Stay Within Professional Boundaries: While ChatGPT can be a valuable tool, it is essential to maintain professional boundaries. Use your clinical judgment to determine when to consult with colleagues, involve specialists, or seek second opinions, as appropriate.

ChatGPT should be utilized to support and enhance clinical practice, but it should differ from human expertise, critical thinking, and ethical decision-making. By leveraging the capabilities of ChatGPT, healthcare professionals can enhance patient care, access information efficiently, and provide valuable support in their daily practice. By embracing AI-powered diagnostic tools and decision support systems, clinicians can enhance diagnostic accuracy, optimize treatment decisions, and improve patient outcomes. However, it is important to continuously evaluate and monitor the performance of AI algorithms to ensure their effectiveness and reliability in clinical practice.

AI in Treatment and Personalized Medicine

AI has the potential to revolutionize treatment plans by leveraging predictive analytics, genomics, and data-driven insights. It offers practical applications that can tailor medical interventions to individual patients, improving treatment outcomes.

Predictive analytics using AI algorithms can analyse vast amounts of patient data, including electronic health records, medical imaging, and genetic information, to identify patterns and trends. By identifying hidden correlations and risk factors, AI can assist clinicians in predicting patient outcomes and suggesting optimal treatment approaches. For instance, AI algorithms can help identify high-risk patients for developing certain diseases, allowing for early intervention and preventive measures.

Genomics is another area where AI can make a significant impact. AI algorithms can analyse genetic data to identify genetic variations, mutations, or biomarkers associated with specific diseases. By combining genomics data with clinical information, AI can assist in customizing treatment plans based on an individual's genetic profile. This enables precision medicine, where therapies can be personalized to maximize efficacy and minimize adverse effects.

Data-driven insights derived from AI analysis can guide treatment decisions. AI can identify treatment responses and outcomes across diverse populations by aggregating and analysing large-scale patient data. This information can inform treatment selection and dosage adjustments based on patient characteristics, such as age, gender, comorbidities, and genetic predispositions. AI can also analyse real-time patient data, monitoring vital signs, symptoms, and treatment progress, to provide timely alerts and recommendations for adjustments in therapy.

Practical applications in clinical practice:

1. Treatment selection: AI algorithms can assist clinicians in selecting the most appropriate treatment options based on patient-specific characteristics, medical history, and clinical guidelines. By considering the patient's unique profile, AI can optimize treatment selection to improve outcomes.
2. Precision dosing: AI algorithms can help determine the optimal dosage of medications based on factors such as patient demographics, genetics, and response patterns observed in similar patients. This personalized approach reduces the risk of adverse effects and enhances therapeutic efficacy.
3. Clinical decision support: AI can provide decision support by analysing patient data, suggesting potential treatment pathways, and offering evidence-based recommendations. Clinicians can leverage AI-driven tools to explore different treatment options and their possible outcomes, thus aiding in shared decision-making with patients.
4. Clinical trials and drug development: AI can accelerate the discovery and development of new therapies by analysing large amounts of biomedical data, identifying potential drug targets, predicting treatment responses, and facilitating more efficient clinical trials.

5. Patient monitoring: AI-powered monitoring systems can continuously analyse patient data, such as vital signs, laboratory results, and symptom patterns, to detect early signs of deterioration or treatment response. This enables proactive interventions and personalized adjustments to treatment plans.

Incorporating AI in treatment and personalized medicine can enhance clinical decision-making, optimize treatment plans, and improve patient outcomes. However, healthcare professionals must actively interpret AI-generated recommendations, consider individual patient preferences, and ensure ethical considerations are upheld throughout the treatment process.

Strategies for Interpreting AI-Generated Recommendations

To navigate the use of AI-generated recommendations effectively and safely in clinical practice, healthcare professionals can adopt several key strategies. Firstly, developing a comprehensive understanding of the AI algorithm being utilized, including its limitations and potential biases, is essential. This knowledge enables clinicians to interpret AI-generated recommendations within the appropriate context.

Secondly, it is crucial to independently validate AI-generated recommendations by cross-referencing them with established clinical guidelines, evidence-based research, and personal clinical expertise. This validation process ensures that decisions are based on robust and reliable information. Additionally, healthcare professionals should prioritize patient preferences and engage in shared decision-making by considering individual patient values, goals, and circumstances alongside AI-generated recommendations. Evaluating each case on its own merits and exercising clinical judgment remains important, as AI systems may not account for unique patient factors or rare and complex conditions.

It is imperative to continuously monitor and provide feedback on AI systems, reporting inaccuracies or ethical concerns to improve performance and address potential biases. Staying informed about the latest advancements in AI technologies, updating knowledge regularly, and adhering to ethical considerations, such as patient privacy and data security, are vital for the responsible and effective use of AI-generated recommendations. Transparent communication with patients about the role of AI in clinical decision-making fosters trust and ensures their active involvement. By employing these strategies, healthcare professionals can effectively interpret AI-generated recommendations, integrate patient preferences, and uphold ethical standards, ultimately optimizing patient outcomes and fostering a collaborative healthcare environment.

AI in Workflow Optimization and Resource Allocation

AI has the potential to revolutionize healthcare workflows by streamlining processes, automating administrative tasks, and enhancing resource allocation. This has practical implications for improving operational efficiency and resource management in clinical practice.

One area where AI can optimize workflows is administrative tasks. For example, AI-powered chatbots and virtual assistants can automate appointment scheduling, patient registration, and billing processes. By handling routine administrative tasks, AI systems free up healthcare professionals' time, allowing them to focus on direct patient care and more complex decision-making. AI can also enhance resource allocation in healthcare settings. For instance, predictive analytics algorithms can forecast patient demand and help allocate staff and resources accordingly. AI can optimize staffing levels, bed utilization, and equipment availability by analysing historical data, patient profiles, and other factors. This ensures that resources are allocated efficiently, reducing wait times, improving patient flow, and maximizing operational capacity.

Another practical application of AI is in clinical decision support systems that optimize treatment pathways. By analysing patient data and medical guidelines, AI algorithms can suggest the most appropriate diagnostic tests, treatment options, and follow-up plans based on individual patient characteristics. This not only enhances the quality of care but also streamlines the decision-making process for healthcare professionals. Additionally, AI-powered image recognition and natural language processing can expedite the analysis of medical images and textual data. AI can accelerate diagnosis and improve workflow efficiency by automating time-consuming tasks such as radiological image interpretation or extracting relevant information from medical records.

Practical applications in clinical practice:

1. Workflow automation: Implement AI systems, such as chatbots or virtual assistants, to automate administrative tasks, including appointment scheduling, documentation, and billing, reducing administrative burdens and improving efficiency.
2. Predictive analytics for resource allocation: Utilize predictive analytics algorithms to forecast patient demand and optimize staff scheduling, bed allocation, and resource

utilization. This ensures resources are efficiently allocated to meet patient needs and minimize wait times.
3. Clinical decision support systems: Incorporate AI-driven tools that analyse patient data and medical guidelines to provide evidence-based recommendations for diagnostic tests, treatment options, and follow-up plans. This streamlines decision-making and enhances care quality.
4. Image and data analysis: Leverage AI algorithms to assist in studying medical images and extracting relevant information from textual data. This accelerates diagnosis, improves accuracy, and enhances overall workflow efficiency.
5. Real-time monitoring and alerts: Implement AI-powered monitoring systems that analyse real-time patient data and provide timely warnings to healthcare professionals, facilitating proactive interventions and optimizing patient care pathways.

There are several platforms and technologies available that can assist with practical suggestions for workflow optimization and resource allocation in clinical practice. Here are a few examples:

1. Workflow Automation and Chatbots:
- Microsoft Healthcare Bot: This platform offers AI-powered chatbots that automate administrative tasks, including appointment scheduling, patient triage, and frequently asked questions (FAQs).
- Google Dialogflow: It provides a conversational AI platform that enables the creation of chatbots and virtual assistants to automate routine tasks and enhance patient interactions.
2. Predictive Analytics for Resource Allocation:
- Qventus: Qventus utilizes AI and machine learning to optimize hospital operations, including patient flow, bed

management, and staff scheduling, improving resource allocation and operational efficiency.
- Hospital IQ: This platform uses predictive analytics to optimize resource utilization, predict patient demand, and provide real-time operational insights for effective resource allocation.
3. Clinical Decision Support Systems:
- IBM Watson Health: Watson for Oncology is an AI-driven clinical decision support system that assists oncologists in personalized treatment recommendations based on patient data and medical evidence.
- VisualDx: It is a diagnostic decision support system that uses AI and image recognition to assist clinicians in accurately diagnosing and treating various skin conditions.
4. Image and Data Analysis:
- Aidoc: Aidoc offers an AI-powered radiology platform that assists in analysing medical images, highlighting potential abnormalities and prioritizing cases for radiologists.
- Natural Language Processing (NLP) tools like Amazon Comprehend Medical or IBM Watson NLP can assist in extracting relevant information from medical records, enabling efficient data analysis.
5. Real-time Monitoring and Alerts:
- EarlySense: EarlySense provides contactless monitoring solutions using AI algorithms to continuously track patient vital signs and provide real-time alerts for early detection of patient deterioration.
- Current Health: This platform offers wearable devices and remote monitoring solutions that use AI to collect and analyse patient data, enabling proactive interventions and timely alerts.

It is important to assess your clinical practice's specific needs and requirements and explore the functionalities and compatibility of these platforms before implementing them. Additionally, compliance of platforms with relevant data privacy and security regulations has to be ensured. By incorporating AI in workflow optimization and resource allocation, healthcare professionals can improve operational efficiency, enhance resource utilization, and ultimately provide patients with more timely and effective care. It is critical to consider the specific needs and context of the healthcare setting when implementing AI solutions and regularly evaluate their effectiveness to ensure continuous improvement in workflow optimization and resource allocation practices.

8.2: AI in Healthcare Research

AI has sparked a revolution in healthcare research, empowering scientists, and researchers with a remarkable array of innovative tools and methodologies to extract valuable insights from vast amounts of data. In the realm of healthcare research, AI presents practical applications that enhance data analysis, expedite discoveries, and drive transformative changes in the field. This chapter embarks on a captivating exploration of the practical implications of AI in healthcare research, unveiling its real-world applications and delving into the benefits and considerations for researchers. By harnessing the immense power of AI, researchers can navigate through complex datasets, unravel hidden patterns, and generate novel knowledge to propel medical science forward. Nevertheless, researchers must grasp the practical aspects of AI adoption, including data privacy, algorithmic transparency, and the indispensable role of human expertise. The purpose of this chapter is to offer practical guidance and insights to researchers, enabling them to effectively leverage AI in healthcare research, thereby fostering scientific advancements and ushering in tangible improvements in patient care.

AI in Data Analysis and Interpretation

With its ability to process and analyse enormous amounts of healthcare data, AI offers practical applications to accelerate research and discovery. This section delves into the practical implications of AI in data analysis and interpretation, showcases real-world examples and discusses the benefits and considerations for researchers.

One area where AI excels is in data mining and knowledge extraction from large-scale healthcare datasets. Traditional manual approaches to data analysis can be time-consuming and prone to human biases. AI algorithms, on the other hand, can efficiently extract relevant information, identify patterns, and uncover hidden insights within complex datasets. For example, AI can assist in identifying disease associations, detecting adverse events, or predicting treatment responses by mining electronic health records and biomedical literature.

Data integration is another crucial aspect of healthcare research where AI plays a vital role. With diverse data sources, including genomics, imaging, clinical records, and wearable devices, integrating and analysing these data streams becomes challenging. AI techniques, such as natural language processing and machine learning, enable the integration of heterogeneous data sources, harmonizing and linking them to provide a holistic view for researchers. This integration facilitates cross-disciplinary collaborations and the identification of new research opportunities.

Practical applications in research:

1. Predictive Analytics: AI algorithms can analyse patient data to predict disease progression, identify high-risk individuals, or forecast patient outcomes. This enables researchers to focus resources on high-risk populations, design targeted interventions, and optimize patient care pathways.
2. Drug Discovery: AI can speed up drug discovery by analysing large-scale molecular databases, identifying potential drug targets, and predicting drug efficacy and safety profiles. This streamlines the identification of promising candidates for further investigation.
3. Clinical Trial Optimization: AI can enhance clinical trial design and recruitment by identifying suitable patient populations, optimizing inclusion and exclusion criteria, and predicting patient response to interventions. This reduces trial costs, accelerates recruitment, and enhances trial success rates.
4. Precision Medicine: AI facilitates personalized treatment strategies by integrating patient-specific data, including genomics, clinical records, and lifestyle factors. This enables researchers to identify subpopulations that may respond differently to treatments, leading to tailored interventions and improved patient outcomes.
5. Data-driven Decision Support: AI-powered decision support systems can assist researchers in interpreting complex data, suggesting hypotheses, and guiding experimental design. This enables evidence-based decision-making and enhances research efficiency.

By incorporating AI in data analysis and interpretation, researchers can unlock valuable insights, accelerate discoveries, and advance medical science. However, it is crucial to address data privacy, algorithmic transparency, and the need for human expertise in interpreting AI-generated results. Through careful integration and utilization, AI has the potential to transform healthcare research, leading to breakthroughs and improved patient care.

AI in Clinical Trials and Drug Discovery

AI has emerged as a game-changer in clinical trials and drug discovery by offering practical applications that enhance efficiency, success rates, and precision in these critical areas of healthcare research. This section explores the practical implications of AI in clinical trials and drug discovery, showcases real-world examples and discusses the benefits and considerations for researchers and pharmaceutical industries alike.

One significant application of AI is improving the efficiency and success of clinical trials. AI algorithms can play a crucial role in patient recruitment by identifying suitable candidates based on specific criteria, accelerating enrolment, and reducing recruitment costs. For instance, AI-powered platforms can analyse electronic health records and other data sources to identify potential participants who meet the study's inclusion criteria. This streamlines the recruitment process, ensuring clinical trials have a diverse and representative participant pool.

AI can also aid trial design by optimizing the study protocol and sample size calculation. By analysing historical clinical trial data, AI algorithms can provide insights into the most effective trial design, including study endpoints, treatment arms, and allocation strategies. This helps to enhance the study's statistical power and validity, leading to more robust results.

In drug discovery, AI offers practical implications for accelerating the development of novel therapies. AI algorithms can analyse vast amounts of molecular data, including genomics, proteomics, and metabolomics, to identify potential drug targets and predict candidate compounds' efficacy and safety profiles. This allows researchers to focus on the most promising drug candidates, reducing the time and costs associated with traditional trial-and-error approaches.

Furthermore, AI contributes to advancing precision medicine by enabling researchers to identify subpopulations that may respond differently to treatments. AI algorithms can identify biomarkers and genetic signatures associated with treatment responses or adverse events by analysing large-scale patient data, including genetic profiles, clinical records, and lifestyle factors. This facilitates the development of targeted therapies and personalized interventions, maximizing treatment effectiveness and minimizing adverse effects.

Practical examples in practice:

1. Clinical trial optimization: AI platforms such as Mendel.ai and Deep 6 AI assist in patient recruitment, using AI algorithms to analyse patient data and identify potential participants who meet specific study criteria. This streamlines the enrolment process and increases the efficiency of clinical trials.
2. Trial design and prediction: Researchers at Stanford University developed an AI algorithm that predicts the success of clinical trials based on various parameters, including study design, target population, and disease characteristics. This helps researchers make informed decisions regarding trial design and resource allocation.
3. Drug discovery: Insilco Medicine, a company focused on AI-driven drug discovery, utilizes deep learning algorithms to

analyse molecular data and predict drug-target interactions, enabling more efficient identification of potential drug candidates.
4. Precision medicine: The NCI-MATCH (National Cancer Institute - Molecular Analysis for Therapy Choice) trial, a precision medicine initiative, utilizes AI to analyse patient genetic data and match patients with targeted therapies based on specific genetic alterations.

By harnessing the power of AI in clinical trials and drug discovery, researchers can streamline processes, improve participant recruitment, optimize trial design, and accelerate the development of novel therapies. However, addressing challenges such as data privacy, regulatory compliance, and the need for interpretability and human expertise in AI-generated results is crucial. Integrating AI in clinical trials and drug discovery holds tremendous potential for advancing medical research, bringing innovative treatments to patients more efficiently and effectively.

8.3 AI in Healthcare Education and Teaching

AI has the potential to revolutionize medical education and training by offering practical applications that enhance learning outcomes, adaptive learning experiences, and personalized curriculum design. This chapter explores the practical implications of AI in medical education and training, showcases real-world examples and discusses the benefits and considerations for educators and learners alike.

One significant application of AI is in adaptive learning, where AI algorithms analyse learner data and adjust educational content based on individual strengths, weaknesses, and learning styles.

Adaptive learning platforms, such as Osmosis and Area9 Rhapsode, utilize AI to provide personalized learning experiences by customizing educational materials and assessments to meet the unique needs of each learner. AI enhances engagement, knowledge retention, and overall educational outcomes by adapting content delivery, pacing, and difficulty levels.

Simulation-based training is another area where AI demonstrates its practical applications in medical education. AI-powered simulators, like those developed by SimX and CAE Healthcare, offer realistic virtual environments that allow learners to practice clinical skills and decision-making in a safe and controlled setting. AI algorithms enable dynamic responses and feedback by adapting scenarios based on learner actions and performance. This enhances learner engagement, critical thinking, and the development of clinical skills.

AI also plays a role in personalized curriculum design by tailoring educational content and resources to individual learners' specific needs and learning objectives. AI-powered platforms like Cognauto and SMARTSITES analyse learner data, including assessments, feedback, and performance metrics, to recommend targeted learning resources and pathways. This personalized approach optimizes learning efficiency and effectiveness to support learners in their educational journey.

Practical examples in practice:

1. Adaptive learning: Osmosis, an adaptive learning platform, utilizes AI algorithms to analyse learner data, provide personalized content recommendations, and deliver spaced repetition techniques to enhance knowledge retention and long-term learning.
2. Simulation-based training: SimX offers AI-powered virtual simulations that simulate realistic clinical scenarios and

adapt based on learner actions and decisions. Learners receive real-time feedback and can practice critical skills in a safe and controlled environment.
3. Personalized curriculum design: Cognauto, an AI-driven learning platform, analyses learner data to provide personalized learning pathways, tailored resources, and adaptive assessments. It optimizes educational content based on learner strengths and weaknesses, facilitating targeted learning experiences.
4. Virtual patient simulations: VR patients and i-Human Patients are AI-driven virtual patient platforms that enable learners to practice clinical skills, diagnostic reasoning, and treatment planning in realistic patient scenarios. AI algorithms adjust patient responses and symptoms based on learner actions and decision-making.

By incorporating AI in medical education and training, educators can enhance learning experiences, customize content to individual needs, and foster lifelong learning. Learners benefit from personalized educational pathways, realistic simulations, and adaptive learning approaches that optimize engagement and knowledge acquisition. However, it is essential to address considerations such as learner privacy, the ethical use of AI, and the importance of human guidance and expertise in the educational process. Integrating AI in medical education holds great potential for transforming how healthcare professionals are trained, ensuring competence, and improving patient care outcomes.

AI in Continuing Professional Development

AI has the potential to revolutionize continuing professional development (CPD) for healthcare professionals by offering practical applications that enhance personalized and adaptive learning experiences. This chapter explores the practical implications of AI in CPD, showcases real-world examples and discusses the benefits and considerations for healthcare professionals seeking ongoing professional growth.

One significant application of AI in CPD is its ability to facilitate personalized and adaptive learning experiences. AI-powered platforms like CME365 and Medscape analyse individual healthcare professionals' learning preferences, knowledge gaps, and performance data to deliver targeted educational content and recommendations. By adapting the learning journey to individual needs, AI enhances engagement, knowledge retention, and the effectiveness of CPD efforts.

AI also plays a crucial role in assessing professional competency and tracking progress in CPD. With AI algorithms, healthcare professionals can undergo automated assessments that evaluate their knowledge, skills, and clinical reasoning. For example, the NEJM Knowledge+ platform utilizes AI to analyse learner responses and adaptively customize assessments, providing immediate feedback and personalized learning plans based on performance. This ensures that professionals can identify areas for improvement and focus their CPD efforts accordingly.

Another practical application of AI in CPD is the enhancement of accessibility to resources. AI-powered platforms can recommend relevant and up-to-date educational materials, journals, and research papers based on individual interests and learning objectives. This helps healthcare professionals stay informed about the latest developments in their field and provides easy access to high-quality CPD resources, fostering continuous learning.

Practical examples in practice:

1. Personalized learning platforms: CME365 uses AI algorithms to analyse healthcare professionals' learning preferences, knowledge gaps, and performance data to deliver personalized educational content and recommendations. This adaptive learning approach optimizes the effectiveness of CPD efforts.
2. Automated assessments and feedback: New England Journal of Medicine (NEJM) Knowledge+ incorporates AI algorithms to analyse learner responses, adaptively customize evaluations, and provide immediate feedback. This allows professionals to track their progress, identify areas for improvement, and receive personalized learning plans.
3. Resource recommendations: Medscape employs AI to recommend relevant educational materials, journal articles, and research papers based on individual interests and learning objectives. This enhances accessibility to high-quality CPD resources and fosters continuous learning.
4. Virtual conferences and webinars: AI-powered platforms like Doximity and Docebo offer virtual conference and webinar experiences, which utilize AI algorithms to personalize content recommendations, facilitate networking opportunities, and track CPD credits.

incorporating AI in CPD, healthcare professionals can benefit from personalized, adaptive, and accessible learning experiences. AI enhances engagement, tracks progress, and facilitates targeted learning efforts, ultimately improving professional competency and patient care outcomes. However, it is important to address data privacy, the ethical use of AI, and the importance of human expertise and reflection in the CPD process. The integration of AI in CPD holds great potential for transforming how healthcare professionals engage in lifelong learning and continuously enhance their knowledge and skills.

8.4 Summary

In conclusion, the practical implications of AI for healthcare professionals in their clinical practice, research, and teaching are profound. AI has the transformative potential to improve healthcare outcomes, drive advancements, and enhance the overall delivery of care. Throughout this book, we have explored various AI applications, highlighting their practical benefits and considerations for healthcare professionals.

AI empowers healthcare professionals with diagnostic support, decision-making tools, and workflow optimization in clinical practice. Real-world examples such as AI-assisted diagnostics and decision support systems demonstrate how AI can enhance accuracy, efficiency, and patient care. Healthcare professionals must embrace AI technologies while maintaining an active role in interpreting AI-generated recommendations. Considering individual patient preferences, ethical considerations, and the need for human expertise ensures responsible integration and the delivery of patient-centred care.

AI's impact on healthcare research is significant. From data analysis and interpretation to clinical trials and drug discovery, AI offers practical solutions for accelerating discoveries, optimizing resource allocation, and personalizing treatment interventions. These applications enable researchers to navigate complex datasets, identify patterns, and uncover new knowledge that drives scientific advancements. Ethical considerations and the need for human interpretation remain important aspects of AI-driven research to ensure data integrity, privacy, and the responsible use of AI-generated insights.

In medical education and teaching, AI revolutionizes learning experiences by providing adaptive learning platforms, simulation-based training, and personalized curriculum design. Healthcare professionals can enhance their educational outcomes, improve clinical skills, and support lifelong learning through AI-driven platforms. However, maintaining human guidance, expertise, and the consideration of ethical implications are crucial in integrating AI into educational practices.

Healthcare professionals need to embrace AI technologies while considering ethical and regulatory considerations. The responsible integration of AI involves ensuring patient privacy, addressing biases, and promoting transparency and explainability in AI systems. Collaboration between healthcare professionals, researchers, policymakers, and AI developers is key to harnessing the full potential of AI in healthcare while upholding ethical standards.

AI holds great promise in transforming healthcare. By embracing AI technologies, healthcare professionals can leverage its practical benefits to improve patient care, advance research, and enhance educational experiences. However, a thoughtful and responsible approach is necessary, considering ethical considerations, regulatory frameworks, and the critical role of human expertise in delivering quality healthcare. Embracing AI while upholding moral and regulatory standards will drive the positive impact of AI in healthcare and shape a future of improved patient outcomes and advancements in the field.

Chapter 9 The Future of AI in Healthcare

The future of artificial intelligence (AI) in healthcare holds tremendous promise to revolutionize patient care, improve clinical outcomes, and transform healthcare delivery as we know it. The increasing availability of vast amounts of healthcare data, advancements in computing power, and breakthroughs in AI algorithms have paved the way for remarkable developments in AI applications across various healthcare domains. This chapter explores the potentially transformative impact of AI in healthcare and examines the key trends and challenges that will shape its future.

The earlier chapters have shown AI's potential to enhance diagnosis and treatment by analysing complex medical data, such as electronic health records, medical images, and genomics. Machine learning algorithms can uncover hidden patterns, detect anomalies, and provide accurate predictions, enabling healthcare professionals to make more informed decisions. From using AI algorithms to aid early disease detection, predict patient outcomes, and assist in personalized treatment planning, AI-driven technologies, such as robotic surgery systems and AI-powered virtual assistants, are also revolutionizing surgical procedures and patient engagement.

The current body of knowledge has shown that the integration of AI in healthcare is wider than in clinical settings. AI can optimize healthcare operations, improve resource allocation, and enhance patient experience. AI-powered predictive analytics can help healthcare organizations anticipate patient demand, optimize staffing levels, and streamline workflows, leading to more efficient and cost-effective healthcare delivery. Moreover, AI technologies enable the development of intelligent healthcare systems, where connected devices and wearables continuously monitor patient health, provide real-time feedback, and enable remote patient monitoring, thus promoting preventive care and patient empowerment.

While the future of AI in healthcare is promising, several challenges and considerations must be addressed. Ethical implications surrounding privacy, data security, and the responsible use of AI algorithms are critical concerns. Ensuring transparency, fairness, and accountability in AI systems is crucial for maintaining patient trust and safeguarding against biases or unintended consequences. Regulatory frameworks must adapt to the rapid pace of AI development, balancing fostering innovation and protecting patient rights.

Additionally, the future of AI in healthcare relies heavily on interoperability and seamless integration with existing healthcare systems. The ability to share and exchange data across different platforms and technologies is essential for harnessing the full potential of AI. Standardization efforts, data governance frameworks, and collaborations between healthcare providers, technology developers, and regulatory bodies are necessary for creating a robust and interconnected AI ecosystem in healthcare.

The future of AI in healthcare will also require a well-prepared workforce equipped with the necessary knowledge and skills to leverage AI technologies effectively. Training programs and educational initiatives must be in place to ensure healthcare professionals are proficient in utilizing AI algorithms, interpreting AI-generated insights, and understanding the limitations and ethical implications of AI in healthcare.

In conclusion, the future of AI in healthcare holds tremendous promise for transforming patient care, clinical decision-making, and healthcare operations. By leveraging the power of AI algorithms, healthcare professionals can access actionable insights, improve diagnosis and treatment, and optimize healthcare delivery. However, to realize the full potential of AI, it is essential to address ethical, regulatory, interoperability, and workforce challenges. With careful consideration, collaboration, and responsible implementation, AI can reshape the future of healthcare and usher in a new era of precision medicine, improved patient outcomes, and enhanced healthcare experiences.

9.1 Emerging Trends and Technologies

Emerging trends and technologies in artificial intelligence (AI) are shaping the future of healthcare, revolutionizing patient care, and enabling innovative approaches to diagnosis, treatment, and healthcare delivery. These advancements can address longstanding challenges in healthcare and drive improvements in patient outcomes. This section explores some of the emerging trends and technologies that are transforming the landscape of AI in healthcare.

1. Precision Medicine and Predictive Analytics: AI is facilitating the shift towards precision medicine, where treatments and interventions are tailored to individual patients based on their unique characteristics and genetic makeup. Machine learning algorithms can analyse large-scale genomic data, clinical records, and other relevant information to identify patterns, predict disease risks, and personalize treatment plans. For example, AI-powered predictive analytics can help identify individuals at high risk of developing specific diseases and enable early interventions for better outcomes.

2. Natural Language Processing (NLP) and Clinical Language Understanding: NLP techniques enable AI systems to understand and process human language, facilitating communication between patients, healthcare professionals, and digital assistants. NLP algorithms can analyse and extract relevant information from unstructured clinical narratives, such as physician notes, radiology reports, and research papers. This technology improves clinical decision support, facilitates medical coding, and enhances information retrieval from healthcare records.
3. Computer Vision and Medical Imaging Analysis: Computer vision algorithms are revolutionizing medical imaging analysis, aiding in the interpretation of radiological images, pathology slides, and other visual data. Deep learning models can detect abnormalities, segment anatomical structures, and diagnose diseases from medical images. For instance, AI algorithms have shown promise in detecting cancerous lesions in mammograms and identifying abnormalities in retinal scans for diabetic retinopathy.
4. Robotics and Surgical Automation: AI-powered robotic systems transform surgical procedures, enhance precision, and improve patient outcomes. Robotic surgical assistants can assist surgeons with complex tasks by offering greater precision and control. Additionally, telerobotic systems enable remote surgery, which allows expert surgeons to perform procedures on patients in remote locations. Such advancements in surgical automation are reducing invasiveness, improving surgical outcomes, and expanding access to specialized surgical care.
5. Internet of Medical Things (IoMT): The integration of AI with the Internet of Things (IoT) in healthcare, known as the Internet of Medical Things (IoMT), is enabling connected

healthcare systems and devices. AI algorithms can analyse data collected from wearable devices, remote monitoring systems, and sensor-equipped medical devices. This allows for continuous monitoring of patient health, early detection of health deterioration, and personalized interventions. IoMT-driven AI technologies are paving the way for proactive and preventive healthcare delivery.

The global market for artificial intelligence in healthcare is expected to reach over USD 187.95 billion by 2030, with a compound annual growth rate (CAGR) of 37% during the forecast period of 2022-2030. The adoption of AI in healthcare goes beyond process automation and data science, and its potential impact is discussed further.[203] These emerging trends and technologies in AI demonstrate the potential to reshape healthcare delivery and enhance patient outcomes. While still evolving, they promise to address healthcare challenges and improve decision-making processes. As these technologies mature, ensuring ethical considerations, patient privacy, regulatory compliance, and responsible implementation.
 are crucial.

Hospitals must undergo a business transformation that leverages technology effectively to fully harness the benefits of implementing technology in healthcare. A paper emphasizes that hospitals must possess a deep understanding of technology to embrace digital and technological advancements successfully. It concludes that acquiring sufficient knowledge of technology is crucial for hospitals to navigate the transformation and fully realize the potential benefits of integrating technology into healthcare practices.[204]

---

[203] 'Artificial Intelligence (AI) in Healthcare Market Size 2022-2030', accessed 21 May 2023, https://www.precedenceresearch.com/artificial-intelligence-in-healthcare-market.
[204] Grazia Dicuonzo et al., 'Healthcare System: Moving Forward with Artificial Intelligence,' *Technovation* 120 (1 February 2023): 102510, https://doi.org/10.1016/j.technovation.2022.102510.

9.2 AI's potential impact on the healthcare workforce

AI technology has the potential to profoundly impact the healthcare workforce by transforming the roles and responsibilities of healthcare professionals and introducing new opportunities for collaboration between humans and machines. AI can enhance efficiency, accuracy, and patient outcomes. By automating administrative tasks and improving diagnostics, AI can free healthcare practitioners to focus more on patient care. However, the successful adoption of AI in healthcare requires accurate data and the development of new digital skills among healthcare personnel. In the potential impact of AI on the healthcare workforce, recognizing that while some jobs may be replaced by automation, new job opportunities can emerge at the intersection of medical and data science expertise. While concerns about job displacement have been raised, AI is more likely to augment the capabilities of healthcare professionals rather than replace them entirely. This section explores the potential impact of AI on the healthcare workforce and highlights the evolving roles that healthcare professionals may assume in an AI-driven healthcare ecosystem.

One significant area where AI can enhance the healthcare workforce is clinical decision support. AI algorithms can analyse vast amounts of patient data, medical literature, and treatment guidelines to provide evidence-based recommendations to healthcare professionals. For example, AI-powered decision support systems can assist physicians in diagnosing complex conditions, determining appropriate treatment plans, and predicting patient outcomes. By leveraging AI-driven insights, healthcare professionals can make more informed decisions and provide personalized, data-driven care.

AI can also alleviate the administrative burden on healthcare professionals, allowing them to focus on patient care. Administrative tasks, such as data entry, documentation, and scheduling, can be automated using AI technologies. Voice recognition and natural language processing can streamline the process of capturing patient information and generating electronic health records, thus reducing the time spent on paperwork and enabling healthcare professionals to allocate more time for direct patient interactions.

Moreover, AI can support healthcare professionals in medical imaging analysis. Radiologists and pathologists can benefit from AI algorithms that assist in image interpretation, detecting abnormalities and improving diagnostic accuracy. For instance, AI-powered algorithms have shown promise in detecting lung nodules in chest X-rays or identifying malignant lesions in histopathology slides. By collaborating with AI systems, healthcare professionals can leverage their expertise while harnessing the analytical power of AI to improve diagnosis and treatment planning.

Another area where AI can significantly impact is remote and personalized healthcare delivery. With AI technologies, telemedicine platforms can enable remote consultations, remote patient vital signs monitoring, and customized treatment recommendations. This allows healthcare professionals to reach underserved populations, provide continuous care, and offer tailored interventions based on real-time data. By leveraging AI-driven tools, healthcare professionals can extend their reach and provide high-quality care to a broader patient population.

While AI presents numerous opportunities for the healthcare workforce, challenges exist. One key challenge is ensuring healthcare professionals have the necessary skills and knowledge to utilize AI technologies effectively. Education and training programs must be in place to equip healthcare professionals with the competencies to collaborate with AI systems, interpret AI-generated insights, and address ethical and privacy concerns associated with AI in healthcare. Continuing education and upskilling efforts are crucial to ensure healthcare professionals remain competent in AI-driven healthcare.

As AI advances, the healthcare workforce must prepare for this transformative shift. In the following section, we explore the steps that healthcare professionals can take to prepare for the implementation of AI in healthcare effectively. From education and training to staying informed and embracing interdisciplinary collaboration, healthcare professionals can position themselves to leverage AI technologies and contribute to improved patient outcomes. By understanding the ethical considerations and embracing lifelong learning, the healthcare workforce can play a pivotal role in harnessing the power of AI to enhance healthcare delivery and shape the future of medicine.

In conclusion, AI has the potential to significantly impact the healthcare workforce by augmenting healthcare professionals' capabilities and transforming their roles. Rather than replacing healthcare professionals, AI technologies can empower them with data-driven insights, streamline administrative tasks, enhance diagnostic accuracy, and enable personalized care delivery. By embracing AI as a collaborative tool, healthcare professionals can leverage its power to improve patient outcomes, increase efficiency, and enhance the overall quality of care.

9.3 Preparing for the future: strategies for health professionals.

Preparing for the future of healthcare requires health professionals to adapt to the evolving landscape shaped by artificial intelligence (AI) technologies. To navigate this changing landscape effectively, health professionals can employ various strategies that equip them with the skills and knowledge needed to leverage AI and ensure optimal patient care. This section explores key strategies for health professionals to prepare for the future of healthcare in an AI-driven era.

1. Lifelong Learning and Continuous Professional Development: Health professionals must embrace a mindset of lifelong learning to keep pace with advancements in AI technologies. Continuous professional development programs and educational opportunities should be leveraged to stay updated on AI applications, data analytics, and ethical considerations. These programs can range from online courses and webinars to attending conferences and workshops focused on AI in healthcare. By engaging in lifelong learning, health professionals can enhance their skills, expand their knowledge base, and adapt to emerging AI trends.
2. Collaboration and Interdisciplinary Cooperation: Collaboration among health professionals, AI specialists, data scientists, and other stakeholders is vital for successfully integrating AI into healthcare. Interdisciplinary teams can work together to develop and implement AI algorithms, address technical challenges, and ensure the ethical and responsible use of AI technologies. By fostering a culture of collaboration and teamwork, health professionals can leverage the expertise of different disciplines to drive

innovation, optimize patient care, and identify AI use cases specific to their healthcare settings.

3. Embracing Data Literacy and Digital Fluency: Health professionals must cultivate data literacy and digital fluency to work with AI technologies effectively. This involves understanding data sources, privacy, security regulations and interpreting AI-generated insights. Health professionals should be able to critically evaluate AI outputs, verify results, and communicate the limitations and uncertainties associated with AI-based recommendations to patients and colleagues. Developing data literacy skills ensures that health professionals can make informed decisions and confidently utilize AI-driven tools.

4. Ethical and Human-Centred Considerations: As AI becomes more integrated into healthcare, health professionals must prioritize ethical considerations and ensure a human-centred approach. This includes addressing bias, fairness, transparency, and privacy issues in AI algorithms. Health professionals should advocate for responsible AI use, actively engage in ethical discussions, and participate in developing guidelines and policies related to AI in healthcare. By placing the well-being and autonomy of patients at the forefront, health professionals can contribute to the ethical and responsible implementation of AI technologies.

5. Cultivating Adaptability and Resilience: The future of healthcare is dynamic and continuously evolving. Health professionals must develop adaptability and resilience to thrive in an AI-driven era. This involves embracing change, being open to new technologies and approaches, and being willing to adapt their practices to leverage the benefits of AI continuously. Health professionals should also stay

informed about emerging AI trends and actively seek opportunities to engage with AI initiatives within their organizations or professional networks.

```
                    Embracing Data
                    Literacy and
                    Digital Fluency
   Collaboration
        and                              Ethical and
  Interdisciplinary                    Human-Centred
     Cooperation                        Considerations


   Lifelong Learning                        Cultivating
   and Continuous      Preparing         Adaptability and
     Professional       for AI              Resilience
     Development
```

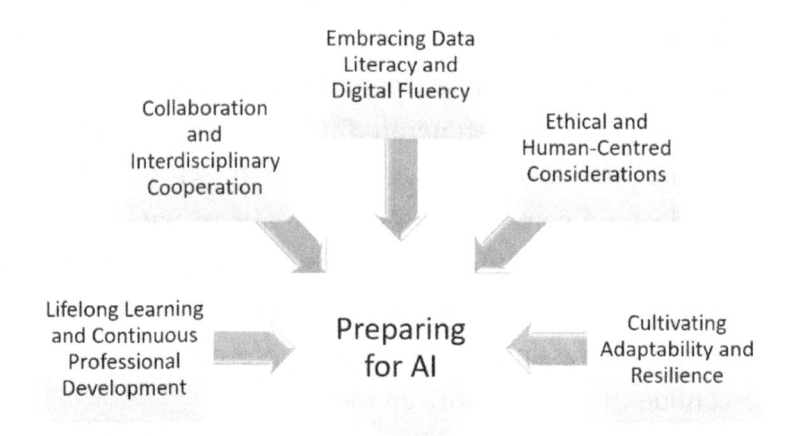

Figure 34. Strategies for Preparing the healthcare workforce for the Future of AI

The practical implications for the healthcare worker to implement in one's practice are as follows. Firstly, they should *prioritize education and training* by pursuing programs focusing on AI, data science, and digital health. This may involve enrolling in courses, obtaining certifications, or pursuing advanced degrees in relevant fields such as medical informatics or health data analytics. *Staying informed about the latest advancements in AI* is essential, and healthcare professionals can achieve this by following relevant journals, attending conferences, participating in webinars, and joining professional networks and organizations dedicated to AI in healthcare.

Developing digital skills is crucial for healthcare professionals to leverage technology tools and platforms effectively. This includes gaining proficiency in electronic health records (EHRs), data analysis tools, and AI-enabled systems. It is imperative to Actively engage in continuous learning and adopt new technologies relevant to their practice.

Collaboration with data scientists and AI experts is also important, as interdisciplinary teamwork and partnerships facilitate the development of innovative solutions and a deeper understanding of the potential and limitations of AI. Healthcare professionals should actively contribute to discussions and *developing ethical guidelines and policies* related to AI in healthcare, considering principles such as transparency, fairness, privacy, and informed consent.

Embracing a mindset of *lifelong learning* is critical in the rapidly evolving field of AI in healthcare. Seeking opportunities for upskilling, attending workshops, and participating in online courses helps healthcare professionals stay updated on new technologies, methodologies, and best practices. Furthermore, *advocating for AI's ethical and responsible use* in healthcare is paramount. Healthcare professionals should actively participate in discussions and decision-making processes to ensure that AI technologies prioritize patient well-being and safety. By taking these steps, healthcare professionals can effectively prepare themselves for integrating AI into healthcare, ultimately enhancing patient care and outcomes.

In summary, health professionals can proactively prepare for the future of healthcare by embracing lifelong learning, collaboration, data literacy, ethical considerations, and adaptability. Health professionals can effectively leverage AI technologies to enhance patient care, contribute to innovation, and navigate this transforming landscape by developing the necessary skills, knowledge, and mindsets.

Chapter 10 Conclusion

The concluding chapter encapsulates the wealth of insights and findings expounded upon in this comprehensive book on AI in healthcare. It serves as a culmination of the diverse topics and perspectives explored, providing a comprehensive overview of the potential and challenges associated with artificial intelligence (AI) in transforming healthcare. Through synthesizing the main themes, drawing overarching conclusions, and offering reflections on the future of AI in healthcare, this chapter solidifies the knowledge acquired throughout the book.

Within these pages, we have embarked on an exploration of the multifaceted applications of AI in various aspects of healthcare, ranging from clinical decision support and diagnostics to patient monitoring and healthcare operations. We have delved into the potential benefits that AI brings, including heightened accuracy, improved efficiency, and personalized care. However, we have also confronted the challenges inherent in the adoption of AI, such as data privacy concerns, ethical implications, and the ongoing necessity for training and education.

Here we consolidate these discussions, highlighting AI's significant impact on healthcare outcomes and the transformational opportunities it presents. We reflect on the ethical, legal, and social considerations accompanying AI technologies' integration in healthcare. The chapter emphasizes the importance of striking a balance between innovation and responsible use of AI, ensuring that patient welfare, privacy, and autonomy remain central in the decision-making process.

Moreover, this chapter delves into the broader implications of AI on the healthcare workforce, examining the evolving roles and skills required of healthcare professionals in an AI-driven era. We discuss strategies for health professionals to embrace lifelong learning, foster collaboration, and navigate the changing landscape of healthcare delivery. The chapter acknowledges the need for a supportive environment that fosters AI adoption and provides the necessary resources and training for healthcare professionals to harness the full potential of AI technologies.

Furthermore, this concluding chapter explores emerging trends and technologies in AI, discussing the future directions and opportunities for AI in healthcare. It reflects on the potential of precision medicine, natural language processing, computer vision, and robotics, among other AI-driven advancements, to shape the future of healthcare. The chapter also emphasizes addressing challenges such as bias, transparency, and interoperability as AI evolves.

In synthesizing these discussions on AI in healthcare, we summarize key insights and conclude the potential impact of AI on healthcare delivery, patient outcomes, and the healthcare workforce. It calls for a balanced and responsible approach to AI adoption, highlighting the need for ongoing education, collaboration, and ethical considerations. The chapter offers reflections on the future of AI in healthcare by encouraging readers to embrace the opportunities presented by AI while navigating the associated challenges and ensuring the human-centric focus of healthcare remains at the core of AI-driven advancements.

10.1 Embracing AI

Embracing AI as a tool for positive change in healthcare holds tremendous potential for improving patient outcomes, enhancing clinical decision-making, and optimizing healthcare delivery. Rather than viewing AI as a disruptive force, healthcare professionals and organizations can adopt a proactive and open mindset toward AI technologies. This section explores the benefits and opportunities of embracing AI as a tool for positive change in healthcare.

One of the key advantages of AI is its ability to augment human capabilities and expertise. AI algorithms can analyse vast amounts of data, identify patterns, and generate insights to inform clinical decision-making. By leveraging AI, healthcare professionals can access evidence-based recommendations, improve diagnostic accuracy, and personalize treatment plans. For example, AI-powered predictive models can assist in identifying patients at high risk for certain conditions, allowing for early interventions and improved outcomes.

Moreover, AI can support healthcare professionals in managing the increasing complexity of healthcare systems. As healthcare data grows exponentially, AI algorithms can efficiently process and analyse this data, enabling healthcare professionals to extract meaningful information promptly. This can lead to more efficient workflows, reduced administrative burden, and improved resource allocation. For instance, AI-driven tools can automate repetitive administrative tasks, allowing healthcare professionals to focus more on direct patient care.

AI also has the potential to address healthcare disparities and improve access to quality care. Telemedicine, enabled by AI technologies, can connect patients in remote or underserved areas with healthcare providers, bridging geographical barriers and increasing access to specialized care. AI-powered decision support systems can assist healthcare professionals in resource-constrained settings, helping them make informed decisions and provide high-quality care even with limited resources.

By embracing AI, healthcare professionals can also contribute to advancing medical research and innovation. AI algorithms can analyse vast amounts of research data, identify novel patterns, and accelerate the discovery of new treatments and interventions. AI can assist in identifying potential drug candidates, predicting drug responses, and uncovering previously unknown correlations in large-scale datasets. This enables researchers and healthcare professionals to develop more targeted and effective therapies, ultimately improving patient outcomes.

However, it is important to emphasize that embracing AI as a tool for positive change requires careful consideration and safeguards. Ethical, legal, and social implications must be considered to ensure responsible and transparent AI deployment in healthcare. Data privacy, security, and algorithmic bias must be addressed to maintain patient trust and protect against potential harm. Collaboration between AI developers, healthcare professionals, policymakers, and regulatory bodies is essential to establish guidelines and frameworks that promote the ethical and responsible use of AI technologies in healthcare.

Embracing AI as a tool for positive change in healthcare can revolutionize patient care, enhance clinical decision-making, and optimize healthcare delivery. By leveraging AI technologies, healthcare professionals can augment their expertise, improve diagnostic accuracy, and personalize treatment plans. AI can address healthcare disparities, increase access to quality care, and contribute to medical research and innovation. However, responsible deployment of AI in healthcare requires careful considerations of ethical, legal, and social implications. By embracing AI with a patient-centric focus and ensuring transparency and accountability, healthcare professionals can harness AI's transformative power to improve healthcare outcomes and patient well-being.

10.2 Lifelong Learning and Adaptability

The importance of lifelong learning and adaptability cannot be overstated in the context of embracing artificial intelligence (AI) in healthcare. As AI technologies advance and shape the healthcare landscape, healthcare professionals must commit to ongoing learning and adaptability to remain at the forefront of their field. This section delves into the significance of lifelong learning and adaptability in the context of AI adoption in healthcare.

Lifelong learning is crucial for healthcare professionals to stay abreast of the latest developments in AI technologies, understand their applications in healthcare, and acquire the skills necessary to leverage AI effectively. As AI algorithms and techniques evolve rapidly, healthcare professionals must engage in continuous professional development programs, attend conferences and workshops, and actively seek educational opportunities focused on AI in healthcare. Lifelong learning enables healthcare professionals to stay informed about emerging trends, best practices, and ethical considerations associated with AI, ensuring they can make informed decisions and provide their patients the highest quality of care.

Adaptability is equally essential in an era of rapid technological advancement. Healthcare professionals must embrace change and be open to adopting new technologies and workflows. AI has the potential to transform traditional healthcare practices, and healthcare professionals must be willing to adapt their roles and responsibilities to harness the benefits of AI technologies fully. This may involve redefining workflows, collaborating with AI systems, and embracing new approaches to patient care. By embracing adaptability, healthcare professionals can navigate the evolving landscape of AI integration in healthcare and proactively leverage AI to enhance patient outcomes and improve healthcare delivery.

Additionally, lifelong learning and adaptability enable healthcare professionals to collaborate effectively with AI systems and algorithms. AI should not be viewed as a replacement for healthcare professionals but as a tool to augment their skills and expertise. Lifelong learning allows healthcare professionals to develop a deep understanding of AI technologies, enabling them to collaborate effectively with AI algorithms in areas such as clinical decision support, diagnostics, and data analysis. By staying updated and adaptable, healthcare professionals can leverage AI technologies as partners in providing optimal patient care, enhancing accuracy, efficiency, and patient outcomes.

Furthermore, lifelong learning and adaptability foster a culture of innovation within healthcare organizations. Healthcare professionals who embrace lifelong learning and adaptability serve as champions for AI adoption, driving change and inspiring their peers to explore the potential of AI in healthcare. They can play a crucial role in advocating for the integration of AI technologies, leading AI-driven projects, and fostering a culture of continuous improvement. By embracing lifelong learning and adaptability, healthcare professionals create an environment that encourages innovation, collaboration, and the responsible use of AI in healthcare.

Lifelong learning and adaptability are essential for healthcare professionals to embrace and leverage AI technologies in healthcare effectively. By committing to lifelong learning, healthcare professionals stay informed about the latest developments in AI, acquire the necessary skills, and understand the ethical implications associated with AI adoption. Adaptability allows healthcare professionals to embrace change, collaborate with AI technologies, and drive innovation in healthcare organizations. By prioritizing lifelong learning and adaptability, healthcare professionals can position themselves at the forefront of AI integration, ensuring high-quality, patient-centred care in the rapidly evolving landscape of AI in healthcare.

10.3 Key takeaways

The key takeaways for AI in healthcare can be summarized as follows. Firstly, AI has great potential to improve patient outcomes, enhance clinical decision-making, optimize healthcare delivery, and address healthcare disparities. It can augment human capabilities, improve diagnostic accuracy, personalize treatment plans, and automate administrative tasks. To harness these benefits, healthcare professionals should prioritize education and training in AI, data science, and digital health, embracing lifelong learning and adaptability to stay updated with the latest advancements. Collaboration between healthcare professionals, data scientists, and AI experts is crucial, which fosters an interdisciplinary approach to developing innovative solutions and translating AI insights into clinical practice.

Ethical considerations are vital in the responsible use of AI. Transparency, fairness, privacy, and informed consent should be prioritized, requiring collaboration with policymakers and regulatory bodies to establish guidelines and frameworks. Additionally, ensuring data quality, security, and interoperability is essential to leverage AI effectively. Healthcare professionals should adopt a patient-centred approach, advocate for AI's ethical and responsible use, and actively participate in discussions and decision-making processes.

Lifelong learning and adaptability are key for healthcare professionals to navigate the evolving AI landscape. By embracing these principles, they can stay informed about emerging trends, acquire necessary skills, and collaborate effectively with AI technologies. Ultimately, a patient-centred approach, responsible adoption of AI, and continuous learning will contribute to improved healthcare outcomes and patient well-being.

Closing thoughts and a call to action are vital components of discussing the future of artificial intelligence (AI) in healthcare. As we conclude our exploration of AI's potential impact, reflecting on the key takeaways and emphasizing the imperative for action is important. This section encapsulates the main insights and presents a call to action for healthcare professionals, policymakers, and stakeholders in the healthcare ecosystem.

The journey through the world of AI in healthcare has highlighted its transformative potential, from improving diagnostic accuracy and treatment outcomes to enhancing operational efficiency and patient experience. We have explored the ethical, legal, and social implications accompanying AI adoption and emphasized the need for responsible and human-centric approaches. The importance of lifelong learning, adaptability, and collaboration among healthcare professionals, AI experts, and policymakers has been underscored as essential for successfully harnessing AI technologies' benefits.

As we stand at the forefront of this AI revolution, there is a call to action for healthcare professionals to embrace AI as a tool for positive change. It is crucial to actively engage in ongoing learning and professional development and stay informed about the latest advancements in AI technologies and their applications in healthcare. By developing AI literacy and expertise, healthcare professionals can play an active role in shaping AI's future in healthcare, ensuring that it aligns with patient needs, ethical standards, and professional best practices.

Furthermore, policymakers and regulatory bodies must proactively establish frameworks that promote responsible and ethical AI adoption in healthcare. Clear data privacy, security, and algorithmic transparency guidelines are essential to build trust and address potential biases or risks associated with AI technologies. Collaboration between healthcare organizations, policymakers, and AI developers is critical to drive innovation while maintaining patient safety, privacy, and ethical standards.

Stakeholders in the healthcare ecosystem must recognize the need for a multidisciplinary approach to AI implementation. Collaboration between healthcare professionals, AI experts, data scientists, and patients is key to ensuring that AI technologies are designed and deployed to address healthcare systems' real-world challenges. By fostering a culture of collaboration and knowledge-sharing, we can collectively leverage AI's potential to transform healthcare and improve patient outcomes.

As we conclude this discussion, it is important to approach the future of AI in healthcare with cautious optimism. AI technologies hold immense promise, but their successful integration requires careful consideration, ongoing evaluation, and constant adaptation. It is crucial to remain mindful of AI adoption's potential risks and limitations and continuously assess the impact on patient care, ethical considerations, and the healthcare workforce.

The journey into the world of AI in healthcare has revealed an array of opportunities, challenges, and ethical considerations. By embracing AI as a tool for positive change, committing to lifelong learning, fostering collaboration, and upholding ethical standards, we can shape a future where AI enhances patient care, empowers healthcare professionals, and improves the overall healthcare ecosystem. The time to act is now as we collectively work towards harnessing the transformative power of AI for the betterment of healthcare outcomes and the well-being of patients worldwide.

RESOURCES

The Art and Science of Qualitative Research

https://tinyurl.com/QUALIRE

Introduction to research in healthcare

https://tinyurl.com/HCARERE

AICHAT BOT FOR Research in healthcare

https://tinyurl.com/HCAREREBOT

AI-Powered Academic Writing   Write Your Research Paper in a Day

https://tinyurl.com/AIAWRITE

AI CHAT BOT for AI_POWERED ACADEMIC WRITING

https://tinyurl.com/AIAWRITEBOT

AI Chatbot for Prompt Engineering

https://tinyurl.com/PROMPTGENIUS

Bibliography

Ajab, Shereen, Emma Pearson, Steven Dumont, Alicia Mitchell, Jack Kastelik, Packianathaswamy Balaji, and David Hepburn. 'An Alternative to Traditional Bedside Teaching During COVID-19: High-Fidelity Simulation-Based Study'. *JMIR Medical Education* 8, no. 2 (May 9, 2022): e33565. https://doi.org/10.2196/33565.

Alaker, Medhat, Greg R. Wynn, and Tan Arulampalam. 'Virtual Reality Training in Laparoscopic Surgery: A Systematic Review & Meta-Analysis.' *International Journal of Surgery* 29 (May 1, 2016): 85–94. https://doi.org/10.1016/j.ijsu.2016.03.034.

'Artificial Intelligence (AI) in Healthcare Market Size 2022-2030'. Accessed May 21, 2023. https://www.precedenceresearch.com/artificial-intelligence-in-healthcare-market.

Bellamy, Rachel, Aleksandra Mojsilovic, Seema Nagar, Karthikeyan Natesan Ramamurthy, John Richards, Diptikalyan Saha, Prasanna Sattigeri, et al. 'AI Fairness 360: An Extensible Toolkit for Detecting and Mitigating Algorithmic Bias'. *IBM Journal of Research and Development*, July 1, 2019. https://doi.org/10.1147/JRD.2019.2942287.

Bera, Kaustav, Kurt A. Schalper, David L. Rimm, Vamsidhar Velcheti, and Anant Madabhushi. 'Artificial Intelligence in Digital Pathology - New Tools for Diagnosis and Precision Oncology.' *Nature Reviews. Clinical Oncology* 16, no. 11 (November 2019): 703–15. https://doi.org/10.1038/s41571-019-0252-y.

Čartolovni, Anto, Ana Tomičić, and Elvira Lazić Mosler. 'Ethical, Legal, and Social Considerations of AI-Based Medical Decision-Support Tools: A Scoping Review.' *International Journal of Medical Informatics* 161 (May 1, 2022): 104738. https://doi.org/10.1016/j.ijmedinf.2022.104738.

Chan, Heang-Ping, Ravi K. Samala, Lubomir M. Hadjiiski, and Chuan Zhou. 'Deep Learning in Medical Image Analysis.' *Advances in Experimental Medicine and Biology* 1213 (2020): 3–21. https://doi.org/10.1007/978-3-030-33128-3_1.

Chan, Kai Siang, and Nabil Zary. 'Applications and Challenges of Implementing Artificial Intelligence in Medical Education: Integrative Review.' *JMIR Medical Education* 5, no. 1 (June 14, 2019): e13930. https://doi.org/10.2196/13930.

Chen, Irene Y., Emma Pierson, Sherri Rose, Shalmali Joshi, Kadija Ferryman, and Marzyeh Ghassemi. 'Ethical Machine Learning in Healthcare.' *Annual Review of Biomedical Data Science* 4, no. 1 (2021): 123–44. https://doi.org/10.1146/annurev-biodatasci-092820-114757.

Cheng, Yang, and Hua Jiang. 'AI-Powered Mental Health Chatbots: Examining Users' Motivations, Active Communicative Action and Engagement after Mass-Shooting Disasters.' *Journal of Contingencies and Crisis Management* 28, no. 3 (2020): 339–54. https://doi.org/10.1111/1468-5973.12319.

Chou, Roger, Jessica C. Griffin, Ian Blazina, Eli Schwarz, Chandler Atchison, and Kim Mauer. 'Literature Update Period: January 22, 2022, through May 6, 202', 2020.

Cohen, I. Glenn, Ruben Amarasingham, Anand Shah, Bin Xie, and Bernard Lo. 'The Legal and Ethical Concerns That Arise from Using Complex Predictive Analytics in Health Care.' *Health Affairs (Project Hope)* 33, no. 7 (July 2014): 1139–47. https://doi.org/10.1377/hlthaff.2014.0048.

Dara, Suresh, Swetha Dhamercherla, Surender Singh Jadav, CH Madhu Babu, and Mohamed Jawed Ahsan. 'Machine Learning in Drug Discovery: A Review.' *Artificial Intelligence Review* 55, no. 3 (March 1, 2022): 1947–99. https://doi.org/10.1007/s10462-021-10058-4.

Dascalu, A., and E. O. David. 'Skin Cancer Detection by Deep Learning and Sound Analysis Algorithms: A Prospective Clinical Study of an Elementary Dermoscope.' *EBioMedicine* 43 (May 1, 2019): 107–13. https://doi.org/10.1016/j.ebiom.2019.04.055.

Davenport, Thomas, and Ravi Kalakota. 'The Potential for Artificial Intelligence in Healthcare.' *Future Healthcare Journal* 6, no. 2 (June 2019): 94–98. https://doi.org/10.7861/futurehosp.6-2-94.

De Cannière, Hélène, Federico Corradi, Christophe J. P. Smeets, Melanie Schoutteten, Carolina Varon, Chris Van Hoof, Sabine Van Huffel, Willemijn Groenendaal, and Pieter Vandervoort. 'Wearable Monitoring and Interpretable Machine Learning Can Objectively Track Progression in Patients during Cardiac Rehabilitation'. *Sensors (Basel, Switzerland)* 20, no. 12 (26 June 2020): 3601. https://doi.org/10.3390/s20123601.

De Cremer, David, and Garry Kasparov. 'The Ethics of Technology Innovation: A Double-Edged Sword?' *AI and Ethics* 2, no. 3 (August 1, 2022): 533–37. https://doi.org/10.1007/s43681-021-00103-x.

De Fauw, Jeffrey, Joseph R. Ledsam, Bernardino Romera-Paredes, Stanislav Nikolov, Nenad Tomasev, Sam Blackwell, Harry Askham, et al. 'Clinically Applicable Deep Learning for Diagnosis and Referral in Retinal Disease.' *Nature Medicine* 24, no. 9 (September 2018): 1342–50. https://doi.org/10.1038/s41591-018-0107-6.

Dias, Pedro, Miguel Cardoso, Federico Guede-Fernandez, Ana Martins, and Ana Londral. 'Remote Patient Monitoring Systems Based on Conversational Agents for Health Data Collection,' 2021. https://doi.org/10.5220/0011011000003123.

Dicuonzo, Grazia, Francesca Donofrio, Antonio Fusco, and Matilda Shini. 'Healthcare System: Moving Forward with Artificial Intelligence.' *Technovation* 120 (February 1, 2023): 102510. https://doi.org/10.1016/j.technovation.2022.102510.

Duraku, Liron S., Lisa Hoogendam, Caroline A. Hundepool, Dominic M. Power, Vaikunthan Rajaratnam, Harm P. Slijper, Reinier Feitz, Jelle M. Zuidam, Ruud W. Selles, and Hand Wrist Study Group. 'Collaborative Hand Surgery Clinical Research without Sharing Individual Patient Data; Proof of Principle Study.' *Journal of Plastic, Reconstructive & Aesthetic Surgery*, 2022.

Esteva, Andre, Alexandre Robicquet, Bharath Ramsundar, Volodymyr Kuleshov, Mark DePristo, Katherine Chou, Claire Cui, Greg Corrado, Sebastian Thrun, and Jeff Dean. 'A Guide to Deep Learning in Healthcare.' *Nature Medicine* 25, no. 1 (January 2019): 24–29. https://doi.org/10.1038/s41591-018-0316-z.

Festor, Paul, Yan Jia, Anthony C. Gordon, A. Aldo Faisal, Ibrahim Habli, and Matthieu Komorowski. 'Assuring the Safety of AI-Based Clinical Decision Support Systems: A Case Study of the AI Clinician for Sepsis Treatment.' *BMJ Health & Care Informatics* 29, no. 1 (July 1, 2022): e100549. https://doi.org/10.1136/bmjhci-2022-100549.

Fiani, Brian, Kory B. Dylan Pasko, Kasra Sarhadi, and Claudia Covarrubias. 'Current Uses, Emerging Applications, and Clinical Integration of Artificial Intelligence in Neuroradiology.' *Reviews in the Neurosciences* 33, no. 4 (June 27, 2022): 383–95. https://doi.org/10.1515/revneuro-2021-0101.

Fjelland, Ragnar. 'Why General Artificial Intelligence Will Not Be Realized.' *Humanities and Social Sciences Communications* 7, no. 1 (June 17, 2020): 1–9. https://doi.org/10.1057/s41599-020-0494-4.

Frank, Darius-Aurel, Christian T. Elbæk, Caroline Kjær Børsting, Panagiotis Mitkidis, Tobias Otterbring, and Sylvie Borau. 'Drivers and Social Implications of Artificial Intelligence Adoption in Healthcare during the COVID-19 Pandemic'. *PLOS ONE* 16, no. 11 (November 22, 2021): e0259928. https://doi.org/10.1371/journal.pone.0259928.

Gaur, Kritika, and Miheer M Jagtap. 'Role of Artificial Intelligence and Machine Learning in Prediction, Diagnosis, and Prognosis of Cancer.' *Cureus* 14, no. 11 (n.d.): e31008. https://doi.org/10.7759/cureus.31008.

Gautam, Nitesh, Sai Nikhila Ghanta, Joshua Mueller, Munthir Mansour, Zhongning Chen, Clara Puente, Yu Mi Ha, et al. 'Artificial Intelligence, Wearables and Remote Monitoring for Heart Failure: Current and Future Applications.' *Diagnostics* 12, no. 12 (December 2022): 2964. https://doi.org/10.3390/diagnostics12122964.

Gu, Yuexing, Yuanjing Xu, Yuling Shen, Hanyu Huang, Tongyou Liu, Lei Jin, Hang Ren, and Jinwu Wang. 'A Review of Hand Function Rehabilitation Systems Based on Hand Motion Recognition Devices and Artificial Intelligence.' *Brain Sciences* 12, no. 8 (August 2022): 1079. https://doi.org/10.3390/brainsci12081079.

Gundersen, Torbjørn, and Kristine Bærøe. 'The Future Ethics of Artificial Intelligence in Medicine: Making Sense of Collaborative Models.' *Science and Engineering Ethics* 28, no. 2 (April 1, 2022): 17. https://doi.org/10.1007/s11948-022-00369-2.

Habehh, Hafsa, and Suril Gohel. 'Machine Learning in Healthcare.' *Current Genomics* 22, no. 4 (December 16, 2021): 291–300. https://doi.org/10.2174/1389202922666210705124359.

Hassan, Mubashir, Faryal Mehwish Awan, Anam Naz, Enrique J. deAndrés-Galiana, Oscar Alvarez, Ana Cernea, Lucas Fernández-Brillet, Juan Luis Fernández-Martínez, and Andrzej Kloczkowski. 'Innovations in Genomics and Big Data Analytics for Personalized Medicine and Health Care: A Review'. *International Journal of Molecular Sciences* 23, no. 9 (January 2022): 4645. https://doi.org/10.3390/ijms23094645.

Higgins, David, and Vince I. Madai. 'From Bit to Bedside: A Practical Framework for Artificial Intelligence Product Development in Healthcare.' *Advanced Intelligent Systems* 2, no. 10 (2020): 2000052. https://doi.org/10.1002/aisy.202000052.

Huang, Kexin, Cao Xiao, Lucas M. Glass, Cathy W. Critchlow, Greg Gibson, and Jimeng Sun. 'Machine Learning Applications for Therapeutic Tasks with Genomics Data.' *Patterns* 2, no. 10 (August 9, 2021): 100328. https://doi.org/10.1016/j.patter.2021.100328.

Huo, Cong-Cong, Ya Zheng, Wei-Wei Lu, Teng-Yu Zhang, Dai-Fa Wang, Dong-Sheng Xu, and Zeng-Yong Li. 'Prospects for Intelligent Rehabilitation Techniques to Treat Motor Dysfunction.' *Neural Regeneration Research* 16, no. 2 (August 24, 2020): 264–69. https://doi.org/10.4103/1673-5374.290884.

Ii, Suzanne Sayuri, Louise Fitzgerald, Megan M. Morys-Carter, Natasha L. Davie, and Richard Barker. 'Knowledge Translation in Tri-Sectoral Collaborations: An Exploration of Perceptions of Academia, Industry and Healthcare Collaborations in Innovation Adoption.' *Health Policy* 122, no. 2 (February 1, 2018): 175–83. https://doi.org/10.1016/j.healthpol.2017.11.010.

Jiang, Fei, Yong Jiang, Hui Zhi, Yi Dong, Hao Li, Sufeng Ma, Yilong Wang, Qiang Dong, Haipeng Shen, and Yongjun Wang. 'Artificial Intelligence in Healthcare: Past, Present and Future.' *Stroke and Vascular Neurology* 2, no. 4 (June 21, 2017): 230–43. https://doi.org/10.1136/svn-2017-000101.

Joachim, Shane, Abdur Rahim Mohammad Forkan, Prem Prakash Jayaraman, Ahsan Morshed, and Nilmini Wickramasinghe. 'A Nudge-Inspired AI-Driven Health Platform for Self-Management of Diabetes.' *Sensors* 22, no. 12 (January 2022): 4620. https://doi.org/10.3390/s22124620.

Kanai, Hideaki, and Akinori Kumazawa. 'An Information Sharing System for Multi-Professional Collaboration in the Community-Based Integrated Healthcare System.' *International Journal of Informatics, Information System and Computer Engineering (INJIISCOM)* 2, no. 1 (June 26, 2021): 1–14. https://doi.org/10.34010/injiiscom.v2i1.4862.

Kavakiotis, Ioannis, Olga Tsave, Athanasios Salifoglou, Nicos Maglaveras, Ioannis Vlahavas, and Ioanna Chouvarda. 'Machine Learning and Data Mining Methods in Diabetes Research.' *Computational and Structural Biotechnology Journal* 15 (January 1, 2017): 104–16. https://doi.org/10.1016/j.csbj.2016.12.005.

Kerasidou, Angeliki. 'Artificial Intelligence and the Ongoing Need for Empathy, Compassion and Trust in Healthcare'. *Bulletin of the World Health Organization* 98, no. 4 (1 April 2020): 245–50. https://doi.org/10.2471/BLT.19.237198.

Kim, Hun-Sung, In Ho Kwon, and Won Chul Cha. 'Future and Development Direction of Digital Healthcare.' *Healthcare Informatics Research* 27, no. 2 (April 2021): 95–101. https://doi.org/10.4258/hir.2021.27.2.95.

Kooli, Chokri, and Hend Al Muftah. 'Artificial Intelligence in Healthcare: A Comprehensive Review of Its Ethical Concerns.' *Technological Sustainability* 1, no. 2 (January 1, 2022): 121–31. https://doi.org/10.1108/TECHS-12-2021-0029.

Kyaw, Bhone Myint, Nakul Saxena, Pawel Posadzki, Jitka Vseteckova, Charoula Konstantia Nikolaou, Pradeep Paul George, Ushashree Divakar, et al. 'Virtual Reality for Health Professions Education: Systematic Review and Meta-Analysis by the Digital Health Education Collaboration.' *Journal of Medical Internet Research* 21, no. 1 (January 22, 2019): e12959. https://doi.org/10.2196/12959.

Laver, Kate E., Belinda Lange, Stacey George, Judith E. Deutsch, Gustavo Saposnik, and Maria Crotty. 'Virtual Reality for Stroke Rehabilitation.' *The Cochrane Database* of *Systematic Reviews* 11, no. 11 (November 20, 2017): CD008349. https://doi.org/10.1002/14651858.CD008349.pub4.

Lee, DonHee, and Seong No Yoon. 'Application of Artificial Intelligence-Based Technologies in the Healthcare Industry: Opportunities and Challenges.' *International Journal of Environmental Research and Public Health* 18, no. 1 (January 2021): 271. https://doi.org/10.3390/ijerph18010271.

Lee, Natalie S., Thai Binh Luong, Roy Rosin, David A. Asch, Christianne Sevinc, Mohan Balachandran, Michael Josephs, et al. 'Developing a Chatbot–Clinician Model for Hypertension Management.' *NEJM Catalyst* 3, no. 11 (October 19, 2022): CAT.22.0228. https://doi.org/10.1056/CAT.22.0228.

Loftus, Tyler J., Patrick J. Tighe, Tezcan Ozrazgat-Baslanti, John P. Davis, Matthew M. Ruppert, Yuanfang Ren, Benjamin Shickel, et al. 'Ideal Algorithms in Healthcare: Explainable, Dynamic, Precise, Autonomous, Fair, and Reproducible.' *PLOS Digital Health* 1, no. 1 (January 18, 2022): e0000006. https://doi.org/10.1371/journal.pdig.0000006.

Manne, Ravi, and Sneha C. Kantheti. 'Application of Artificial Intelligence in Healthcare: Chances and Challenges.' SSRN Scholarly Paper. Rochester, NY, April 24, 2021. https://papers.ssrn.com/abstract=4393347.

Menon, Ashwin, Shiv Gaglani, M. Ryan Haynes, and Sean Tackett. 'Using "Big Data" to Guide Implementation of a Web and Mobile Adaptive Learning Platform for Medical Students.' *Medical Teacher* 39, no. 9 (September 2017): 975–80. https://doi.org/10.1080/0142159X.2017.1324949.

Mese, Ismail. 'The Impact of Artificial Intelligence on Radiology Education in the Wake of Coronavirus Disease 2019'. *Korean Journal of Radiology* 24, no. 5 (May 1, 2023): 478–79. https://doi.org/10.3348/kjr.2023.0278.

Min, Xu, Bin Yu, and Fei Wang. 'Predictive Modeling of the Hospital Readmission Risk from Patients' Claims Data Using Machine Learning: A Case Study on COPD.' *Scientific Reports* 9, no. 1 (February 20, 2019): 2362. https://doi.org/10.1038/s41598-019-39071-y.

Mittelstadt, Brent Daniel, Patrick Allo, Mariarosaria Taddeo, Sandra Wachter, and Luciano Floridi. 'The Ethics of Algorithms: Mapping the Debate.' *Big Data & Society* 3, no. 2 (December 1, 2016): 2053951716679679. https://doi.org/10.1177/2053951716679679.

Miyashita, Yohei, Tatsuro Hitsumoto, Hiroki Fukuda, Jiyoong Kim, Takashi Washio, and Masafumi Kitakaze. 'Predicting Heart Failure Onset in the General Population Using a Novel Data-Mining Artificial Intelligence Method.' *Scientific Reports* 13, no. 1 (March 16, 2023): 4352. https://doi.org/10.1038/s41598-023-31600-0.

Narindrarangkura, Ploypun, Min Soon Kim, and Suzanne A. Boren. 'A Scoping Review of Artificial Intelligence Algorithms in Clinical Decision Support Systems for Internal Medicine Subspecialties.' *ACI Open* 05, no. 2 (July 2021): e67–79. https://doi.org/10.1055/s-0041-1735470.

Neureiter, Daniel, Eckhard Klieser, Bettina Neumayer, Paul Winkelmann, Romana Urbas, and Tobias Kiesslich. 'Feasibility of Kahoot! As a Real-Time Assessment Tool in

(Histo-)Pathology Classroom Teaching'. *Advances in Medical Education and Practice* 11 (2020): 695–705. https://doi.org/10.2147/AMEP.S264821.

Novelli, Claudio, Mariarosaria Taddeo, and Luciano Floridi. 'Accountability in Artificial Intelligence: What It Is and How It Works.' *AI & SOCIETY*, February 7, 2023, 1–12. https://doi.org/10.1007/s00146-023-01635-y.

Nwoye, Ephraim, Wai Lok Woo, Bin Gao, and Tobenna Anyanwu. 'Artificial Intelligence for Emerging Technology in Surgery: Systematic Review and Validation.' *IEEE Reviews in Biomedical Engineering* 16 (2023): 241–59. https://doi.org/10.1109/RBME.2022.3183852.

Obermeyer, Ziad, and Ezekiel J. Emanuel. 'Predicting the Future — Big Data, Machine Learning, and Clinical Medicine.' *New England Journal of Medicine* 375, no. 13 (September 29, 2016): 1216–19. https://doi.org/10.1056/NEJMp1606181.

Obermeyer, Ziad, Brian Powers, Christine Vogeli, and Sendhil Mullainathan. 'Dissecting Racial Bias in an Algorithm Used to Manage the Health of Populations. *Science (New York, N.Y.)* 366, no. 6464 (October 25, 2019): 447–53. https://doi.org/10.1126/science.aax2342.

Patra, Braja G, Mohit M Sharma, Veer Vekaria, Prakash Adekkanattu, Olga V Patterson, Benjamin Glicksberg, Lauren A Lepow, et al. 'Extracting Social Determinants of Health from Electronic Health Records Using Natural Language Processing: A Systematic Review.' *Journal of the American Medical Informatics Association* 28, no. 12 (December 1, 2021): 2716–27. https://doi.org/10.1093/jamia/ocab170.

Patrício, Lia, Daniela Sangiorgi, Dominik Mahr, Martina Čaić, Saleh Kalantari, and Sue Sundar. 'Leveraging Service Design for Healthcare Transformation: Toward People-Centered, Integrated, and Technology-Enabled Healthcare Systems.' *Journal of Service Management* 31, no. 5 (January 1, 2020): 889–909. https://doi.org/10.1108/JOSM-11-2019-0332.

Pietris, James, Antoinette Lam, Stephen Bacchi, Aashray K. Gupta, Joshua G. Kovoor, and Weng Onn Chan. 'Health Economic Implications of Artificial Intelligence Implementation for Ophthalmology in Australia: A Systematic Review.' *The Asia-Pacific Journal of Ophthalmology* 11, no. 6 (December 2022): 554. https://doi.org/10.1097/APO.0000000000000565.

Price, W. Nicholson, and I. Glenn Cohen. 'Privacy in the Age of Medical Big Data.' *Nature Medicine* 25, no. 1 (January 2019): 37–43. https://doi.org/10.1038/s41591-018-0272-7.

Pugliese, Raffaele, and Stefano Regondi. 'Artificial Intelligence-Empowered 3D and 4D Printing Technologies toward Smarter Biomedical Materials and Approaches'. *Polymers* 14, no. 14 (January 2022): 2794. https://doi.org/10.3390/polym14142794.

Pushpakom, Sudeep, Francesco Iorio, Patrick A. Eyers, K. Jane Escott, Shirley Hopper, Andrew Wells, Andrew Doig, et al. 'Drug Repurposing: Progress, Challenges and Recommendations.' *Nature Reviews Drug Discovery* 18, no. 1 (January 2019): 41–58. https://doi.org/10.1038/nrd.2018.168.

Qiu, Hang, Shuhan Ding, Jianbo Liu, Liya Wang, and Xiaodong Wang. 'Applications of Artificial Intelligence in Screening, Diagnosis, Treatment, and Prognosis of

Colorectal Cancer.' *Current Oncology* 29, no. 3 (March 2022): 1773–95. https://doi.org/10.3390/curroncol29030146.

Rajkumar, Alvin, Eyal Oren, Kai Chen, Andrew M. Dai, Nissan Hajaj, Michaela Hardt, Peter J. Liu, et al. 'Scalable and Accurate Deep Learning with Electronic Health Records.' *Npj Digital Medicine* 1, no. 1 (8 May 2018): 1–10. https://doi.org/10.1038/s41746-018-0029-1.

Reddy, Sandeep, Sonia Allan, Simon Coghlan, and Paul Cooper. 'A Governance Model for the Application of AI in Health Care.' *Journal of the American Medical Informatics Association* 27, no. 3 (March 1, 2020): 491–97. https://doi.org/10.1093/jamia/ocz192.

Rogers, Michael P., Anthony J. DeSantis, Haroon Janjua, Tara M. Barry, and Paul C. Kuo. 'The Future Surgical Training Paradigm: Virtual Reality and Machine Learning in Surgical Education.' *Surgery* 169, no. 5 (May 1, 2021): 1250–52. https://doi.org/10.1016/j.surg.2020.09.040.

Ruberto, Aaron J., Dirk Rodenburg, Kyle Ross, Pritam Sarkar, Paul C. Hungler, Ali Etemad, Daniel Howes, et al. 'The Future of Simulation-Based Medical Education: Adaptive Simulation Utilizing a Deep Multitask Neural Network.' *AEM Education and Training* 5, no. 3 (2021): e10605. https://doi.org/10.1002/aet2.10605.

Samoili, Sofia, Montserrat Lopez Cobo, Emilia Gomez, Giuditta De Prato, Fernando Martinez-Plumed, and Blagoj Delipetrev. 'AI Watch. Defining Artificial Intelligence. Towards an Operational Definition and Taxonomy of Artificial Intelligence'. Monograph. Joint Research Centre (Seville site), 2020. https://publications.jrc.ec.europa.eu/repository/handle/JRC118163.

Sarbadhikari, Suptendra N., and Keerti B. Pradhan. 'The Need for Developing Technology-Enabled, Safe, and Ethical Workforce for Healthcare Delivery.' *Safety and Health at Work* 11, no. 4 (December 1, 2020): 533–36. https://doi.org/10.1016/j.shaw.2020.08.003.

Schoeb, Dominik, Rodrigo Suarez-Ibarrola, Simon Hein, Franz Friedrich Dressler, Fabian Adams, Daniel Schlager, and Arkadiusz Miernik. 'Use of Artificial Intelligence for Medical Literature Search: Randomized Controlled Trial Using the Hackathon Format.' *Interactive Journal of Medical Research* 9, no. 1 (March 30, 2020): e16606. https://doi.org/10.2196/16606.

Schork, Nicholas J. 'Artificial Intelligence and Personalized Medicine.' *Cancer Treatment and Research* 178 (January 1, 2019): 265–83. https://doi.org/10.1007/978-3-030-16391-4_11.

Shah, Anjan, Christine L. Mai, Ronak Shah, and Adam I. Levine. 'Simulation-Based Education and Team Training.' *Otolaryngologic Clinics of North America* 52, no. 6 (December 1, 2019): 995–1003. https://doi.org/10.1016/j.otc.2019.08.002.

Shaheen, Mohammed Yousef. 'AI in Healthcare: Medical and Socio-Economic Benefits and Challenges.' *ScienceOpen Preprints*, September 25, 2021. https://doi.org/10.14293/S2199-1006.1.SOR-.PPRQNI1.v1.

Shaw, James A., and Joseph Donia. 'The Sociotechnical Ethics of Digital Health: A Critique and Extension of Approaches From Bioethics.' *Frontiers in Digital Health* 3 (2021). https://www.frontiersin.org/articles/10.3389/fdgth.2021.725088.

Sheikhalishahi, Seyed Mostafa, Riccardo Miotto, Joel T Dudley, Alberto Lavelli, Fabio Rinaldi, and Venet Osmani. 'Natural Language Processing of Clinical Notes on Chronic Diseases: Systematic Review.' *JMIR Medical Informatics* 7, no. 2 (April 27, 2019): e12239. https://doi.org/10.2196/12239.

Shen, Yiqiu, Farah E. Shamout, Jamie R. Oliver, Jan Witowski, Kawshik Kannan, Jungkyu Park, Nan Wu, et al. 'Artificial Intelligence System Reduces False-Positive Findings in the Interpretation of Breast Ultrasound Exams.' *Nature Communications* 12, no. 1 (September 24, 2021): 5645. https://doi.org/10.1038/s41467-021-26023-2.

Singh, Rishi P., Grant L. Hom, Michael D. Abramoff, J. Peter Campbell, Michael F. Chiang, and on behalf of the AAO Task Force on Artificial Intelligence. 'Current Challenges and Barriers to Real-World Artificial Intelligence Adoption for the Healthcare System, Provider, and the Patient.' *Translational Vision Science & Technology* 9, no. 2 (August 11, 2020): 45. https://doi.org/10.1167/tvst.9.2.45.

Somashekhar, S. P., M.-J. Sepúlveda, S. Puglielli, A. D. Norden, E. H. Shortliffe, C. Rohit Kumar, A. Rauthan, et al. 'Watson for Oncology and Breast Cancer Treatment Recommendations: Agreement with an Expert Multidisciplinary Tumor Board'. *Annals of Oncology: Official Journal of the European Society for Medical Oncology* 29, no. 2 (February 1, 2018): 418–23. https://doi.org/10.1093/annonc/mdx781.

Stallard, N., L. Hampson, N. Benda, W. Brannan, T. Burnett, T. Friede, P. K. Kimani, et al. 'Efficient Adaptive Designs for Clinical Trials of Interventions for COVID-19'. *Statistics in Biopharmaceutical Research* 12, no. 4 (October 1, 2020): 483–97.

Stern, Ariel Dora, Avi Goldfarb, Timo Minssen, and W. Nicholson Price II. 'AI Insurance: How Liability Insurance Can Drive the Responsible Adoption of Artificial Intelligence in Health Care.' *NEJM Catalyst* 3, no. 4 (March 16, 2022): CAT.21.0242. https://doi.org/10.1056/CAT.21.0242.

Stokes, Jonathan M., Kevin Yang, Kyle Swanson, Wengong Jin, Andres Cubillos-Ruiz, Nina M. Donghia, Craig R. MacNair, et al. 'A Deep Learning Approach to Antibiotic Discovery.' *Cell* 180, no. 4 (February 20, 2020): 688-702.e13. https://doi.org/10.1016/j.cell.2020.01.021.

Sun, Yuanxi, Long Bai, and Dianbiao Dong. 'Editorial: Lighter and More Efficient Robotic Joints in Prostheses and Exoskeletons: Design, Actuation and Control.' *Frontiers in Robotics and AI* 10 (March 7, 2023): 1063712. https://doi.org/10.3389/frobt.2023.1063712.

Tai, Michael Cheng-Tek. 'The Impact of Artificial Intelligence on Human Society and Bioethics.' *Tzu-Chi Medical Journal* 32, no. 4 (August 14, 2020): 339–43. https://doi.org/10.4103/tcmj.tcmj_71_20.

Tang, Jie, Rong Liu, Yue-Li Zhang, Mou-Ze Liu, Yong-Fang Hu, Ming-Jie Shao, Li-Jun Zhu, et al. 'Application of Machine-Learning Models to Predict Tacrolimus Stable Dose in Renal Transplant Recipients.' *Scientific Reports* 7, no. 1 (February 8, 2017): 42192. https://doi.org/10.1038/srep42192.

Teo, Zhen Ling, and Daniel Shu Wei Ting. 'AI Telemedicine Screening in Ophthalmology: Health Economic Considerations.' *The Lancet Global Health* 11, no. 3 (March 1, 2023): e318–20. https://doi.org/10.1016/S2214-109X(23)00037-2.

Tursunbayeva, Aizhan, and Maarten Renkema. 'Artificial Intelligence in Health-Care: Implications for the Job Design of Healthcare Professionals.' *Asia Pacific Journal of Human Resources* n/a, no. n/a. Accessed May 21, 2023. https://doi.org/10.1111/1744-7941.12325.

Upadhyayula, Venkata K. K., Venkataramana Gadhamshetty, Kavitha Shanmugam, Nabil Souihi, and Mats Tysklind. 'Advancing Game Changing Academic Research Concepts to Commercialization: A Life Cycle Assessment (LCA) Based Sustainability Framework for Making Informed Decisions in Technology Valley of Death (TVD).' *Resources, Conservation and Recycling* 133 (June 1, 2018): 404–16. https://doi.org/10.1016/j.resconrec.2017.12.029.

Vamathevan, Jessica, Dominic Clark, Paul Czodrowski, Ian Dunham, Edgardo Ferran, George Lee, Bin Li, et al. 'Applications of Machine Learning in Drug Discovery and Development.' *Nature Reviews. Drug Discovery* 18, no. 6 (June 2019): 463–77. https://doi.org/10.1038/s41573-019-0024-5.

Wartman, Steven A., and C. Donald Combs. 'Reimagining Medical Education in the Age of AI.' *AMA Journal of Ethics* 21, no. 2 (February 1, 2019): 146–52. https://doi.org/10.1001/amajethics.2019.146.

Weng, Chunhua, and James R. Rogers. 'AI Uses Patient Data to Optimize Selection of Eligibility Criteria for Clinical Trials.' *Nature* 592, no. 7855 (April 2021): 512–13. https://doi.org/10.1038/d41586-021-00845-y.

Williams, Simon, Hugo Layard Horsfall, Jonathan P. Funnell, John G. Hanrahan, Danyal Z. Khan, William Muirhead, Danail Stoyanov, and Hani J. Marcus. 'Artificial Intelligence in Brain Tumour Surgery—An Emerging Paradigm.' *Cancers* 13, no. 19 (October 7, 2021): 5010. https://doi.org/10.3390/cancers13195010.

Wolff, Justus, Josch Pauling, Andreas Keck, and Jan Baumbach. 'The Economic Impact of Artificial Intelligence in Health Care: Systematic Review.' *Journal of Medical Internet Research* 22, no. 2 (February 20, 2020): e16866. https://doi.org/10.2196/16866.

Yap, Marie Bee Hui, Pamela Doreen Pilkington, Siobhan Mary Ryan, and Anthony Francis Jorm. 'Parental Factors Associated with Depression and Anxiety in Young People: A Systematic Review and Meta-Analysis.' *Journal of Affective Disorders* 156 (March 2014): 8–23. https://doi.org/10.1016/j.jad.2013.11.007.

Yin, Zugang, Chenhui Yao, Limin Zhang, and Shaohua Qi. 'Application of Artificial Intelligence in Diagnosis and Treatment of Colorectal Cancer: A Novel Prospect.' *Frontiers in Medicine* 10 (March 8, 2023): 1128084. https://doi.org/10.3389/fmed.2023.1128084.

Zhavoronkov, Alex, Yan A. Ivanenkov, Alex Aliper, Mark S. Veselov, Vladimir A. Aladinskiy, Anastasiya V. Aladinskaya, Victor A. Terentiev, et al. 'Deep Learning Enables Rapid Identification of Potent DDR1 Kinase Inhibitors'. *Nature Biotechnology* 37, no. 9 (September 2019): 1038–40. https://doi.org/10.1038/s41587-019-0224-x.

Zhou, Na, Chuan-Tao Zhang, Hong-Ying Lv, Chen-Xing Hao, Tian-Jun Li, Jing-Juan Zhu, Hua Zhu, et al. 'Concordance Study Between IBM Watson for Oncology and Clinical Practice for Patients with Cancer in China.' *The Oncologist* 24, no. 6 (2019): 812–19. https://doi.org/10.1634/theoncologist.2018-0255.

Index

3D printing, 39
4D printing, 39
academia, 131, 132
access, 4, 8, 19, 34, 35, 36, 37, 49, 53, 58, 61, 67, 68, 71, 78, 103, 110, 111, 113, 114, 116, 124, 125, 128, 130, 132, 135, 141, 142, 143, 128, 132, 133, 141, 142
accessible, 8, 9, 17, 25, 35, 37, 42, 79, 108, 111, 113, 129
accountability, 3, 7, 22, 104, 108, 111, 117, 118, 119, 120, 121, 122, 125, 143, 131, 142
adaptability, 40, 67, 137, 138, 142, 143, 142
adaptable, 5, 27, 37, 48, 143
administrative, 3, 6, 16, 21, 23, 44, 45, 70, 112, 133, 146, 122, 134, 135, 141, 143
adverse effects, 58, 144, 125
agent, 5, 32, 119
AI Fairness 360, 117
Aidoc, 122
algorithm, 4, 6, 12, 14, 16, 17, 23, 29, 34, 38, 50, 51, 54, 60, 63, 72, 75, 116, 118, 122, 132, 145, 126
algorithmic transparency, 121, 125
algorithms, 4, 5, 7, 8, 11, 12, 13, 14, 15, 16, 17, 20, 23, 25, 26, 27, 29, 30, 36, 37, 38, 39, 40, 44, 47, 48, 52, 53, 59, 60, 62, 63, 65, 66, 67, 69, 71, 74, 76, 77, 78, 79, 80, 104, 114, 116, 117, 118, 120, 121, 122, 124, 128, 130, 132, 133, 135, 136, 138, 139, 141, 142, 143, 144, 146, 122, 123, 124, 125, 126, 127, 128, 129, 131, 132, 133, 134, 136, 141, 142, 143
analytics, 11, 15, 16, 19, 42, 43, 62, 69, 72, 132, 143, 144, 146, 122, 131, 132, 136, 137
anonymization, 23, 53
Application Programming Interfaces (APIs)., 53
applications, 1, 3, 5, 10, 16, 17, 19, 22, 23, 25, 26, 34, 35, 37, 74, 113, 114, 115, 124, 125, 131, 133, 135, 138, 140, 142, 143, 144, 146, 123, 124, 125, 126, 127, 128, 129, 131, 136, 142
Area Under Curve (AUC) of the Receiver Operating Characteristic (ROC) Curve (AUC-ROC), 74
Area9 Rhapsode, 126
artificial intelligence, 1, 3, 5, 7, 10, 11, 13, 15, 26, 42, 59, 62, 69, 72, 78, 102, 103, 104, 113, 116, 118, 121, 132, 131, 132, 133, 136, 142
artificial neural networks, 4, 11, 15
Augmented Reality (AR), 54
automated, 7, 44, 63, 65, 79, 112, 128, 134
autonomous, 5, 59
autonomy, 102, 104, 121, 122, 133, 143, 136, 139
barriers, 1, 67, 78, 124, 125, 126, 127, 128, 134, 137, 142, 141
bed utilization, 146
beneficence, 102, 103, 122, 143
best practices, 58, 68, 114, 126, 133, 142, 143, 138, 142
bias, 1, 4, 7, 12, 21, 22, 23, 28, 34, 41, 64, 70, 72, 104, 116, 117, 122, 133, 136, 139, 142
big data, 45, 52
Big data, 44, 45
billing, 3, 146
bioethics, 103, 104
black box, 19
CAE Healthcare, 127
cancer, 6, 12, 14, 16, 17, 18, 26, 27, 32, 38, 69, 77, 141
Central Processing Unit (CPU), 52
certification, 23, 137
challenges, 1, 7, 10, 12, 18, 21, 23, 25, 32, 34, 35, 59, 64, 69, 70, 78, 82, 111, 112, 113, 114, 115, 118, 120, 124, 125, 126, 127, 128, 129, 130, 134, 140, 126, 131, 132, 133, 135, 136, 139, 140, 143
chatbot, 37, 128
chatbots, 6, 37, 48, 67, 80, 128, 146, 122
ChatGPT, 142, 143
claims, 6, 21, 75
clinical notes, 20, 76, 78

235

clinical practice, 25, 58, 140, 142, 143, 145, 129
clinical records, 124, 132
clinical trial, 7, 76, 77, 78, 124, 125
clinical trials, 4, 69, 77, 138, 144, 125, 126, 129
cloud computing, 114, 138
cloud-based, 71, 124, 128, 135
clustering algorithms, 74, 75
CME365, 128
Cognauto, 127
collaboration, 1, 7, 47, 49, 70, 72, 78, 79, 80, 82, 110, 112, 125, 126, 127, 128, 129, 130, 133, 138, 132, 134, 135, 136, 138, 139, 140, 143, 142, 143
collaborative learning, 55, 66
communication, 1, 7, 34, 35, 42, 52, 59, 70, 78, 80, 82, 105, 108, 127, 128, 133, 142, 145, 132
complications, 38, 39, 56
Computed Tomography (CT), 6, 69
computing, 4, 16, 69, 128, 138, 131
concerns, 4, 7, 34, 41, 59, 82, 111, 113, 114, 116, 117, 124, 125, 126, 127, 128, 134, 145, 131, 134, 135
confidentiality, 82, 113, 116, 121, 143
conscientization, 103
consent, 1, 8, 53, 58, 104, 114, 121, 122, 134, 143, 138, 142
continuing professional development (CPD), 66, 128
Continuous Professional Development, 136
convolutional neural networks, 4
Copilot, 82
cost savings, 3
course development, 45
Covidence, 72, 73
crisis, 131, 137
Cultural resistance, 127
Current Health, 123
curricula, 42, 45, 47, 62, 63, 133
curriculum, 1, 44, 45, 47, 62, 63, 64, 65, 132, 126, 127, 130
customization, 33, 132
cybersecurity, 54, 111, 122, 139
da Vinci Surgical System, 38
data, 1, 3, 4, 6, 7, 11, 13, 14, 15, 16, 18, 19, 21, 22, 23, 25, 26, 27, 28, 29, 30, 31, 33, 34, 35, 36, 37, 40, 42, 48, 50, 52, 53, 54, 58, 62, 63, 64, 66, 67, 69, 70, 71, 72, 73, 74, 75, 76, 77, 78, 79, 80, 82, 102, 103, 104, 105, 109, 111, 113, 114, 115, 116, 117, 121, 122, 124, 125, 128, 129, 130, 132, 133, 134, 135, 138, 139, 140, 141, 143, 144, 145, 146, 122, 123, 124, 125, 126, 127, 128, 129, 131, 132, 133, 134, 135, 136, 137, 138, 141, 143, 142, 143
data breaches, 7, 114
data centre, 52
data integrity, 44, 129
data mining, 45, 60, 74, 135, 124
data privacy, 23, 28, 30, 32, 35, 68, 69, 113, 115, 116, 122, 125, 138, 125, 126, 143
data scientists, 54, 59, 115, 129, 133, 136, 139, 136, 138, 142, 143
data security, 35, 58, 114, 145
data storage, 53, 135
data transparency, 121
databases, 29, 30, 52, 61, 72, 73, 77, 124
datasets, 3, 7, 29, 63, 69, 74, 79, 114, 115, 117, 122, 124, 138, 124, 129, 141
decision making process, 30
decision support systems, 1, 11, 25, 124, 141, 142, 143, 146, 124, 129, 134, 141
Decision Support Systems, 11, 12, 28, 29, 30, 32, 122
decision-making processes, 23, 102, 104, 118, 120, 121, 122, 141, 133, 138, 142
Deep 6 AI, 126
deep learning, 4, 11, 15, 16, 17, 18, 19, 27, 29, 58, 76, 77, 135, 126
Deep Learning, 4, 10, 13, 16, 17, 25, 32, 34, 77
deep neural networks, 4
DeepMind, 20, 25, 70
dermatologist, 16, 17
developers, 45, 54, 113, 117, 118, 120, 121, 126, 130, 132, 142, 143
devices, 6, 15, 23, 27, 29, 35, 36, 37, 39, 41, 61, 62, 113, 120, 136, 123, 124, 131, 133
diagnoses, 3, 14, 26, 36, 54, 116, 130, 132
diagnosing disease, 3

diagnosis, 3, 14, 16, 17, 18, 19, 23, 34, 69, 102, 118, 125, 133, 135, 140, 142, 146, 122, 131, 132, 135
diagnostics, 1, 6, 25, 26, 28, 67, 69, 116, 140, 141, 129, 134, 143
Differential Privacy, 115
discrimination, 104
DistillerSR, 71, 72, 73
Docebo, 129
Doximity, 129
drug discovery, 7, 15, 16, 21, 23, 33, 69, 76, 77, 78, 124, 125, 126, 129
early disease, 23, 131
EarlySense, 123
economic impact, 134, 135
education, 1, 5, 7, 34, 35, 42, 43, 44, 45, 46, 47, 48, 49, 50, 52, 53, 54, 56, 57, 58, 59, 60, 61, 62, 64, 65, 66, 108, 110, 119, 124, 127, 131, 132, 133, 134, 142, 126, 127, 130, 135, 137, 140, 143
efficacy, 22, 30, 39, 58, 76, 120, 139, 144, 124, 125
efficiency, 3, 5, 14, 15, 23, 25, 38, 43, 44, 47, 71, 72, 73, 76, 78, 82, 125, 128, 130, 140, 146, 122, 123, 124, 125, 126, 127, 129, 134, 135, 143, 142
electronic health records, 124, 125
electronic health records (EHRs), 27, 76, 124, 137
Encryption, 114
engagement, 34, 37, 40, 41, 42, 45, 47, 60, 62, 63, 65, 66, 105, 128, 129, 133, 142, 126, 127, 128, 129, 131
engineers, 54, 129, 136, 139
environment, 5, 22, 23, 42, 43, 44, 45, 48, 49, 52, 54, 55, 56, 57, 59, 65, 68, 105, 111, 127, 129, 145, 127, 139, 143
equipment availability, 146
errors, 4, 45, 71, 81, 118, 120
ethical, 1, 3, 4, 8, 21, 22, 23, 28, 30, 41, 69, 102, 105, 108, 110, 111, 112, 116, 118, 120, 121, 122, 124, 125, 126, 127, 131, 132, 134, 140, 143, 145, 127, 129, 130, 132, 133, 135, 136, 138, 139, 140, 142, 143, 142, 143

ethical, legal, and social implications (ELSI), 102, 112
ethics, 23, 102, 110, 111, 122, 132, 138
explainability, 120, 121, 130
F1 score, 74
faculty, 42, 47, 48
Federated Learning, 115
feedback, 5, 7, 29, 31, 34, 40, 42, 43, 44, 45, 47, 48, 49, 51, 54, 55, 56, 57, 58, 60, 61, 62, 63, 64, 65, 66, 67, 133, 145, 127, 128, 131
financial considerations, 1, 135
financial constraints, 127
Food and Drug Administration, 23, 120
framework, 23, 47, 62, 106, 108, 110, 111, 112, 122, 129, 133, 134, 136, 137
funding, 124, 136, 137, 138
GDPR, 22, 53, 113, 125
General Data Protection Regulation, 22, 113, 125
genetic, 6, 12, 14, 21, 27, 33, 75, 76, 144, 125, 126, 132
genomic, 29, 33, 76, 78, 113, 132
genomics, 21, 27, 69, 77, 143, 144, 124, 125, 131
Google Dialogflow, 122
Graphical Processing Units (GPUs), 52
guidelines, 8, 22, 23, 29, 30, 31, 41, 80, 81, 103, 111, 112, 113, 118, 120, 121, 125, 126, 139, 141, 142, 143, 144, 145, 146, 134, 136, 138, 142, 143
harm, 8
Heads-Up Display (HUD), 49
health assistants, 21
Health Insurance Portability and Accountability Act (HIPAA), 19, 22, 35, 113, 125
health monitoring, 3, 6, 15
high-performance computing (HPC), 135
HIPAA, 19, 22, 35, 53, 113, 125
history, 6, 12, 13, 14, 19, 40
Hospital IQ, 122
i-Human Patients, 127
image, 4, 5, 11, 15, 17, 18, 146, 122, 134
images, 6, 12, 14, 16, 17, 20, 25, 26, 30, 35, 38, 39, 69, 113, 146, 122, 131, 133
individualized, 7, 40, 42, 43, 45, 141

237

information filtering system, 50
informatization, 41
informed decisions, 6, 14, 29, 73, 103, 122, 132, 140, 126, 131, 134, 136, 141, 142
infrastructure, 12, 52, 58, 113, 124, 127, 128, 134, 135, 136, 138
Infrastructure, 52, 138, 139
innovation, 1, 22, 23, 80, 109, 115, 126, 127, 128, 129, 130, 137, 138, 140, 131, 136, 138, 139, 141, 142, 143
Insilco Medicine, 126
integration, 3, 4, 19, 25, 32, 37, 38, 41, 47, 57, 61, 68, 69, 70, 78, 102, 108, 110, 111, 113, 114, 118, 122, 124, 126, 127, 128, 129, 131, 132, 133, 134, 138, 140, 141, 124, 125, 126, 127, 129, 130, 131, 133, 136, 138, 139, 143
integration of artificial intelligence, 3, 124, 127, 129, 131
Intelligent Tutoring System (ITS, 44
internet, 53, 110, 113
Internet of Medical Things (IoMT), 133
interoperability, 124, 125, 126, 127, 128, 138, 131, 132, 139, 142
intervention, 3, 6, 14, 27, 34, 55, 58, 69, 144
investment, 12, 134, 135, 136, 138, 139
IRIS.AI, 80
Java, 53
job displacement, 8, 112, 127, 134
Just-In-Time (JIT), 49, 61
Kahoot!, 60
Labii ELN & LIMS, 80
laws, 22, 23, 35
Legacy systems, 128
legal, 1, 4, 30, 109, 112, 116, 118, 120, 125, 126, 139, 142
legislators, 22, 23
Legislators, 22, 23
liability, 1, 4, 7, 22, 23, 109, 118, 120, 122, 125, 126, 127
liability insurance, 120, 126, 127
lifelong learning, 9, 61, 134, 127, 129, 130, 135, 136, 138, 139, 142, 143
Limitless-Arity Multiple-testing Procedure (LAMP), 26
literacy, 124, 127, 142, 136, 138, 142
literate, 4, 8

machine learning, 4, 5, 11, 13, 14, 15, 19, 29, 31, 37, 38, 52, 53, 54, 62, 64, 69, 71, 73, 74, 75, 79, 80, 115, 131, 133, 136, 122, 124
Machine learning, 11, 13, 14, 15, 25, 63, 67, 69, 70, 76, 77, 114, 131, 132
Machine Learning, 4, 10, 13, 14, 15, 19, 26, 27, 40, 59, 75, 76, 77
Magnetic Resonance Imaging (MRI), 6, 69
Maintenance, 74, 139
medication, 21, 35, 61
Medscape, 128, 129
Mendel.ai, 126
Microsoft Healthcare Bot, 122
model, 17, 18, 29, 31, 32, 33, 42, 46, 47, 49, 50, 73, 74, 82, 105, 108, 109, 115, 121, 142
models, 4, 14, 18, 19, 27, 30, 31, 38, 54, 69, 70, 71, 74, 75, 76, 77, 105, 111, 114, 115, 116, 117, 136, 138, 133, 141
monitoring, 4, 19, 21, 28, 34, 35, 36, 37, 38, 39, 40, 50, 54, 67, 108, 120, 128, 139, 142, 144, 145, 122, 123, 131, 133, 135
Multiple Linear Regression (MLR), 75
natural language processing, 5, 32, 64, 65, 67, 71, 78, 80, 131, 146, 124, 134, 139
Natural language processing, 20, 76
Natural Language Processing (NLP), 44, 49, 122, 132
NCI-MATCH (National Cancer Institute - Molecular Analysis for Therapy Choice) trial, 126
network, 52, 135
New England Journal of Medicine (NEJM) Knowledge+, 128
non-maleficence, 102, 103, 122
operational capacity, 146
Ophthalmology, 37, 125, 135
organizational transparency, 121
organizations, 3, 113, 116, 117, 118, 120, 124, 126, 127, 128, 129, 130, 131, 132, 133, 135, 136, 131, 137, 141, 143
Orthopaedic, 60
Osmosis, 60, 126, 127
outcomes, 4, 7, 12, 21, 23, 24, 26, 27, 30, 31, 34, 38, 40, 41, 48, 54, 58, 59, 60, 63, 64, 67, 69, 70, 76, 77, 78, 103,

104, 108, 110, 113, 117, 118, 119, 120, 122, 127, 128, 143, 144, 126, 127, 129, 130, 131, 132, 133, 138, 139, 141, 142, 143
over-fitting, 18
PathAI, 26
pathologists, 26, 134
Pathology, 26, 60
patient care, 3, 6, 8, 12, 13, 14, 15, 20, 21, 23, 24, 30, 32, 34, 59, 61, 62, 75, 76, 80, 105, 124, 128, 133, 140, 142, 143, 146, 122, 124, 125, 127, 129, 130, 131, 132, 134, 136, 138, 141, 142, 143
patient data, 12, 14, 19, 35, 37, 76, 114, 115, 142, 144, 146, 134
patient engagement, 3, 133
patient outcomes, 3, 11, 16, 17, 21, 25, 26, 27, 31, 32, 38, 40, 57, 59, 73, 75, 78, 82, 102, 116, 129, 131, 134, 140, 142, 143, 144, 145, 124, 130, 131, 132, 133, 134, 135, 140, 141, 143
patient privacy, 115, 116, 143, 145, 133
patient record management, 3
pattern recognition, 7, 140
patterns, 3, 4, 10, 13, 14, 15, 16, 17, 26, 27, 29, 37, 44, 45, 48, 62, 63, 69, 70, 74, 76, 77, 78, 135, 140, 144, 145, 124, 129, 131, 132, 141
payer, 3
permission, 3
personalization, 5, 21, 47, 51, 66
personalized, 7, 12, 21, 23, 25, 27, 32, 33, 34, 38, 39, 40, 41, 42, 43, 44, 45, 47, 48, 52, 55, 58, 59, 60, 61, 62, 63, 64, 65, 67, 69, 75, 76, 79, 129, 130, 140, 141, 142, 144, 145, 122, 124, 125, 126, 127, 128, 129, 130, 131, 133, 134, 135
personalizing treatments, 3
plain radiographs (X-rays), 6, 69
platforms, 34, 36, 42, 43, 59, 60, 61, 63, 67, 73, 78, 79, 80, 82, 110, 136, 137, 122, 123, 125, 126, 127, 128, 129, 130, 131, 135, 137
Policymakers, 23, 113
practice, 1, 5, 7, 9, 23, 25, 35, 41, 54, 55, 56, 57, 60, 64, 67, 102, 103, 120, 121, 126, 133, 140, 141, 142, 143, 144, 146, 122, 123, 126, 127, 128, 129, 137, 142
precision, 4, 21, 25, 33, 38, 41, 74, 76, 144, 125, 126, 132, 133, 139
Precision, 26, 47, 144, 124, 126, 132
prediction, 7, 14, 17, 25, 31, 38, 70, 73, 74, 75, 76, 126
predictions, 4, 11, 13, 14, 18, 27, 29, 73, 74, 75, 76, 122, 131
prescriptions, 35
preventive, 19, 144, 131, 133
privacy, 1, 3, 4, 7, 12, 19, 20, 21, 22, 23, 24, 34, 35, 42, 53, 58, 64, 102, 109, 111, 113, 114, 115, 121, 122, 125, 134, 135, 123, 127, 129, 130, 131, 135, 136, 138, 139, 142
procedures, 1, 4, 7, 12, 21, 25, 38, 41, 43, 48, 54, 55, 60, 119, 121, 142, 131, 133
prognosis, 25, 26, 27
provider, 3, 23, 35, 128
Python, 53
quality, 3, 5, 8, 18, 23, 40, 45, 72, 102, 104, 113, 115, 118, 125, 126, 128, 130, 134, 135, 138, 146, 122, 128, 129, 130, 135, 141, 142, 143, 142
Qventus, 122
radiologists, 14, 68, 132, 141, 122
Rayyan, 71
real-time, 4, 7, 17, 21, 27, 35, 37, 39, 40, 43, 46, 48, 49, 54, 56, 60, 61, 62, 63, 65, 69, 74, 78, 79, 80, 81, 142, 144, 122, 123, 127, 131, 135
records, 6, 14, 16, 19, 20, 21, 27, 29, 30, 33, 35, 67, 69, 76, 77, 78, 112, 113, 135, 144, 146, 122, 124, 125, 131, 133, 134
recurrent neural networks, 4
Regression Tree (RT), 75
regulation, 8, 21, 22, 23, 111, 118
regulations, 19, 22, 30, 53, 110, 111, 112, 113, 125, 126, 137, 138, 143, 123, 136
regulators, 22, 23
rehabilitation, 12, 25, 38, 39, 40, 41
remote, 4, 34, 35, 36, 37, 38, 43, 110, 142, 123, 131, 133, 135, 141
research, 1, 3, 5, 7, 9, 12, 19, 20, 23, 29, 30, 32, 33, 39, 48, 58, 69, 70, 71, 72, 74, 76, 78, 79, 80, 81, 82, 115, 121,

239

129, 130, 133, 135, 136, 138, 140, 141, 142, 143, 145, 123, 124, 125, 126, 128, 129, 130, 132, 141, 142
resources, 7, 15, 32, 43, 45, 47, 48, 49, 50, 55, 60, 61, 65, 66, 67, 72, 82, 103, 110, 116, 124, 126, 127, 128, 129, 130, 131, 132, 134, 135, 136, 138, 146, 124, 127, 128, 129, 139, 141
responsibility, 22, 23, 104, 109, 111, 118, 120
right to be forgotten, 53
rights, 23, 103, 109, 113, 134, 131
risk management, 120
robot-assisted, 40
robotic, 38, 39, 131, 133
robotics, 11, 21, 139
safety, 7, 20, 22, 23, 24, 30, 32, 37, 54, 59, 77, 78, 109, 118, 120, 126, 131, 139, 124, 125, 138, 143
sample size calculation, 125
scheduling, 3, 6, 21, 112, 146, 122, 134
SciSpace, 82
Scite, 80
screening, 17, 36, 72, 135
security, 7, 19, 35, 41, 42, 53, 69, 82, 102, 111, 113, 114, 115, 116, 122, 125, 128, 138, 139, 123, 131, 136, 142, 143
Semantic Scholar, 80
sepsis, 32
service design, 129
Service Design, 129
shared decision-making, 105, 106, 107, 121, 122, 144, 145
side effects, 6, 14, 21, 61, 69, 76
simulation, 43, 50, 54, 55, 56, 59, 130
simulations, 7, 40, 48, 56, 58, 67, 68, 127
SimX, 127
smart content, 44, 45, 47
SMARTSITES, 127
social justice, 102, 104, 111, 122
staffing, 15, 146, 131
stakeholders, 22, 110, 111, 117, 118, 122, 125, 126, 127, 128, 129, 130, 136, 142
statistical power, 125
study protocol, 125
Substitution, Augmentation, Modification, and Redefinition (SAMR), 46
supervised learning, 74

Support Vector Machines (SVM), 74
surgery, 12, 37, 38, 39, 48, 59, 131, 133
talent, 128, 134, 136, 139
telehealth, 34, 35, 113
telemedicine, 1, 4, 25, 36, 37, 38, 110
Telemedicine, 12, 34, 36, 37, 135, 141
telemonitoring, 37
Tensor Processing Units (TPUs), 52
tool, 1, 3, 7, 8, 14, 18, 19, 21, 28, 32, 39, 49, 58, 60, 64, 68, 71, 72, 73, 77, 80, 82, 113, 142, 143, 135, 141, 142, 143, 142, 143
Touch Surgery, 43
training set, 17, 74
transformation, 3, 19, 42, 44, 45, 46, 129, 133
transparency, 1, 3, 8, 23, 30, 32, 41, 68, 108, 110, 117, 118, 120, 121, 122, 125, 142, 143, 130, 131, 136, 138, 139, 142, 143
transparent, 5, 72, 111, 142
treatment, 3, 6, 7, 11, 12, 14, 17, 21, 23, 27, 31, 32, 33, 34, 36, 39, 40, 41, 69, 74, 76, 78, 102, 116, 117, 118, 122, 125, 130, 133, 140, 141, 142, 143, 144, 145, 146, 122, 124, 125, 127, 129, 131, 132, 134, 135, 141, 142, 143, 142
trends, 1, 3, 45, 62, 63, 70, 71, 78, 144, 131, 132, 133, 136, 137, 139, 142
Trial Pathfinder, 77
Typeset.io, 80, 81, 82
unstructured data, 16, 20, 76, 78
Unsupervised Learning, 75
upskilling, 112, 132, 136, 135, 138
validation, 19, 74, 75, 118, 122, 137, 138, 139, 145
virtual assistants, 16, 146, 122, 131
virtual reality, 7, 40, 43, 50, 54, 58
Virtual Reality (VR), 56
VisualDx, 122
Voice recognition, 134
wait times, 146
Watson, 32, 33, 141, 122
wearables, 15, 21, 35, 131
workforce development, 1, 131, 132, 133

ABOUT THE AUTHORS

Dr Vaikunthan Rajaratnam graduated from the University of Malaya and is an accredited hand surgeon, medical educator and instructional designer and has practised and taught over the last four decades in Malaysia, UK, and Singapore. He regularly conducts teaching and training programs in Malaysia, Bangladesh, Sri Lanka, and Cambodia apart from his current place of practice, Singapore. He has developed and maintains open online educational programs for Hand Surgery and Medical Education.

Dr Ang Mu Liang is a certified orthopaedic surgeon, subspecialising in endoscopic spine surgery, and involved in the implementation of Next Generation Electronic Medical Records at National Healthcare Group, Singapore. His contribution in the offices of Clinical Informatics and Research help clinicians, administrators, and researchers to deliver data-driven value-based care. He graduated from National University of Singapore and has received multiple teaching awards for his role as Clinical Faculty.